YOU'RE NOT
DONE YET

ALSO BY B. JANET HIBBS, M.F.T., Ph.D.
AND ANTHONY ROSTAIN, M.D., M.A.

The Stressed Years of Their Lives

YOU'RE NOT DONE YET

Parenting Young Adults
in an Age of Uncertainty

B. JANET HIBBS, M.F.T., Ph.D.
AND ANTHONY ROSTAIN, M.D., M.A.

ST. MARTIN'S PRESS
NEW YORK

First published in the United States by St. Martin's Press,
an imprint of St. Martin's Publishing Group

YOU'RE NOT DONE YET. Copyright © 2024 by B. Janet Hibbs, M.F.T., Ph.D.,
and Anthony Rostain, M.D., M.A. All rights reserved. Printed in the United
States of America. For information, address St. Martin's Publishing Group,
120 Broadway, New York, NY 10271.

www.stmartins.com

Library of Congress Cataloging-in-Publication Data

Names: Hibbs, B. Janet, author. | Rostain, Anthony L., author.
Title: You're not done yet : parenting young adults in an age of uncertainty /
    B. Janet Hibbs, M.F.T., Ph.D. and Anthony Rostain, M.D., M.A..
Other titles: You are not done yet
Description: First edition. | New York : St. Martin's Press, 2024. | Includes
    bibliographical references and index.
Identifiers: LCCN 2023038136 | ISBN 9781250283238 (hardcover) |
    ISBN 9781250283344 (ebook)
Subjects: LCSH: Parent and adult child. | Parenting. | Adult children.
Classification: LCC HQ755.86 .H533 2024 | DDC 306.874—dc23/eng/20231106
LC record available at https://lccn.loc.gov/2023038136

Our books may be purchased in bulk for promotional, educational, or
business use. Please contact your local bookseller or the Macmillan
Corporate and Premium Sales Department at 1-800-221-7945, extension
5442, or by email at MacmillanSpecialMarkets@macmillan.com.

First Edition: 2024

10 9 8 7 6 5 4 3 2 1

To Earl and life's meaning in growing together
and growing up as we raised our sons.

—B. Hibbs

To the memory of my beautiful son, Julian Edmond Rostain, whose presence on earth brought joy and love to his family and friends. He will live forever in our hearts.

—A. Rostain

Contents

PART ONE

The Age of Uncertainty

INTRODUCTION

A New Era for Parents

> Negative Capability, that is, when a man is capable of being in uncertainties.
> —*John Keats (1817)*

SCOTT AND ELAINE MILLER, A COUPLE IN THEIR FIFTIES, WERE FRUSTRATED when their twenty-six-year-old refused their entreaties to get help. Early on in the Covid pandemic, Tyler lost his job and returned to his parents' home to live. Online gaming soon filled his time, while his persistent lack of motivation to look for a job gradually eroded his parents' warm welcome. Their concerns about his stalled progress led them to seek guidance. In our offices, they told us their stories, underscoring recent disagreements and mutual discouragement.

The Millers typify many of the uncertainties and challenges that today's parents and young adults confront, even before a global pandemic interrupted all of our lives.* Parents who have been intensively involved in their children's lives face a predicament following the end of K–12 schooling. On the very cusp of their adolescent's young adulthood, and arguably the most decisive decade of their life, the roster of expert advice evaporates, leaving parents adrift. This guidance gap mirrors the enduring but outdated cultural storyline that adulthood starts at eighteen—when children are up and out of the nest, off to a job

---

* The stories and names of clients and their family members have been modified, and other identifying details changed, to preserve privacy and confidentiality.

or college and the rest of their life.[1] Paradoxically, the longest stage of parenting unfolds during these years: the mature relationship between parent and adult child. While once a parent, always a parent, today's young adults are increasingly turning to their parents for needed support to deal with the numerous tumultuous transitions in their personal and professional lives. In our era of stunning advances and rapid disruptions, developing a tolerance for uncertainty can enrich decision-making and build needed resilience for parents and young adults alike.

The years between the ages of eighteen to thirty carry the weight of great hopes and exhaustive parental preparation, leading up to a young adult's claim on a fulfilling and satisfying life. This stage lays the foundation for completing education, obtaining a job and settling into a career, living independently, finding a partner, and becoming a parent—what sociologists have defined as the five markers of adulthood. Yet there is no magical age for becoming an adult. It's neither the eighteenth birthday nor the twenty-first; not college entry or graduation; not the first "real" job or even the once-defining thirtieth birthday. Parenting now extends well past these milestones. Adult maturation is a process with false starts and detours along the way. Invalid notions about when adulthood begins only amplify parental worries. During this decade-plus of emerging independence, parents may house their young adults and also assume the roles of financiers, emotional sounding boards, and even career advisors. These days, the generational baton-pass into adulthood takes longer than it used to. Whether pleasantly surprised or mildly alarmed by this unexpected extension of parenting, parents discover that they're not done yet.

Like the Millers, today's parents contend with many uncertainties: "Why is it so hard for kids now, and why are they taking so long to grow up? We did so much to support them. Did we do too much? Why are more young adults anxious, depressed, or discouraged? I'm not sure what we're supposed to do anymore. Let go? Be there? It can't be normal. We don't understand." And still others ask, "Where do we go for help?"

THE GUIDANCE GAP

This book addresses the dilemma that parents face and fills the guidance gap. We offer parents a game plan that provides reassurance and constructive direction when things don't go as smoothly as planned. The majority of books about twentysomethings focus almost entirely on the young adult's struggles, giving parents the courtesy of a walk-on role, often cast in sadly familiar tropes: hovering, overbearing, and even harmful, from whom the young person must recover. We aim to debunk and discard these stereotypes as we emphasize the shared generational mission: completing a child's complicated developmental transition to adulthood. We extend a helping hand to both generations. You can become a partner to your young adult; your relationship can allow for a component of friendship that is welcome to you both.

That helping hand begins with a new definition of normal parental involvement, because young adulthood now is markedly different from what parents experienced during their own time.

THE NEW NORMAL FOR PARENTS

For the first time in over a century, parents and families have returned to the position of primary safety net for their young adults. The default position for half of young adults—from eighteen through their early thirties—is multigenerational living in their parents' home rather than with a spouse or partner in their own household.[2] Yet parents often feel a bit sheepish acknowledging the extent to which they are helping. Likewise, young adults are embarrassed to admit how much financial and emotional support they need and receive from their parents, as if it were a sign of immaturity. However, the centuries-old historical record reflects the reality that parents have always helped their children gain a firm footing in adulthood. Whether it's a hundred years ago or today, parents giving their young adults help is not only sometimes necessary but also common, even though it goes against our long-held assumption regarding the normal, on-time arrival of full adulthood. This assumption contributes to the current reluctance by parents to talk openly about their level of assistance. They anticipate judgment from the shaming court of popular opinion, which is equally disparaging of the overinvolved helicopter or child-centered parents, as it is of their dependent kids-turned-young-adults. Both older and younger generations need to more freely ask for input and guidance, receive healthy support, and strengthen their connections. Rather than blame or stereotype, we reveal the complicated realities behind the skewed generational portrayals.

When you talk to parents, you'll hear a blend of silver linings alongside concern and frustration:

- "We're not empty nesters—we're open nesters, letting them come and go."
- "It was rocky through the college years until they got jobs. Then we enjoyed having them at home, where they could save money."
- "We argued about how much dope he was vaping. We worried, 'Was it stress, depression, poor coping, or a phase he'd outgrow before it got worse?'"

These comments are sprinkled with complicated questions:

- "What advice should we give them for major life decisions?"
- "What does it take to get a good job? Is it still college, or on-the-job skills training, or online certifications?"
- "How do we help them get back on track? Are they ever going to grow up?"

In a similar vein, ask a group of twentysomethings about their generation, and you'll detect a high degree of closeness with their parents.* When living independently, they text or call their parents frequently and are often grateful for their financial backup. Many who return home to live aren't thrilled with what can feel like a regression to childhood dependency. As we'll show, this doesn't need to be the case. Their parent-child relationship can grow up too.

Though appreciative of parental support, many young adults express cynicism about their own futures and the world they've inherited from the "OK boomer" and the "not-woke" Gen X generations. They are understandably defensive about stereotypes of their slow "adulting" and are well aware of their tags. In classrooms they were "snowflakes" and "excellent sheep" who required trigger warnings before some discussions. In the workplace, they became the norm-defying, goblin mode, Big Quit and Quiet Quitter generations, with decidedly different expectations than their bosses or parents.† In turn, they

---

* Given the morphing shape of families today, our use of the term *parents* throughout this book refers to any adult who has raised a young person. The term includes biological and adoptive parents; relatives such as grandparents, aunts, and uncles; and other parenting figures such as stepparents, foster parents, and close family friends.
† Throughout this book, we'll use the following approximate (and overlapping) birth years to delineate the four generations we'll be discussing the most: baby boomer, 1945–1965; Gen X, 1966–1979; millennials, 1980–1995; Gen Z, 1996–2010. Definitions are from Sarah

sometimes make jarring accusations of societal and economic burdens that their parents' generations have shifted to them.

Problematically, each generation holds stereotypes of "What's wrong with kids today?" (the parents ask) and "You've ruined everything; we inherited your mess" (the kids assert). Because cross-blaming increases in times of large-scale social change, today's families need to do even more to improve communication.

To develop mature parent–young adult relationships, parents can initiate change and relate more collaboratively by moving from correcting to responding, from talking to listening, and from offering unsolicited advice to becoming a safe sounding board. These shifts enable young adults to seek parental guidance when needed and build upon their autonomy and competency. But when a bump in the road becomes a young adult's off-road excursion, parents may be challenged as never before to know how to help. We'll explore how parents can be a guide and help their young adults manage these uncertain times and avoid the sometimes-costly mistakes of early adulthood. As family systems therapists, we have advised many parents and young adults alike who are confused by the unexpected changes and who lacked the support they needed to chart a path ahead. We're here to share those stories and solutions with you.

WHO WE ARE

We are well-established national experts in lifespan psychiatry and in family psychology. Dr. Rostain has devoted his career to fostering resilience in vulnerable youth and their families and made it his mission to find solutions for youth and parents alike. He is a department chair and professor of psychiatry and pediatrics at Cooper Medical School of Rowan University with expertise in treating youth with neurodevelopmental disorders. He's also professor emeritus at the University of Pennsylvania, having cochaired the President's and Provost's Task Force on Student Psychological Health and Well-Being. Dr. Hibbs has dedicated her career to intergenerational family ethics in her roles as psychologist, family therapy supervisor, educator, and author. Together and

Brown, "How Generations X, Y, and Z May Change the Academic Workplace," *Chronicle of Higher Education*, September 17, 2017, https://www.chronicle.com/article/how-generations -x-y-and-z-may-change-the-academic-workplace/.

separately, we have helped parents and young adults cope in demanding and crisis-laden times.

As parents of nascent adults, we've had front-row seats to observe the changes and challenges posed to both generations. Our children taught us what we didn't know about how much harder growing up had become and how youthful anxieties and the pressures of college and its alternatives, jobs, careers, and even romantic relationships had swerved from the expectations of the prior half-century. Our deep thanks to them, from whom we learned to embrace the experience "You're not done yet."

Across our religious, cultural, and familial differences, our own childhoods belong to an era of economic stability and safety. Childhood was more free-wheeling and carefree, for kids and for their parents too. Our divergent passages to young adulthood, amid social and political upheavals, shared comforting commonalities. Unlike today, a middle-class job used to be equally attainable with or without a college degree. A college education was affordable. Few questioned the labor market value that a degree would hold or whether it would afford a "good life." The way it was for us is not how it is for youth today.

We will bring our personal perspectives and professional experiences to bear as we return to the Millers. We'll revisit this family at various places throughout Part I of the book, as they epitomize a variety of intergenerational concerns, to which we provide practical strategies, support, and hope. When their conflict reached a peak, the parents, Scott and Elaine, consulted us for help with Tyler. We proposed a family therapy session. This was more than Tyler's problem—and would take a team to solve it.

THE MILLERS: THREE'S A CROWD

When we first met the Millers, Tyler's anger at his parents was apparent. While avoiding their eye contact, he told us that he was furious with them for making him the problem. His complaints echoed many of his generation. "I'm sick of them harping about how I'm wasting my time online and why don't I get a job." He fumed, "They just don't get it. I can't even get a living-wage job with my college degree. My generation got screwed. You guys wonder why we're so stressed? For starters, there was 9/11, where we watched over two thousand people die on TV with hourly replays; then we got to practice shooter drills in our 'safe' schools; then we saw polar bears starving from climate change; then the economy collapsed—again. Then Covid. So if we'd known the headlines really meant 'News flash: your future will get worse,' we might have been better prepared. Today's a lot harder."

After a pause, his mother, Elaine, murmured sympathetically, "Honey, this will get better, I promise."

Tyler snapped, "Mom, stop trying to bright-side this."

"Don't give your mother that," his father, Scott, said. "What? I should say, 'I'm sorry for how hard your mother and I worked to provide for your comfortable childhood and college'? Give me a break."

Predictably, their exchanges devolved into a heated crossfire of blame and accusations.

Compounding the family tensions, the parents disagreed about what to do. Scott accused Elaine of babying Tyler, while Elaine discouraged Scott from his tough-love threat to show Tyler the door. Elaine was in danger of enabling Tyler's stall through understanding alone, while Scott issued ever-expiring deadlines.

It was evident from the session that both parents and son had significant changes to make. Our work with them would entail best practices for productive conversations, challenges to their generational expectations, and encouragement to rethink their stereotypes. Parental shifts would precede and facilitate Tyler's acceptance of changes he needed to make and support his motivation to rebuild his adult life. They could resolve their differences and promote sturdier family relationships. We began with their contradictory stories about normal young adulthood.

Rethinking Our Stories

The Millers believe three different versions of what's normal, what's gone wrong, and who's to blame. Tyler's story is of outdated expectations and broken promises for achieving adulthood; Elaine's story is of a worried mother, her son's source of emotional support, who questions their parenting; Scott's story is one of a father who provided more for his son than he ever got and who faults Tyler for not "growing up." Each generational view is limited by its singular perspective. Despite their differences, both generations agree that young adulthood is not shaking out as expected. It's not normal. No one told them that reaching adulthood today is more difficult.

The stories we tell ourselves attempt to make sense of and protest changes that we don't understand. The contradictions between generational stories create stereotypes and tensions that inevitably lead to confusion and unhappiness for both parents and their young adults. Parents may second-guess their child-rearing practices when their young adults have not hit the big five adulthood markers. Or they might fault their kids. Young people, too, may either blame themselves for falling behind on "adulting" or accuse the older generations of screwing up their chances. In the tug-of-war between the competing views of who's at fault, something's gotta give. So, do we need to change the kids, the parents, or their stories?

Each family's story is different, each person's perspective is unique, and like the Millers, each family's efforts—no matter how ineffective—must be understood and respected.[3] Yet a single story told from only one generation's perspective is polarizing and precludes our understanding of the other's experience. We advise parents and young adults alike to combine their perspectives and incorporate the partial realities that each story holds. Toward this goal, we nudge each generation to rethink their approach, regulate their reactions, and build their resilience to ambiguities. That begins by considering a broader explanation to the question "How did we get here?"

How Did We Get Here? It's Not All in the Family

Parents and young adults themselves face a problem much bigger than family communication. In a recent Pew survey, young people (eighteen to twenty-nine years old) and adults over fifty were asked if young adults today have it harder than their parents' generation did. The younger group overwhelmingly affirmed that it's harder to buy a home, save for the future, and pay for college. The older respondents were the least likely to say these measures were harder for younger generations to reach.[4]

These generations have had very different experiences of young adulthood. In the 1950s, sociologists defined the classic markers of adulthood. The numbers tell the story. From the late 1940s through the 1980s, between 65 and 70 percent of young adults reached the five adult milestones in their late teens or early twenties or, at the latest, by age thirty.[5] In 2020, only 24 percent of young adults, by age thirty-four, had completed the adulting marathon of "finish your education, get a job, live independently, settle down with a partner, and become a parent."[6]

If we interpret these facts according to the ethic of American self-reliance and individualism, we have the perfect setup to censure the shortcomings of the younger generation. Rather than assuming that our first conclusion is correct, let's remain open to additional information. The numbers themselves exist within a historical context. After all, it's been seventy years since sociologists time-stamped adulthood markers. They are long past their expiration date.

Historians of family life remind us that our beliefs about the past are often idealized. The way we wish it were is usually how it never was, the rough edges of the good old days gradually eroded by time.[7] An account of the post–World War II years provides an explanation for why becoming an adult was relatively easy in the United States from the mid-twentieth century through the early 1980s. That period coincided with a unique national growth blip. While much of Europe, Japan, and the rest of Asia were rebuilding from WWII, the United States reigned as the world's dominant manufacturer and political superpower. Living wages and middle-class jobs were plentiful—and most required no college degree. For many young adults, an early marriage and parenthood were the norm and the ticket for leaving home. Although this thirty-five-year period of exceptional economic boom is the extreme historical outlier of an early and straightforward path to young adulthood, that era continues to influence our current beliefs. It's past time to change the clock on our expectations for "adulting."

A New Era and a Shared Story

A shared generational storyline expands our understanding behind the numbers. The likelihood that most twentysomethings will have a predictable, undeviating path to adulthood is inconsistent with current economic and social realities. The 1980s heralded a turn to growing inequalities and harsher competition that crashed into the twenty-first century in what first seemed a once-in-a-century storm, only to be followed by others.

Our young adults have witnessed and grown up with shock after historic shock: terrorism brought home by 9/11, the 2008–2010 financial crisis, a global recession with a flat-line recovery, political extremism at home and abroad, the transformational breakthroughs of the information age, and the era-defining effects of the Covid-19 pandemic. Although many parents took a hit from these universal events, the future economic, mental health, and educational damages more deeply affected twentysomethings than they did other groups. Young adults at the start of their lives and careers will carry the aftereffects far longer, resulting in delayed adulthood goals.[8]

In an unusual twist, the financial vulnerabilities of this period impacted both generations. Parents and young adults suffered long-standing labor market insecurities. The brunt force fell on the middle to lower socioeconomic classes, as well as on women and minority households. Along with heightened caregiving demands and financial liabilities, parents had fewer social and health-care safety nets. The insidious creep of these factors landed most heavily on parents born in the late 1960s and 1970s and then on their children, today's twentysomethings.

The long-playing impact of these socioeconomic and health threats have converged with mental health concerns. The kids are not all right. Neither are their parents.

Mental Health: The Kids Are Struggling, So Are the Parents

Prior to the pandemic, the term "youth mental health crisis" was in common usage and denoted a sharp and decades-long rise in anxiety and depression. With the pandemic's onset, a high percentage of young adults dropped out of college or failed to enroll due to online learning difficulties or the need to financially support their families. Others quit or lost their jobs. Gen Z sustained the highest number of job losses across the working generations.[9] Their collective loss of a purposeful life, combined with peer isolation, contributed to a historic incidence of youth mental health problems and substance abuse. The urgent need for mental health services for this generation is recognized as a trend for years to come.

Often overlooked in our concern for youth mental health is the parallel consideration: How are the middle-aged parents doing?* Their mental health has also gotten worse. Their seeming generational ease (less educational debt, more job and housing security) is contradicted by the large numbers who are experiencing historically greater declines in their mental health, even more so in the U.S. than in other high- and middle-income countries.[10] Post-Covid, their situation doesn't seem to be improving. In December 2022, 37 percent of Americans rated their mental health as only "fair" or "poor," up from 31 percent in 2021.[11]

---

* We are using the traditional definition of middle age for parents from forty to sixty-five. At this writing, it includes those born between 1957 and 1982.

The worsening mental health trend among the parent generations has multiple causes brought on by two core challenges: changing intergenerational dynamics and financial vulnerabilities. Intergenerational dynamics have converged to exponentially expand parents' caregiving responsibilities.[12] During the harrowing early years of Covid's onset, from 2020 to 2022, middle-aged parents bore two crucial caregiver roles. They prematurely shouldered the emotional, social, and medical-advocacy needs of their locked-down, aging parents amid death, medical scares, and reduced social support. Concurrently, they experienced the second challenge of financial insecurities. Job losses befell both parents and their young adults. Despite this, middle-aged parents provided a wide safety net for the delayed and lost educational, social, financial, and career opportunities for their young adults. The opportunity losses took a heavy emotional toll on both generations. One mother commented on her daughter's setbacks, "It's heartbreaking to watch," and a young adult tearfully commented, "I know my parents are worried about me. They have reason to be." Parents' caregiving roles included mental health assistance to both older and younger generations. Their individual heroic efforts occurred while most of them continued full-time jobs.

HOW THIS BOOK CAN HELP

You're Not Done Yet picks up the trail of expert and practical guidance for parents and their young adult children. We show how to strengthen your relationships, drawing on our decades of clinical experience and applying our knowledge from family theory, social science, clinical science and practice, and firsthand interviews. True-to-life vignettes illustrate how to break free of unhealthy patterns of thinking, feeling, and acting.

This book addresses the many uncertainties that beleaguer parents today. Why did an entire generation of young adults depart from the supposedly normal model? When did the markers of adulthood shift? Why did they shift? How does the thinking and framing of individual and familial perceptions, beliefs, and behaviors shape our relationships? What societal forces and family patterns do we need to understand and change to become better parents and to better guide young adults?

Whether your young adult has experienced relatively smooth sailing or rough seas, you are still their guide to a safe harbor. You may be understandably perplexed about what expectations are reasonable and what constitutes sufficient support when you no longer know what's normal. You and your adult child need a new storyline for normal young adulthood and, in parallel, practical guidance.

Our prescription for parenting young adults in an age of uncertainty invites both generations to accept a nonlinear path to adulthood. We refute outdated beliefs about normal and take the pressure off young adults and parents alike. Before considering the personal dimension of your relationships, you'll want to recognize that your concerns may reflect the trends of our times and the common misinterpretations of generational differences. We ask you to rethink the stereotype of parents as neurotic enablers from whom young adults must recover and to reconsider the bias that delayed young adult milestones reflect a generational character flaw. As you reflect on your own family situation, we will provide plenty of practical tips for managing challenging conversations, as well as for coping with transient or more serious mental health concerns that arise during this time of life.

This book underscores the importance of healthy family dynamics that counterbalance recent and rapid societal changes and provide a safety net for the enormous developmental challenges ahead. Parents who have relied on formal and informal guidance to boost their child's outcomes now wonder how to thread the needle between just enough but not too much help and for how long. There is a new normal for young adulthood and a new opportunity for parents to deepen and strengthen their relationships with their young adults for this longest era of parenting.

How This Book Is Organized

In the chapters ahead, we make suggestions to parents to support the multi-year process of a young adult's autonomy. We organize the book in two parts. Part I offers a framework to promote your understanding of the changed realities for young adults. We begin by redefining their new normal. Next, parents take the lead by rethinking generational biases and stereotypes. You'll learn about different kinds of thinking: open mindsets and closed mindsets. Along the way, you'll gain an important lesson from how children think and add it to your own adult repertoire.

As we move from individual understanding to interpersonal relating, we embrace a new era of parenting: parents as collaborative partners to their young adults. When parents witness the growing pains, miscues, surprising decisions, and sometime desolation of their young adult, it's hard not to relapse into old advice-giving ways. We offer tips for parents to manage their understandable distress. Both generations can learn to relate more effectively and then enjoy the closeness that emerges.

Part I concludes with a chapter on the changing world of credentialing and jobs. Covid's seismic shocks have altered traditional pathways in education and employment. As more young adults question the social-mobility dream that college has long held, parents want to help. We follow five families as they discover new educational and career pathways.

Part II of the book takes you behind the scenes to the lives of parents and twentysomethings who have stumbled over commonly experienced mental health challenges of delayed executive functioning, anxiety, overuse of screen time or substances, and depression. Through true-to-life vignettes, we'll help parents and young adults discern when delays in adulthood are the result of temporary and age-related problems and when they are indicators of mental illness. We hope to better prepare today's parents and those of tomorrow—who are facing the rising youth incidence of anxiety, depression, and preventable deaths. Education about mental health and stigma reduction is key to prevention, treatment, and recovery. We'll offer strategies for parents and their young adults as they strive toward the mental well-being needed for the increased demands of adulthood. Part II concludes with resources to help parents and young adults identify when, how, and from whom to get help. Beyond the usual parental tropes to be understanding or practice self-care, we offer practical skills.

Why We Wrote This Book

Most advice books encourage parents to step back—as if the problems for young adults will be solved if parents don't hover or shower with praise. Whatever your child-rearing style was, a young adult's self-sufficiency always benefits from healthy family dynamics. Though individual lives are complicated, we are convinced that by daring to challenge old assumptions and ways of relating, you and your young adult will discover effective ways to support their progress in our complex society.

We share a deep interest in helping both generations. Parents and families, who are tasked with so much, remain at the heart of the concentric circles of support for their young adults. Our goal in writing this book is to connect and empower parents as their adult children build the resilience they need to reach autonomous adulthood. We thank the many young adults, parents, and educators who so generously lent their stories to this book. We owe a debt of thanks to the many families that we have treated and learned from. We feel privileged to have been part of their lives.

We hope to speed and smooth your path and to create the best possible relationship between you and your young adult. Despite geographical or emotional distance, fraught disconnects, or loss, parents and children share a deep bond. Your relationship is entering its longest phase yet. *You're Not Done Yet* builds a sturdy bridge across generational differences while strengthening emotional connections. We're on the same mission. You are not alone.

1

The New Normal

Time to Reset Your Thinking

> If you truly want to understand something, try to change it.
> —*Kurt Lewin*

KURT LEWIN, THE 1940S FOUNDER OF MODERN SOCIAL PSYCHOLOGY, DIDN'T HAVE parents' expanded role, generational stereotypes, or this book in mind, yet his timeless aphorism aptly sums up our task.[1] To understand the new normal for parenting young adults, we must first evaluate, understand, and then possibly change our thinking. Formerly, parents relied on their own young adult experiences to adequately guide their twentysomethings. But the recent size and scope of economic, social, and pandemic disruptions has profoundly influenced the expectations of parents and their young adults alike. We begin with the thorny question of what we mean by *normal* and why we care so deeply about it.

WHAT'S *NORMAL*?

Look around. Things are definitely not what they once were for young adults. Six years is the new four years to attain a college degree.[2] A college degree no longer guarantees a living-wage job. Financial independence often means living with roommates and eating ramen to manage student debt. "Text me when you get home" is the new umbilical cord. Marriage, if it occurs, is postponed and may be decoupled from parenthood. Many of these socioeconomic and cultural changes that delayed full adulthood were underway long before the pandemic. Without a path to the "good life," young adults now run a gauntlet of uncertainties and find themselves in a bind of either trying against the odds or—as our friend Tyler was doing—not trying. And like Tyler, twenty-somethings no longer refer to themselves as adults but consider themselves kids who poke fun at "adulting."

Beyond the misery of Tyler's floundering, his story acquaints us with a generational reality. Some of this parent-and-young-adult struggle isn't new. The transition from adolescence to adulthood has often been fraught with anxiety, especially in times of economic strain. The third decade of life has long been recognized, written about, and bemoaned by its current inhabitants as one of the most tumultuous periods of life. One young man summed up the general consensus: "The twenties are like the hardest online game of *Elden Ring*. You play it but only understand what you've done wrong in hindsight. It's fun but punishingly hard. There is no guide. You learn by making costly mistakes." Paradoxically, most of its tasks sound joyful—make your own money, get your own place, date and partner up—even enviable in the abstract.

So in this hardest game of young adulthood, what do we even mean by normal? Its definition depends on which expert you ask. Statisticians explain normal as a distribution of scores in the usual range—such as the average for a particular population. Doctors refer to a disease model. Mental health professionals talk about culturally accepted behavior as an indication that a person is mentally healthy and has no psychological disorder. Historians who study family life remind us of the past cultural, societal, religious, and moral expectations for intergenerational relationships. But when parents are wondering if their child is normal, they most want to hear from an expert on child development.

Earlier, parents turned to pediatricians for reassurance that their child was on track. Eventually, though, teens outgrow their pediatricians. Parents also looked to educators to tell them whether their kids were on target academically and socially. Parents once assumed that a college degree implicitly confirmed that their work was done. Presumably, diploma in hand, the young adult was ready for prime-time adult life. The truth is parents are not done. Normal has lost its center.

Let's try another set of experts for an understanding of normal—twenty-somethings. According to one young adult, "Normal is nothing more than the average of man's eccentricities." Another jokes, "Normal is just a setting on a dryer," while a young man ridicules the premise, "No one has a normal childhood. There is no such thing as normal." These young adults haven't read Freud, but their answers express his century-old assertion that normality is "an ideal fiction" and that "every normal person, in fact, is only normal on the average."[3]

Parents are not so glib. They care deeply about a child's expectable, safe trajectory to maturity. It's in their job description found on page one of evolution's survival guide: "Protect your child from danger and raise them to thrive." Of course, today's dangers are rarely the mortal illnesses or diseases that claimed the lives of so many children in the premodern millennia. Yet, our brains do not read textbooks to detect danger but to scan our bodies. When our brain senses heightened physical distress, it triggers a fight-or-flight rush of adrenaline that creates a long and sustained release of the stress hormone cortisol. High levels of cortisol are linked to parenting stress, which begins to increase in expectant and new parents and boosts their responsiveness toward infants. Just the "right amount" of cortisol keeps parents alert for problems that they may misinterpret as dangers. A parent's elevated level of cortisol persists throughout childrearing, rising more during the adolescent years and then, if all goes well, slowly ebbing in the transition to young adulthood.

The parents of twentysomethings remain on alert, wondering: *If normal is no longer normal, and if I'm not done yet, then what am I in for?* Worrisome stress can signal a slow leak in a parent's own resilience. One mom fretted, "I was looking forward to being an empty nester. But we didn't even get five years between their college graduations and needing to help my elderly parents." Parents might also resent the unexpected extension of the two-decades-long tour of duty. One dad protested: "I didn't sign up for this." Another added: "What if we aren't prepared to be there emotionally or can't finance another decade of support?" A young adult's delayed independence translates into an individually borne emotional and financial burden for their parents, whose own tasks of middle age are deferred.

We share a secret hidden in plain sight: *Normal* is difficult to define. Chasing normal does little to help us guide our twentysomethings into full adulthood. Despite our best efforts to be good parents and to help our children flourish, we can achieve only a partial measure of control, no matter how much we try. Rather than pressure ourselves or our kids even more, we might release ourselves from the stressful performance-driven striving for normal and send youth a reassuring message: "You will be okay, even if you weren't accepted by your dream college, even if that special job didn't work out, and even if your original life plans haven't materialized yet."

But even if you or your adult child wants to believe this message, even if your own experiences bear it out, embracing future uncertainty feels like a leap of faith, perhaps a foolish or even dangerous one. You are contending with both the conscious and the largely unconscious resistance to change—a change that could upend your beliefs about what's normal in young adulthood—and middle-aged parenting.

The search for the new normal takes us to the first of five resets to our thinking. We begin with the premise that normal is on a continuum and sometimes it's okay to not be okay, no matter your age.

Reset 1: Defining a New Normal of Emerging Adulthood

The phrase "the new normal" isn't new. It was first used to describe the period of societal settling following the crisis of World War I. Over the next hundred years, the new normal has repeatedly tagged postcrisis eras: the September 11, 2001, terrorist attacks; the 2008 financial meltdown and global recession; and the Covid-19 pandemic. Recent and repeated societal and economic upheavals have impacted the realities of young adults and their parents.

In today's new normal, our first reset requires accepting a developmental progression in young adulthood that is not mired in the past. This new developmental stage is flexible and dynamic, with interludes of dependence and independence. It also has a new name—*emerging adulthood*.

Psychologist Jeffrey Arnett defines emerging adulthood as a stage between adolescence and adulthood. It is as an in-between period of delayed adulthood that features multiple job changes, career restarts, and deferred decisions about marriage and children up to and often past age thirty.[4] The delays of better-resourced twentysomethings are often on behalf of prolonged education with ongoing financial reliance on parents. Young adults with limited access to these opportunities typically experience milestone delays due to insufficient education or skills training. In either case, emerging adulthood is no longer age-defined by stable, linear markers. There is no clear rite of passage but rather a highly individual experience where adulthood relies on the subjective feeling of self-sufficiency.[5] Yet advice to parents about how to respond to the stops, starts, and stalls in their young adult's progress has been limited. Even the guidance that does exist is confusing and even contradictory.

For many years, parents have been encouraged to help their young adult grow up by letting go and have been chastised for being too involved. Now they're being advised, "Hold tight; they're not ready yet." Parents grapple with a range of topics influencing their involvement and relationship with their young adult children. Who's to say what advice to follow? Popular opinion, even expert opinion, has become a support-your-own-bias hunt that ultimately questions both a parent's choices and their motivations. For every talk-show guest, op-ed writer, or researcher who says that young people need more parental support today than they received historically, there are others who advise us to beware of our smothering tendencies and who mock egregious examples of helicopter parenting, which was once viewed as a corrective to the prior generation's more hands-off style.

Our advice? Don't fault yourself. It's a confounding time for parents, because much of what affects all our lives is beyond our control. What we can control is our response to unfolding events and uncertainties and how we relate to each other.

To gain clarity, allow yourself to ask deep questions about your general assumptions and beliefs about young adulthood. Among the broad questions you might ask are these:

- How different are my adult child's experiences from that time in my life?
- Do I need to give them more parental or adult guidance than I got?
- Do I think of my adult children as kids or adults?
- Do I judge myself, or them, if they're not flourishing?
- Is this delay in growing up a period of self-discovery—or self-indulgence?
- What signs of progress should I expect to see?

There are no one-size-fits-all answers. For now, allow yourself some understandable confusion. Chapter 2 explores how these aspects of emerging adulthood play out in the daily lives and challenges of parents and their young adults. The shift from old beliefs about adulthood to new information about emerging adulthood takes us to Reset 2: how we make up and change our minds and our beliefs.

Reset 2: Making Up and Changing Our Minds

Once we've made up our minds, it's hard to change them. As parents, we must make up our minds about what's good for our children. Our parenting beliefs inform our decisions that become rules for the basics of bedtime, nutrition, table manners, behavior, and grades. Later, we make age-appropriate determinations for chores, screen time, and smartphone use. By the time a child becomes an adolescent, parents set new rules for curfew, driving, dating, and alcohol use, among many others. Educationally, parents make decisions that are scattered throughout the childhood and teenage years. Over time, parents gradually ease up on their rules and trust that their earlier guidance and their implicit values have taken hold. With all these decisions, parents make up their minds and rely on their beliefs.

Yet we only have to look back a few decades to see that certain beliefs, regarding what children need and what parents should do, are changeable. We pivot from "Babies should be picked up and coddled" to "Let babies cry it out and self-calm." We've exchanged "Children should be seen and not heard" for "Listen to kids so they'll talk to you." We've reframed "Video games are harmful" to "Video games can be okay and promote social bonding." More recently, we've debated striving for the brand-name college against "Performance stress is the path to burnout."[6]

These shifts in attitudes clearly show that our beliefs are not absolute truths but rather rest on a particular construction of a socially shared reality. We often think of reality in the cause-and-effect terms of physics. The apple falls from the tree to the ground, according to Newton's law of gravitation. Physical reality is predictably stable. Social reality is not. Social reality, or the relationships and understandings among people, is a communicated and inherently unstable belief construction. Yet when people make up their minds, they call it reality. Polarization and mistrust often result when people argue their conflicting versions of reality. Family life is the proving ground for the ability to talk about and resolve our differences, rethink our misunderstandings, and strengthen our relationships. But how do parents and young adults constructively discuss, or even consider, opposing beliefs when they've made up their minds?

When the Mind Is Closed

When your mind, full of firm beliefs, is made up, we call it a mindset. The very term *mindset* contains the word *set*, suggesting convictions, thoughts, and ideas that are resistant to change. Mindsets matter. Mindsets inform our understanding of others and shape our behaviors that underpin all of our relationships, including our relationship to ourselves. Though most of us enjoy novelty, when it comes to how we organize our thinking, individuals prefer the consistency of familiar, predictable beliefs. We are comfortably stuck. When our beliefs are fixed, we're less open to entertaining other perspectives. We have a *closed mindset*.

The upside of a closed mindset is its efficiency. We arrive at one answer (or belief) and can stop looking for another answer. The downside to this efficiency is a learning trap that abruptly halts the exploration we need for creative problem-solving. Closed mindsets are vulnerable to distortions that reduce reality to all-or-nothing thinking. People with closed mindsets cling to unevaluated, rigidly held beliefs that are often self-defeating.

Returning to young adulthood, one example of a closed mindset is the belief in a linear, on-schedule arrival to adulthood. When parents and twentysomethings hold on to this color-by-numbers, age-based mindset, the likely result is disappointed expectations. This closed mindset, which is most often based on a parent's own experiences, leads to an unrealistic anticipation of a similar time line for their twentysomething. When reality falls short of expectations, a closed mindset makes things worse for both generations.

For instance, when a young adult flubs a test, the closed parental mindset settles on its first fault-finding answer: "You didn't study enough." Closed-minded thinking does not allow curious or empathic exploration. Our closed-mindset reactions can feel reasonable in the moment, though they may neither meet the goals of improved family relationships nor support a young adult's competencies. Instead, a parent's open-mindset response in this example might be: "Gee, that's tough. What do you think was going on for you?" The young adult then has a chance to share: "I studied, but I got so nervous that I blanked on some answers."

Closed mindsets, though quick to react, are not always critical or blaming. Parents may overreact protectively with increased control and monitoring of a young adult's progress. Parents may also reflexively urge their children to "fail forward" for success and turn mistakes into future stepping stones. While the good intention is for growth, it goes awry when a parent's feedback is limited to achievement markers (grades, scores, and accomplishments) over mastery and learning.

Authors Belle Liang and Tim Klein describe the emphasis on achievement as a closed, performance mindset.[7] It incentivizes children and young adults to minimize mistakes rather than learn from them. Instead of fostering resilience in a changing, increasingly competitive world, the performance mindset sends the message that success is a zero-sum game—you only win by beating others. This pressured focus often backfires by generating anxiety and depression in emerging adults, especially in those who are already struggling.[8]

Returning to the Millers, we see how their closed-mindset approach results in Tyler's resistance. Early on in the family therapy, his parents led with pressured advice or judgment. "You need to get a job and move out. Smoking this much can't be good for you." And just as predictably, Tyler reacted furiously: "Even with a crummy job, I can't afford to move out. And don't you think I know that smoking is poison? But at least I enjoy it. Just leave me alone."

Knowing what his parents expect hasn't motivated him. Though their expectations (if not their presentations) are reasonable, their performative pressure has backfired. Feeling valued only if he measures up to their standards, Tyler feels worthless, becomes more defensive, and angrily disengages.

We introduced them to an open-mindset approach, with conversational tips to avoid meltdowns. They needed both prevention and repair skills. Prevention relies on respectful, open-ended questions that show curiosity rather than judgment. Repair skills include naming feelings, asking for time to calm down, and owning up to blaming or critical responses.

**OPEN MINDSET TIPS FOR CHALLENGING TALKS
WITH YOUNG ADULTS**

- Ask open-ended questions that show curiosity.
- Remember that unsolicited advice is often unwanted.
- Give the benefit of the doubt.
- Ask questions in a nonjudgmental and respectful manner.

Now using an open-mindset approach, Scott asked Tyler, "If you're willing to talk with me about your job loss, I promise I won't give unsolicited advice. Can you tell me what it's been like for you?" Tyler replied, "It has been really hard to be dependent on my parents again."

When parents relate with an open mindset, they show appreciation for the courage it takes for a young adult to own up to their difficulties. In this way parents instill the valuable life trait of conscientiousness, or taking responsibility for one's actions.[9] This parental approach, known as positive parenting, combines high warmth and low psychological control[10] while incorporating rules with reasonable expectations.[11]

Even when a parent or young adult has an initial knee-jerk reaction, they can repair their misstep and get back on course with a few repair tips.

REPAIR TIPS

- Name your feelings: "I feel pressured. Can we take a time-out?"

- Own up: "I'm sorry that I got agitated."

- Show appreciation: "Thanks for being willing to talk with me about this."

Yet changing a closed mindset to an open mindset is easier said than done. Let's explore what's involved.

When the Mind Is Open for Business

When mindsets are flexibly open, we can hold certain beliefs while remaining open to new information. An open mindset incorporates beliefs that are adaptable to evaluate new or complicated material. We welcome challenging feedback to better guide decisions. The ability to evaluate our thinking promotes the creative exploration of ideas and solutions. The reset to an open mindset—which seems like a simple thing to do—is to just be open. Yet Einstein's insight reminds us that no problem can be solved with the same level of consciousness that created it. An open mindset requires a different level of thoughtful awareness.

Remember, we are deeply invested in our beliefs. And change can feel especially threatening because loss precedes gains. You must lose your existing closed system of thinking and organizing experiences before you can gain an open mindset with a more nuanced way of thinking. For that reason, resets to what we think and believe are initially disorienting and distressing.[12] We turn to early childhood for an example that is quite familiar to parents.

The "terrible twos" illustrate the process of a developmental tug-of-war between losses and gains in closed/open self-awareness. This stage earned the prefix "terrible" because of the tantrums of *No!* However, they can become the terrific twos when we understand the remarkable cognitive growth manifested in a child's battle to cling to the closed-minded but reassuring and fixed belief in their own omnipotence. It's a "world revolves around me and my needs" mindset from infancy. Cry and you get comforted. Cry and you get fed. Fuss and you get jollied. Though short-lived, it must feel like being the center of the universe. However, soon it comes into conflict with a toddler's growing awareness of separateness from their parents. When a child emerges from this earliest mindset, they have lost the belief in their sense of ultimate power, gained a more complex understanding and control over their impulses, and accepted the self as an individual who can now make their needs known verbally. In the bargain, they protest, then learn their parents' limits.

This incredible evolution allows for a more realistic understanding of the world. That's what developmental-stage change is: a self-evolution in awareness. A leap in self-awareness is repeated when a child of five or six first grasps the concept of secrets. Another advance occurs with an adolescent's growing self-reliance and sometimes-rebellious autonomy from parents. Beyond adolescence, advances in self-evolution and open mindset are voluntary.

Beginning in young adulthood, into middle age and later, neurocognitive development is no longer biologically driven. You must decide to be open to take in new information, to reevaluate, and to possibly change your mindset. In that process we can expect to experience anew the terrible twos of distress at the loss of our old set of beliefs, followed by remarkable gains in our conscious awareness.

Before we see how mindset change works in family life, let's attempt mindset change by rethinking generational stereotyping. In times of profound and rapid change, members of the older generation are not as prepared as they would like to be to offer constructive guidance to young people. Instead, they may resort to a closed mindset that stereotypes the younger generation. The third reset invites you to practice open-mindedness as we evaluate true generational differences from stereotypes.

Reset 3: Becoming Open-Minded About Generational Differences

Generational differences do exist and accrue with age. The problem lies with stereotypes that misinterpret these differences. This reset asks you to be open-minded as we search for accurate explanations of generational differences. No doubt you're familiar with the most common generational stereotypes: Gen Z:

#Materialistic and #TechSavvy. Millennials: #Adulting and #MillennialProblems. Boomers: #OKBoomer and #ClimateChangeDeniers. One journalist suggests that Gen X gets off easier because they're a small group and "so irrelevant that people can't even be bothered to hate them."[13] But beyond the misinterpretation of differences and eternal gripes about each other, the perpetual resistance of older generations to the changing of the guard, and the younger generation's resentment of them, what's the problem with generational stereotypes?

Negative stereotypes emphasize differences and lead the generations to blame one another rather than solve mutual and pressing problems. An example of this is the very close alignment between older and young generations regarding their shared concerns about the climate.[14] If this fact surprises you, you've fallen for a polarizing belief, hardened by negative generational stereotyping that only the younger generations care about climate change.

We turn to expert British social researcher and author Bobby Duffy to help us sort generational truths from stereotypes. He explains that there are three factors that explain generational differences: period effects, life-cycle effects, and cohort effects.

1. Period effects are experiences that affect everyone, regardless of age. The Covid-19 pandemic is an example.
2. Life-cycle effects refer to changes that occur when people age. For example, our natural hair color changes to gray or white with age. Life-cycle effects are also seen in developmental milestones, such as leaving home, getting married, having children, and retiring.
3. Cohort effects describe the attitudes, beliefs, and behaviors common to people of a particular generation. For example, younger generations are quicker to accept changing cultural norms pertaining to race, immigration, sexuality, marriage, and gender identity. They are early adopters of new technology and innovators in current fashion trends, hairstyles, and musical tastes.

Yet, seen through the lens of divisive generational stereotypes, everything is a cohort effect. It makes an ageist disinformation sweep that ignores period and life-cycle effects. Not long ago, academics were the only ones who studied age-cohort differences. Now they're a marketing ploy—a shorthand way to communicate trends to promote products and brands targeting specific age groups. Over and over again, we fall for clickbait stereotypes to explain our generational differences. Why?

Clickbait gives us the quick feeling of truth with simplified, lazy but age-cohort explanations of our differences that are better attributed to the historical period or developmental life-cycle effects.[15] Today's feeling-based labels go viral with the boosts they get from social media. Catchy hashtags and partial truths are tough to dispel. The stickiness of stereotypes relies on thinking that what I *feel* makes it true. But feelings are not facts. Resetting generational biases is key to open-minded communication, as it focuses us on our commonalties and shared understanding.

Regrettably, most of us carry negative stereotyping into our family relationships. Let's look in on the Millers and observe their efforts to evaluate their generational stereotyping and change their closed-mindset beliefs to better guide Tyler.

The Millers Work to Reset Their Mindsets

In couples sessions focused on parenting, we encouraged Scott and Elaine to reconsider their ideas about what had led to Tyler's stall and what might help. We were inviting them to change their minds. Mindset change initially entails confusion, defensive rejection of new information, and frustration. Scott and Elaine have turned on each other and doubled down on their differing beliefs. Their resistance to change was evident as the shame-blame game commenced.

"We didn't do enough," Elaine said to Scott. "We were too busy to have consistent family meals. I didn't spend enough time with him. You didn't, either."

"Hold up there, Elaine," Scott said. "Times were hard when I was that age too, and I figured it out without running home to Mommy. I don't get why he's so stressed, except that you overindulged him. You're still doing too much for him, like those helicopter moms. Time for you to stop babying him and making all these excuses. Tyler and his generation of whiners just aren't interested in growing up."

Elaine gets him back, replying, "If I was hovering, it was to counter your Tiger Dad. We know how well that worked."

Elaine and Scott hold implicit "hers and his" stereotypes in the ping-pong of cross-blaming. She blames him for not spending enough time with their son and Scott for being too harsh; Scott blames her for coddling Tyler and blames Tyler and his generation for their struggles to get adult lives. Blaming is a toxic brew, whether it bubbles up in a marriage or in a parent-child relationship. It creates defensiveness, which prevents the self-awareness necessary for mindset change. The couple is stuck in a closed mindset that precludes creative problem-solving and signals their sense of helplessness. They don't know what to do. The trio of shame, blame, and helplessness is a barrier to an open mindset. Defusing this dynamic will be a crucial reset in our upcoming sessions with Scott and Elaine.

As the Millers' struggle illustrates, a mindset change involves taking a close look at your family relationships. That change can begin with open-ended self-questioning that emphasizes our efforts, minus the judgment: "In hindsight, what have I come to understand about my child, now young adult? What have I learned about myself as a parent? Were my expectations a reasonable match for their educational and employment goals?" These questions often have complicated and uncomfortable answers. We encourage you as a parent to step away from guilt feelings, blaming stereotypes, or recriminations and choose the openness that allows you to learn from your reflections. Becoming open to new information can also include understanding how wider societal changes have altered once-stable patterns in young adult development and in parenting.

The Millers are among millions of others in the United States and worldwide who were impacted by societal forces outside of their control that amplified the stressors on both twentysomethings and their parents. Our fourth reset takes you behind the scenes to our offices, where we observed the impact of societal disruptions that changed the course of normal for parents and youth.

Reset 4: Understanding the Disruptions

We first observed a significant uptick in the frequency and intensity of parental anxiety in our clinical practices in the late 1990s. We were accustomed to seeing worried parents with children and adolescents in tow. American parenting has typically pulsed with more anxiety than its European counterpart.[16] Still, the universality of parental stress, across a wide class and ethnic strata, felt palpably different to us. Soon the signs of stress were apparent in children and adolescents as well.

Early on, we reassured parents that they didn't need to sweat the small stuff—such as whether they allowed sweets, set strict bedtimes, or let their child play games online. We weren't bright-siding these worries; we were simply telling them about the research of renowned psychologist and philosopher Alison Gopnik, who reports, "It is very difficult to find any reliable, empirical relation between the small variations in what parents do . . . and the resulting adult traits of their children."[17] Parents do play a significant role in enduring trait development that contributes to a child's life success—such as personality, intelligence, and conscientiousness—but not through focusing on the small stuff. Yet, as we scratched the surface, we understood that parents' anxious efforts to control the small stuff covered their growing uneasiness about the large-scale changes that they could not influence.

With increased awareness and urgency during this period, parents sought mental health treatment for their kids. "Do they have ADHD [attention-deficit/ hyperactivity disorder]?" parents would ask us. "Or a learning difference? A neurodevelopmental delay? Are they on the autism bubble? Is their worry an anxiety disorder? How problematic is my child's screen-time use?" Next up came their concerns about their adolescent and college-aged students: "Is their substance use abnormal? Has their dieting gone too far? What happened to our competent kid who came back from college depressed?" As we listened to these parents, we wondered whether there was a contagious effect of stress and anxiety between the generations. And was it a one-way street or a feedback loop?

By the time the Millers consulted us, we were well aware of the profound historical changes that brought them to our offices. What was once considered normal for young adulthood had come unmoored from the lived experience of three generations. Many young people were scared that the promised path to the good life would slip from their grasp. They were disillusioned, if not cynical, anxious, or depressed, as a result of their experiences of delayed adulthoods. With self-deprecating humor, these young people captured adulthood with memes like "Adulting in 456 easyish steps."

Neither generation understood why youthful hopes, dreams, and expectations had suddenly become so much harder to reach. The world today is radically different in certain ways, even from the recent past. There are increased demands on parents and a rise in youth mental health problems. The widespread and persistent generational anxieties coincided with wider gaps between have and have-not lives and fiercer competition for scarce resources. A unique, postindustrial, information-age economic shift was underway that resulted in health, wealth, and educational inequities. Public opinion mistook the headwinds of this once-in-a-century storm for generational causes that stereotyped parents and youth alike. Two predominant stories took hold.

Two Generations, Two Stories

One story blamed the neurotic helicopter parent whose child-rearing style overprotected, overscheduled, overvalued, and so thwarted their child's emerging autonomy. The second narrative cast an entire generation as the #MeGeneration of entitled kids and excellent sheep who were unable to manage their lives. To counter the bias toward pathology, we thought of a benign explanation. Perhaps there was a shared storyline that reflected a rationally anxious parent who senses danger and becomes more fearful and protective of their child, who in turn feels more pressured to gain access to the narrowing path to the good life.

As the storm warnings grew, negative generational stereotyping became even more deeply ingrained. By 2000, "helicopter parent" was a commonly used pejorative. Despite being stereotyped, parents continued to exert more and more control over young people's lives. Middle and high school counselors, along with parents, joined in the growing chorus of concern as mental health problems were detected at younger ages. Alarms blared with reports of drastic increases in mental health problems and suicides on campus.[18]

By 2010, colleges across the country had ramped up their counseling services, only to find that they could not staff their way out of the mental health epidemic. In addition to increased treatment outreach, the focus shifted to prevention through wellness programs, mental health apps, text help, and telehealth.

Soon we began to hear from more parents who sought help for their floundering young adults. Instead of easing, the stressors on young adults and their parents only intensified after college graduation. Though better educated than any prior generation, they were also underemployed, if employed at all. So many U.S. college grads returned home to live with their families that by 2014, they had acquired the nickname boomerang kids. The same phenomenon was observed in all of Western Europe and other high-income countries.[19] "What's wrong with their lack of motivation?" parents asked us. "How much help should parents give? When will they grow up? When should we show them the door? We did all the right things; how did things go wrong?" The answers were lost in the fog that preceded the storm's landing.

A Fog Settles In

It was as if a dense fog had settled into the flight path of young adulthood, delaying the scheduled arrival by nearly a decade. There were conflicting and accusatory explanations for the delay that defied the expectations of the prior half-century. Despite parents' best efforts to get it right and provide a good foundation, their twentysomethings entered a crowded waiting area with other young millennials, who were quickly joined by an influx of new arrivals from Gen Z, almost all accompanied by fretful parents. The long wait for the fog to lift was disorienting.

Then we saw it. An economic tsunami had been forming since the late 1980s. Invisible for decades, slowly creating for all but the very wealthiest, a true earnings nosedive. The downturn encompassed globalization, the loss of manufacturing jobs, debts incurred by lengthy foreign wars, the housing bubble, the global financial crisis of 2008–2011, rising student debt, and an ever-shrinking middle class. Time-honored blue-collar jobs no longer meant a living wage. Those without a college education, and racial groups and minorities who had experienced systemic bias, suffered the greatest losses. The tsunami crashed in on parents first, then on the younger generations.

The problems of twentysomethings came under closer public scrutiny. A news article from 2010 summarizes some of the changed habits of young adults: "The 20s are a black box, and there is a lot of churning in there. . . . Forty percent move back home with their parents at least once. They go through an average of seven jobs in their 20s, more job changes than in any other stretch. Two-thirds spend at least some time living with a romantic partner without being married. And marriage occurs later than ever."[20]

At the time, we believed that the global economic crash and recession was the era-defining shock-and-scar event that would shadow youth's entry into adulthood. And then Covid-19 hit.

The Pandemic's Big Reveal

As much of the world moved online and we moved to telehealth, our sessions bore witness to the home impacts of the coronavirus pandemic shutdown. At a personal level, families experienced overwhelming health vulnerability among older adults, while parents were stressed with juggling jobs and online schooling for their younger children. In parallel, young adults experienced significant educational and job disruptions. Covid's early lockdowns immediately compounded the unhealed scars of long-term wage stagnation and job loss, as it put health at risk for frontline workers. The amplification of economic forces, already burdening young adults, left them drifting into adulthood.

Although many larger trends preceded the pandemic, its global shock highlighted problems that deserve our understanding and focus. The pandemic years starkly revealed the flimsiness of young adult financial independence, as it normalized multigenerational living. The well-publicized return of young adults to the security of childhood homes was wrapped around job losses, college-enrollment declines, and dropouts. For the third year in a row (2020, 2021, and 2022), colleges experienced huge drops in attendance.[21] The largest decrease of 13 percent (at least one million fewer students in 2021 and 2022) came from enrollment at community colleges,[22] where the record number of 2022 job openings caused many to opt for work over a degree. Most who dropped out did not return but were saddled with debt. The Some College, No Credential (SCNC) population reached thirty-nine million as of July 2020.[23] Though educational hybrid and online models became more common, this change did not result in a better completion rate. Educational setbacks affected future earnings and the ability to pay off student debts, and limited the option of independent housing with a partner rather than a parent.

Many young adults felt unmoored as their parents remained on standby to provide continued financial and emotional support. Their years of careful planning for a young person's orderly progression into adulthood went unrealized. And what's to blame? We need only look at the rapid, chaotic changes that have taken place across socioeconomic, cultural, political, and health fronts in a single generation. The pandemic's impact will not be fully tallied or absorbed for years. Yet this universal trauma continues to resound with confusion and disorientation across the generations.

Facing these challenges, parents remain perplexed. Acting in the best interests of the young adult is a high-wire act. From parents who can afford to support a young adult's extended period of exploration, we hear a host of doubts: "When does our support tip into a floundering adulthood that creates a dependency trap? When should parents hold firm or pull back in order to meet their own midlife needs? When does setting firm limits inadequately protect young adults at a vulnerable period of their lives?" A wrong turn in either direction, with too much or too little support, can feel oppressively consequential. The ongoing challenge for parents lies in understanding what level of support is individually appropriate.

Just as there is no formulaic post-pandemic new normal, there is no uniform answer to "What should I do so my kid will be okay?" A parent's answer will be individually based on the resources, needs, limits, and values of both parent and young adult. The assessment of a young adult's need for support can be compounded with the emergence of a mental health problem. Our final reset asks parents to evaluate their beliefs and attitudes surrounding mental illness.

Reset 5: Recognizing Mental Health Concerns

Despite more involved parenting, mental health problems among young people have surged. One-quarter of the lifetime prevalence of mental illness occurs by age fourteen, when parents can still "eyeball" their child for signs of worrisome behavioral or emotional changes. By age twenty-six, 75 percent of the lifetime prevalence of mood and substance disorders occurs. Parents are understandably confused by how to discern transient and age-related mental health problems from those that are more serious. They often wonder how to help and when to intervene. Many parents whose teens were asymptomatic before they left home are stunned, if not in outright denial, by the young adult onset of a mental illness.

Unsurprisingly, a pandemic-driven spike in anxiety and depression significantly impacted the mental health of the younger generation amid their transition to adulthood. In 2020, cases of major depressive disorders for young adults increased globally by 28 percent, and major anxiety disorders by 26 percent.[24] A 2021 Pew Research Center survey reported high levels of psychological distress among 32 percent of eighteen- to twenty-nine-year-olds compared with the overall adult rate of 21 percent.[25] Covid's enduring emotional wallop, called the inner pandemic, refers to the long-term mental health hangover following remote education, workplace shifts, social isolation, loneliness, anxiety, depression, substance misuse, and stress.

Covid reminded us of what we already knew. Parents can neither control nor protect their young adults from setbacks. Yet parents can preventatively alert teens and young adults to the mental health problems that run in the family. Hopefully, a young adult will dodge a heritable mental illness. It helps young people to know what "runs in the family." Those who are educated about mental health, illness, and treatment are better prepared if they confront these concerns. The good news today is that Gen Z and millennials are often open to the crucial step of seeking help as they rely on their parents as an important part of their support network.

Curiously, despite the widespread interest in genealogy, we're much less inclined to have family discussions about our common heritable mental health problems or chemical and behavioral addictions. Perhaps it feels disloyal, as if we're throwing shade on a beloved family member or calling them names. We encourage you to get in touch with whatever sense of shame or stigma this reset brings.

Allow yourself the uncomfortable tally of emotional disorders on both sides of the family. Include family members, one or two generations back, who might have been thought of as "nervous, weird, a drinker, or downright crazy." In the recent past, mental illness was highly stigmatized, and unlike today, effective treatment was quite limited. The first step in getting mental health treatment requires a recognition of a problem, and then an accurate professional assessment. That first step was a problem for the Millers.

What Runs in the Miller Family

The Millers, like many parents, didn't see it coming. There were no warning signs. After all, Tyler hadn't lived at home for years. In an early parents' session, they reported that Tyler's adolescent and college years seemed relatively smooth. Or at least that's what Tyler presented, and what Elaine and Scott believed at the time. However, when Tyler returned home to live, they became aware of his pack-a-day cigarette habit, his excessive online gaming, his binge drinking, and his irritable and depressed mood. Like many struggling young adults, he resorted to age-typical coping behaviors: overconsumption of junk food, poor sleep patterns, procrastination, avoidance of challenges such as job searching, and increased screen time and substance use. In combination, the result was Tyler's profound lack of motivation to get going.

It's tricky to know what to do or say when you see signs of poor coping in your adult child. Before a problem can be solved, it must be talked about in a constructive manner. Sometimes a parent may feel more empathy by recalling times of their own poor coping, whether as a teen, a young adult, or even now. Parents don't have to approve of poor coping habits to extend a helping hand. Lectures about cringe-worthy habits won't accomplish your goal. Scott and Elaine Miller had learned that the hard way.

Shaking the Family Tree

To sort problem coping from a mental disorder, we take a routine mental health history. We call this "shaking the family tree." Most often, a combination of both nature and nurture plays a leading role in the drama of mental illness and substance abuse tendencies. We are preloaded with familial, heritable risk vulnerabilities, which can get activated by negative interactions at home, at school, or in the community during childhood through adulthood. Very often, parents like Elaine try to locate the cause of a mental health problem in the outside world rather than in the interior world of our genetics. Elaine wondered if Tyler's sluggishness could be blamed on the last blip to appear on their radar. "Is this Covid fatigue?" she hopefully asked us, wishing that Tyler's malaise would vanish with the virus. We affirmed that Tyler had sustained several economic and social setbacks that were precipitated by Covid and common among young adults. Yet we needed to rule out an adulthood onset of a mood or substance misuse disorder. We asked the parents to tell us about their family mental health history.

Scott, sounding offended, rebuffed the request, saying, "This isn't about some wacky uncle or cousin twice removed. We came to find out why Tyler is doing so little with all that we've provided." Scott's anger was interspersed by Elaine's defenses of their son's depressed and irritable mood.

The parents' initial reluctance to answer the routine mental health history signaled underlying stigma and a sense of threat. Assessing for heritable physical conditions doesn't carry the negative self-stigma for parents as their child's emotional illness does. A child's mental illness attacks a parent's very sense of self and creates fears that a child or young adult is not normal and will not be okay. Yet our brain's neurological wiring and neurochemistry are vulnerable to genetics and environmental influences, just as our bodies are. Complicating the diagnostic and treatment process, the environment isn't simply around us but resides in and between us, in the culture of family life.

Shaking the Millers' family tree meant examining any mental illness stigma, checking for unhelpful beliefs, and accepting the important parental role of emotional safety net and treatment connector for Tyler. Like each reset from a closed to an open mindset, loss is followed by gain.

Addressing the Millers' resistance to talking about their families' mental health histories, Dr. Hibbs validated their discomfort: "This is such a tough discussion for many parents, who worry, *What if it turns out to be something from 'my side'? Or maybe I see some of my younger self in his behavior?* Parents sometimes blame

Shaking the Family Tree

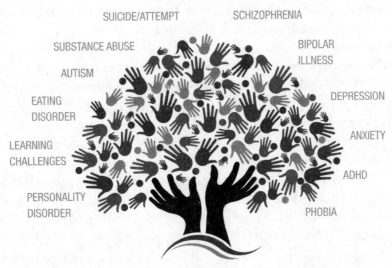

Consider the heritable genetic traits and mental disorders that "run" in the family when a young adult has concerning changes in mood, behavior, or coping.

themselves, or worry that the other parent will feel ashamed if it's from 'their side.' " Hibbs ended with this reassurance: "There's no judgment here. We're all on the same side of wanting to help you know how to help Tyler."

A long silence ensued. She'd hit a nerve.

Thus reassured, Scott and Elaine shared their histories. With a collective deep breath, they revealed the mental health problems that ran on both sides of the family: alcohol misuse, smoking, anxiety, and depression. Scott's father was a problem drinker, so Scott kept to a strict rule of two drinks a day. Elaine's mother was a chain-smoker before cigarette addiction was understood as an over-the-counter self-medication to cope with anxiety and depression. They thought these problems were in the past and so hadn't informed Tyler of his own susceptibility. We'll return to the Millers in Chapter 4 as they learn best practices to boost open-minded conversations with Tyler as he reclaims his independent adulthood.

Like Scott and Elaine, many parents are in denial about the possibility of mental illness when it's too close to home. They are dismayed when their formerly happy-seeming kid shows up deeply miserable. However fortunate our circumstances, we inevitably pull nature/nurture joker cards from our life deck. Setbacks in young adulthood, such as college rejections, being passed over for a desired job, or the loss of a friendship or romance can precipitate anxiety or depression. These early-adult letdowns are painful, yet with the encouragement of family and friends, we can recover from life's disappointing losses and boost our future resilience.

Occasionally, a depression may emerge in adulthood that seems disproportionate to the present situation. A recent event can tap into a well of unresolved painful memories. These are post-traumatic, time-lapse releases of childhood or adolescent experiences with two distinct pathways. One is event-driven, such as a one-time violent incident; the other is cumulative, caused by ongoing relationship problems. The event-driven-trauma pathway is akin to a severe blast of radiation; the other is like a prolonged release of low-level ionization. The lingering sights, smells, or memories of the most negatively adverse childhood events may arise from community or domestic violence, exposure to war, childhood neglect, sexual abuse, or the burden of racial and gender identity trauma.[26] Less obviously damaging is the steady drip of cumulative experiences that occurs within day-to-day relationships. For instance, being bullied in school, or at home, is more often a daily and chronic experience than a single event. The home environment, including parent, sibling, and extended family relationships, can contribute to a sense of safety or an experience of distress. That seems intuitive. Counterintuitively, even the commonly perceived good of years of academic achievement can add to the adverse-event count when there are ever-higher levels of continuous demands.[27] Fortunately, despite different trauma-induced pathways, there are effective treatments.

Whether the culprit in the story of a mental illness is shaped more by biology, environment, negative social media exposures, or life events, parenting is never done until these problems are identified, resolved, and treated. Part II returns to mental health concerns in depth with resources to help a parent recognize and respond to these stumbling blocks of young adulthood.

• • •

Dealing with uncertainty is our new normal. Today's youth, like the generations before them, share the eagerness of making it in the world, looking ahead to the future, and hoping to achieve dreams they've cultivated. As this chapter shows, the new normal no longer follows the more direct time line of earlier generations. The open-minded approach we've described here is what best promotes the resilience that each generation needs. We continue to build upon the resets of Chapter 1 throughout the book. With that in mind, Chapter 2 describes the characteristic features of emerging adulthood, as both young adults and parents grapple with its unexpected pathways. Two families bring these struggles to life and recount how they resolve their conflicts to navigate this unfamiliar era.

2

Emerging Adulthood
as a Developmental Stage

If we ever think of the freedom we possessed and have lost, the freedom for self-chosen tasks, for unlimited, far-flung studies, we may well feel the greatest yearning for those days and imagine that if we ever had such freedom again, we would fully enjoy its pleasures and potentialities.

—*Hermann Hesse,* The Glass Bead Game *(1943)*

WHAT WE TAKE FOR GRANTED ABOUT THE THIRD DECADE OF LIFE DOESN'T QUITE match up with what emerging adulthood is like in the twenty-first century. Times have changed, for better and for worse. In some ways, the generations have always been in conflict. After all, our own parents' lives were different from ours, and we were constantly reminded of this difference as we entered adolescence and challenged their transmitted wisdom about the ways of the world. If nothing else, adolescence is defined by the need of youth to challenge parental teachings and to figure things out for themselves.

But what happens during the next developmental stage? How do young adults go about preparing for and achieving independence and maturity? How much is universal about this phase of life, and how much is historically unique? As our children never cease to point out, we had no computers or internet when we were their age. We didn't have to deal with the Covid pandemic, and school shootings and climate change were barely on the radar when we were growing up. So how do we find common ground for talking with young people about the developmental challenges they are facing in this brave new world? In this chapter, we will review the salient features of emerging adulthood and, through case illustrations, learn how parents can adapt their mindsets to better support their twentysomethings as they navigate the rough seas of this important life stage.

EMERGING ADULTHOOD: FIVE COMMON FEATURES

Jeffrey Arnett, professor of psychology at Clark University, describes five defining features of emerging adulthood: identity exploration, feelings of instability, self-preoccupation, feeling oneself in between life stages, and a sense of possibilities (or general optimism about the future).[1] These defining aspects of young adulthood were derived from extensive interviews he conducted with eighteen-to-twenty-nine-year-old American youths in the late twentieth and early twenty-first centuries, which have been validated by other researchers.[2]

Identity Exploration

Identity exploration has long been recognized as the most significant feature of this age. Renowned developmental psychologist and psychoanalyst Erik Erikson observed that successful resolution of the crisis posed by this stage of life (identity versus confusion) requires young people to explore multiple social roles without committing to any one of them until they have achieved what they believe to be an authentic self-identity.[3] In Erikson's notion of a "psychosocial moratorium," society allows young people the freedom to defer taking on the responsibilities of adulthood: "The freedom for self-chosen tasks, for unlimited, far-flung studies," to which Herman Hesse alludes.

In today's harsh economic climate, when opportunities to explore without committing may seem too risky to many emerging adults, identity exploration may be prematurely curtailed. Young people may feel trapped or pressured into less-than-optimal roles or remain confused about their identity. Parents may unwittingly play into this dynamic by insisting that their young adults choose a career path by the time they declare a major in college. Most experts agree that it's extremely hard to find a firm career path by age twenty.

Feelings of Instability

A young adult's feelings of instability are related to the difficulty in defining a lifelong career path at this age. Emerging adults commonly experience a pervasive sense of vulnerability and uncertainty. They may appear indecisive and may behave in erratic and unpredictable ways, such as moving in with friends only to move out and return home for various periods of time. Your child may seem moody or touchy when you question them about their plans. According to Arnett and others, this behavior is quite normal.[4]

Self-Preoccupation

The self-preoccupation of young adults is considered a necessary component of this life stage because it helps them concentrate their energies on resolving their quest for identity. This self-focus, however, is often viewed by parents, teachers, employers, and others as evidence of immaturity, a lack of empathy, or narcissism. Their apparent self-centeredness becomes especially contentious when young adults are living at home with their parents, who may feel disrespected or mistreated. In our clinical encounters with youth and families, we often see this conflict between the adult child's necessary self-absorption and the parents' perception of it as disrespect. We'll address this issue further in the next chapter.

Feeling In Between

Across most modern cultures, young adults distinctly feel in between adolescence and adulthood. They recognize they are more responsible for their own decisions and actions than they were as adolescents, but they also know they haven't reached full adult status. They are not yet financially independent, they don't live on their own, a committed long-term relationship is still far off, and they have not yet become parents. This in-between feeling can be linked to ambivalence about growing up and may manifest itself through a lack of initiative in finding gainful employment, reluctance to move out of the family home, resistance to do household chores, or periodic regressions into adolescent risk-taking behaviors. However, we must consider another interpretation. Ambivalence may also reflect resignation about the new realities facing Gen Zers. Both parents and emerging adults agree that the younger generation will have a harder time affording an education, a home, and other necessities of adult life and will not be better off financially than the generation coming of age in the 1980s.

By resisting power struggles, which tend to worsen the young person's ambivalence and associated rebelliousness, parents can avoid making matters worse. As a rule, the more parents assume a critical and controlling stance, the greater the likelihood of negative reactions from, and constant conflicts with, the young adult child. Adopting a more neutral and dispassionate stance often helps the young adult resolve this stage of development.

A Sense of Possibilities

The final feature of emerging adulthood, the sense of possibilities and general optimism about the future, may no longer be broadly applicable to today's youth. Whereas a decade ago, the overwhelming majority (77 percent) of young adults agreed with the statement "I believe that, overall, my life will be better than my parents' lives have been," this attitude no longer predominates. An October 2021 poll by the Pew Research Center finds that 55 percent of eighteen-to-twenty-nine-year-olds say finding a job is harder for them than it was for their parents, 52 percent believe it's harder to find a spouse or partner, and 72 to 70 percent believe it will be harder to save for the future, pay for college, and buy a home.[5] Moreover, there are distinct class and racial differences in the sense of optimism expressed by emerging adults in the United States. Interestingly, a spring 2021 poll by the Harvard Kennedy School's Institute of Politics found that young adults' hopefulness about America's future was higher than in 2017 and that young adults of color were more optimistic than whites.[6]

At this moment, would you say that you are more hopeful or fearful about the future of America?

Percent who responded "hopeful"

■ 2017 ■ 2021

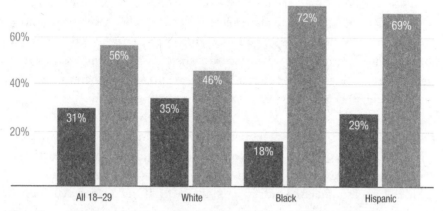

Source: Harvard IOP Youth Poll, Spring 2021, https://iop.harvard.edu/youth-poll/41st-edition -spring-2021.

Finally, young people's outlook on the future is closely tied to their personality profile. Researchers at the University of Florida studied emerging adults' view of the future during the Covid pandemic and identified two distinct personality types: forgers and reflectors.[7] These personalities had different outlooks. Forgers had higher conscientiousness, agreeableness, extraversion, resilience, gratitude, and internal control than did reflectors, who tended to be less assertive and more introspective and introverted. Not surprisingly, forgers reported a brighter outlook toward the future and had fewer concerns about the impact of the pandemic on their chances for a good life.

BALANCING UNDERSTANDING, EMPATHY, AND RESTRAINT

Why should we as parents understand these five features of emerging adulthood? First, they can remind us that the journey through this phase of life is neither linear nor smooth. If we reflect on our earlier selves, we can doubtlessly identify moments when the search for our identity was fraught with uncertainty, anxiety, disorientation, confusion, and even a sense of loss. Later in this chapter, we present an exercise to help you remember those unsettling times so that you can better appreciate what your twentysomething is now going through. The sense of being in between and the feeling of instability that Arnett and others describe is a commonplace aspect of our children's experience. To paraphrase Kermit the Frog, "It ain't easy being in-between." This insight allows us to situate their struggles in a broader context.

While we can certainly empathize with their difficulties with envisioning their future selves or defining their life goals, we must not overidentify with our children. Doing so risks our ability to stay as objective and as nonintrusive as possible. While young people may want to understand what it was like for us when we were their age, it's wise to wait until asked before sharing our experiences.

The same can be said for the numerous pieces of advice we are tempted to offer when we see our kids struggling with career choices, friendships, intimacy, money management, or the demands of life in the Covid world. Watchful attentiveness and mindful nonintervention are useful concepts to guide our responses.

SOME INSIGHTS FROM REAL-LIFE FAMILY CONFLICT

The following two clinical vignettes offer examples of how parents can apply the developmental perspective of emerging adulthood to accomplish the five resets that we outlined in Chapter 1: (1) redefine normal, (2) remain open, (3) refute stereotypes, (4) view things through a historical lens, and (5) recognize mental health concerns. Although the names and details have been changed for confidentiality, the counseling sessions are similar to the ones we conducted recently with clients. In the first vignette, you'll meet parents who take a second look at their biases and expectations for their son's career trajectory. The second family illustrates an important question regarding the distinction between normal development and a mental health concern. In each situation, parents learn an important lesson about balancing the impulse to help against the harm of controlling a young adult's emerging sense of competence and autonomy. In the process, both generations learn to tolerate the anxious uncertainty that is part of the emergence into adulthood.

John: College, Interrupted

John, age twenty-one, and his parents, Lynda and Carl, sat close together in their living room, shifting uncomfortably in their seats. This Zoom appointment was not something John was particularly looking forward to. In fact, as he made clear from the outset, he was only here because "My parents are threatening me either to get my act together or go back to college, which is a complete waste of time at this point." Asked to explain further, John described how he'd become completely fed up with online college classes that were not worth his time or his parents' money. "Covid has killed my enthusiasm for college," he exclaimed, "and my folks seem to think all I need to do is reenroll in school and everything will be fine. But nothing could be further from the truth. They just can't appreciate that everyone in my age group is turned off to college." With that comment, he glared at his parents and folded his arms across his chest as if to say "I'm done with all this."

"It must be tough to be sitting here against your will," we replied. "But given that you've decided to participate, perhaps you can say a little more about how you decided that college isn't for you."

John described how he had gone off to college about two years earlier with hopes of eventually applying to medical school. He found the premed courses—especially chemistry and biology—in his first semester to be very challenging. He had difficulty studying because he spent a lot of time making friends and hanging out with them, playing video games. He also found it hard to concentrate in the large lecture halls where his classes took place. To make matters worse, he began missing classes and avoided going to the recitation sections of his science classes. After midterms, he was given warning notices in chemistry and biology, something he never mentioned to his parents. Eventually, he failed those two courses and was placed on academic probation.

At this point in his narrative, John paused to look over at his parents, who were seated quietly and looking away from him. "I know you were upset with me for not telling you more about what was going on," he said, "but it's not my fault I didn't pass those classes. They were much harder than I expected, and the teachers weren't very good. You thought I wasn't trying hard enough, but that's not true!"

Lynda shook her head slowly and interjected, "John, we've been through this a hundred times. We don't blame you for having a hard time academically. We're just disappointed that you never trusted us enough to keep us in the loop. We might have been able to help you."

"Yeah, right," John said. "You claim you didn't blame me, but I don't buy that for one minute. Neither of you had any trouble in college, and you both got into medical school on your first try! You just don't get what it's like for me!"

After a moment, we offered John a suggestion: "Maybe it was hard to tell your parents about your struggles with school because you didn't want to disappoint them. And maybe you were disappointed in yourself because you had plans to go to medical school and these courses are mandatory. That must have been very rough for you to deal with. Please tell us what happened next."

John, now very engaged in the session, explained how he returned for the second semester of his first year, determined to study harder and to attend all his classes. Just as he was getting into the swing of things and learning how to manage the academic rhythms of college, the pandemic shut down his campus and he was forced back home to finish the semester. This sudden change of circumstances—leaving his friends, switching to online classes, and being in lockdown mode with his family—was extremely difficult for John. He disliked online learning, he became bored with the altered format and content of his courses, and he found it hard to stay motivated enough to complete his assignments on time. Missing his friends and the freedom and activities of campus living, he became increasingly annoyed with his parents and younger sister, who were doing their best to be cheerful in the face of the pandemic. Eventually, John dropped his two science courses and managed to pass his two other classes. Subsequently, his college strongly recommended that he take an academic leave of absence for one year.

John continued: "I was bummed out for most of the summer, but then I realized that since school was going to be happening completely online, I wasn't going to miss much on leave. It's fine with me that I wasn't in school, because none of my friends were enjoying their time in college. The worst part of it all is being stuck at home when I'd rather be hanging out with my friends. But I'm okay with things for now. I'm in no rush to get back. I've enrolled in an EMT [emergency medical technician] course, and it's a lot of fun. In a few months, I'll be eligible to get certified, and I'll be able to get a job. My biggest stress right now is that my parents disagree with my decision, and they want me to go back to college. I just don't see the point. It's my choice, not theirs."

We affirmed John's basic assertion, but we were interested in understanding more about why he and his parents were at odds. We turned to Lynda and Carl and asked, "So what's wrong with this picture from your point of view? What concerns you about John's plan of action?"

Lynda hesitated, but Carl jumped right in. "There's nothing wrong with being an EMT," he said, "but it's not a suitable long-term career for John. He's very smart, and he could easily get good grades in college if he gets motivated to study. We're convinced he's capable of doing more with his life, like being a nurse or even a doctor. He's just giving up on himself too easily. Lots of people have trouble in their first year of college and manage to find a way to succeed. He shouldn't sell himself short. We just want what's best for him."

What is going on with John and his parents? Clearly, he is not meeting their expectations to return to college and pursue a career they believe is suitable for him. The family has come for therapy because Lynda and Carl haven't been able to change John's mind and he hasn't been able to change theirs.

From a developmental perspective, John is experiencing four of the five defining features of emerging adulthood: He is *experimenting with identity formation* by trying a different path to adulthood than the one his parents would have him choose. He is *self-preoccupied* and feels "neither here nor there" (*in between*) since taking a break from college. For his future career, he is also *sensing many possibilities* that his parents don't yet recognize as valid or valuable.

For a better understanding of John's experiences, his parents need to consider four of the five resets from Chapter 1. They could reset their view of normal young adulthood (Reset 1) and learn to be more open-minded about John's approach to his future (Reset 2). They could also challenge the negative stereotypes they may have about how he and his peers are adapting to the current world situation (Reset 3). Finally, they'll want to better appreciate the historical context that's affecting him, including the Covid pandemic (Reset 4). We'll learn how John and his parents resolve this conflict following the next family's dilemma.

Amy: There's No Place Like Home

Amy, age twenty-three, and her parents, Julie and Brad, came in to discuss concerns about their older daughter's lack of close friendships. Amy is a college grad living at home and working as a receptionist and an administrative assistant at a local community health center. She enjoys her job but is considering taking graduate courses in health management to advance her career. Although she is friendly with people at work, they are all older than she is, and she doesn't socialize with them after hours. Apart from going to work, Amy seems content to spend time at home, reading books, checking her favorite YouTube channels, and watching TV shows.

"I guess you could say I'm a homebody," Amy began. "I've never really wanted to be anywhere else. When I was at college, I was homesick to the point where I came home almost every weekend instead of staying on campus. I got along okay with my roommates, and I had some friends, but I never felt all that comfortable being away from my family. As far as I'm concerned, things are going fine for me. I mean, I know I should have friends to spend time with, but it doesn't really bother me all that much. You could say I just like being alone more than hanging out with people. My parents are worried, though, and I suppose I could use some help with finding friendships. I don't know. . . ."

After thanking Amy for being so honest and direct, we commented, "It sounds like it's hard for you to feel comfortable in social situations. The social scene at college must have been a bit stressful for you. Can you describe more about what it was like for you?"

Amy frowned slightly and leaned forward in her chair. "I guess I just never felt like I fit in with the crowd. Most of the girls I knew enjoyed going to parties on weekends, and many of them joined sororities. I hate parties. They're just not my thing. They're loud, everyone drinks a lot, and people are just trying to impress each other. Unfortunately, at my school, parties are the main social event on weekends, which is why I preferred to come home."

We asked Amy how things went for her during the pandemic.

"I had no problem with it at all," she replied. "In fact, it was great because I got to stay at home, which was just fine with me. I got better grades in school, and I didn't mind being quarantined. It felt fine to be together with my family. We all got along well. I helped with the chores, and we had fun together playing board games, doing jigsaw puzzles, and watching Netflix movies. Isn't that true, Mom?"

At this point, Julie smiled and said, "Yes, it was relatively easy for us to be together during lockdown. Although I must admit, I was looking forward to you going back to school at some point. And your sister was miserable not seeing her friends and missing out on campus life."

We asked Amy to describe how she felt when the lockdown ended and she returned to college.

"It was awful," she replied. "I mean it. I just couldn't get used to being back at school.

"Everything was strange—people wearing masks everywhere and having to keep social distance in class. I got more homesick than ever, and eventually I decided to live at home and take all online classes. My academic advisor at school tried to convince me to stay on campus, and I even went to see a counselor at the student center. But nothing helped. I was so anxious that I couldn't concentrate on my classwork, and I couldn't fall asleep. I was having multiple panic attacks daily, so I requested a medical leave. Eventually, they gave me a medical excuse to take all my classes virtually. I ended up getting excellent grades that last semester."

We asked Amy if she feels she missed out on having a social life at college.

She replied, "I guess so, but it really doesn't bother me that much. I could've tried harder to make friends, but it just didn't seem worth it to try to fit in with the social life. I know my sister is very comfortable in social situations. She always makes lots of friends wherever she goes. But I'm different. I'm choosy about who I make friends with. I mean, I have two friends from school that I'm in touch with on Instagram, but I never get to see them because they live over two hours away from me."

We asked Amy's parents for their input.

Julie said that Amy always had a great deal of social anxiety and trouble making close friends: "She was very shy and fearful in new settings. Eventually, she'd find someone to talk to, but it wasn't something that came easy to her. When she was in middle school, she was afraid to speak up in class, and she went for therapy to learn how to be less fearful in social situations. We're pretty sure she was teased a bit back then, but she didn't really tell us much about it. We learned about it from her school counselor. In high school, she managed to find a few girlfriends who shared her interests in Harry Potter and fantasy fiction. She got together with them at their invitation but always drew the line about sleepovers. In fact, the first time she was ever away from home alone was when she went off to college. We weren't sure it was going to work for her, but she did manage to keep it together for the first few years. You could say Amy has never had a strong need for close friendships and she's used to doing things on her own or with the family. We're just concerned that as we are getting older, we want her to have a full life with peers instead of just hanging out with her parents. It's been hard to know how to get her to move in that direction, because she insists that she likes her life the way it is. So, that's why we're here. We need to figure out what more we can do to motivate Amy to explore friendships."

After a pause, Brad added, "We love having Amy around. She's a wonderful young woman. We wonder if she's lonely and just isn't telling us about her true feelings. We're not pressuring her to be someone she's not. We just want her to be happy." At this point, both Julie and Brad gazed at Amy, who was trying to avoid looking at them. There were unmistakably sad expressions on all their faces. We told them it was important for them to find a way to talk about this painful and complicated topic and that they'd come to the right place to do so.

Julie and Brad are seeking to understand Amy's pathway through emerging adulthood—a path that seems atypical for a young person her age. They are expecting her to develop close friendships, but she is not especially invested in this pursuit. She is exploring her identity in her own way and is somewhat self-preoccupied and ambivalent (in between) about her readiness to find meaningful relationships outside the family. Her parents need help with challenging their stereotypes about normal young adulthood (Reset 3). They also need to relate less anxiously and more collaboratively. Amy is quite resistant to their fearful concerns about her risk of having a mental health problem that may need treatment (Reset 5).

WHEN THE DEFINING FEATURES OF EARLY ADULTHOOD ARE STALLED

These clinical vignettes illustrate the complexity of family dynamics that unfold as young people face obstacles and detours in their paths toward adulthood. As we've already outlined, the milestones of adulthood in the current era include finishing one's schooling, launching a career, gaining financial independence, leaving home, forming attachments, committing to a partner, and becoming a parent.

But as much recent literature shows, even under optimal circumstances, the timing of these developmental signposts has been delayed by several years over the past few decades.[8] Today's parents can expect one or more of their children to be living with them for several years beyond the completion of college or other postsecondary education. The dual challenge parents face in such instances is learning how to coexist with their young adult "roommate" and figuring out how to provide support when they perceive their child is having trouble moving ahead in the quest to separate and individuate from the family.

Follow-Up for John: The Confidence and Freedom to Choose His Own Path

John's parents were primarily concerned about his decision to drop out of college to pursue an alternative career to nursing or medicine. They're troubled that he had opted out of the best path toward a professionally and financially fulfilling occupation. They were also worried that his initial setbacks in college convinced him that he couldn't succeed there, despite their beliefs to the contrary. Lynda and Carl saw it as their responsibility to challenge John's negative views of himself and convince him to go back to school. They feared that if he didn't return soon, chances were low that he would ever do so.

By contrast, John thought his parents were too negative about his decision to pursue EMT certification. He resented their insistence that he return to college, seeing them as controlling and as acting out their needs rather than his. He accepted their good intentions, but he was angry that they didn't accept his rationale for following this path. He believed that because Lynda and Carl were both physicians, they were biased toward other health-care workers. And he was upset with them for insisting he speak to mental health professionals, as if his choice were an indicator of a mental disorder.

From our perspective as family systems therapists, it's always important to approach this type of family conflict with compassion and respect for every family member. Each person has a valid reason for seeing the situation from their own vantage point. No one has a monopoly on truth. Lynda and Carl had a valid concern that John might not be making the best decision to forgo college for the moment. But John was justified in insisting that he—not his parents—should be the decision-maker.

Our initial intervention in this family's conflict involved reframing the discussion from one focused on right versus wrong to one that recognized the many paths toward autonomy. We acknowledged that John took the initiative to enroll in an EMT certification program, and we endorsed his wish to become a responsible adult who planned to make a difference in the lives of patients entrusted to his care. As Mark McConville, Ph.D., points out in his book *Failure to Launch*, becoming responsible is the first skill young adults need on their path toward independence.[9] They need to feel they are capable and are being taken seriously by others. John was disturbed by his parents' dismissal of his choice of career because this attitude implied that they didn't take him seriously.

On the other hand, Lynda and Carl were worried that their son was giving up on himself and believed they needed to persuade him to make another go at college. In their efforts to be encouraging, they were unwittingly heightening John's sense of vulnerability and shame for having messed up his academic record.

We finished our initial session with this family by telling them that all three family members were trying to do their best and that they needed to find a middle ground on which to discuss this disagreement. We recommended that they put the conversation on hold for a few months while John began his EMT training course. This way, he'd have the opportunity to see how he liked the work and how well he could perform in the program. Once this "probation period" was over, everyone would be more likely to look at the situation more objectively.

John, Lynda, and Carl returned three months later to report on how things had been going. John was doing extremely well in his EMT course and had already started going on ambulance rides with his program. His parents were impressed with his enthusiasm for the classes and the seriousness with which he applied himself to learning topics such as airway management, patient assessment, medical emergencies, and trauma emergencies. They were very pleased when John peppered them with questions about the material he was studying—their dinner conversations had taken on a positive tone as they heard about medical emergencies he'd been learning to manage. Clearly, they now saw John as responsible and capable. They'd spent time reflecting on their biases about his career plans and realized they were projecting some of their own needs and desires on John. By letting go of their narrative for him, they allowed John to begin to take charge of his life.

When queried about his plans, John replied that he hoped to finish his training course in a few months, work for a year as an EMT, and eventually return to college to resume his premed studies. "I love what I'm doing," he said. "I'm feeling more confident in myself, and I'm glad my folks have supported me in choosing this path toward my future. I know they were really worried that I was giving up on myself. But now they realize that I'm in a much better place to get back on track and find my way toward a medically related career."

Lynda and Carl nodded, big smiles on their faces. Carl added, "I'm so thrilled for John because he loves what he does, and he's so motivated to learn. It's a relief to see how he's taking charge of his life." We ended the session by emphasizing how impactful it was that John's parents had started to see him both as an adult who can make good decisions on his own and as someone who still valued their opinions and needed their support.

Follow-Up for Amy: Working on Relationship Skills

Amy's parents, by contrast, were extremely worried about her failure to form meaningful attachments outside the family. They weren't sure what to make of this situation or what they could or should do about it. On the one hand, they understood that their daughter had little motivation to go out and make friends. From all outward appearances, she was accepting of her solitary life and didn't seem concerned with finding a romantic partner. Yet at the same time, they wondered if her social isolation was based on social anxiety and avoidance of situations that made her uncomfortable. If that was the case, they wanted to see her learn to overcome these barriers and eventually find real friendships and even a romantic relationship. They were seeking advice about how to proceed.

Amy and her parents were stuck at an impasse that was difficult to comprehend and resolve. From Julie and Brad's perspective, their daughter wasn't reaching an important milestone of young adulthood and didn't seem to be especially concerned about it. They didn't understand why she wasn't bothered by not having friends, and worried they were overlooking what might be a treatable mental health condition, such as social anxiety disorder or avoidant personality disorder. They'd had concerns about Amy's social anxiety before, but their efforts to get her to talk about it had never gotten very far. And whenever they suggested that she reach out to friends and try to get together with them, she became indignant and defensive, as if they were accusing her of not making enough of an effort. It was clear to them that raising the issue of friendship caused Amy to feel bad about herself—a reaction they were loath to provoke. But after several years of unsuccessfully trying to get her to address this problem, Julie and Brad concluded they needed to push her (and themselves) out of their comfort zone. So they were seeking formal professional help.

Amy always found it hard to express her feelings and even harder to explain them. She readily acknowledged she was nervous talking in front of other people, but she also explained that she was used to feeling anxious and didn't really let it bother her "that much." She said she had enough friends with whom she stayed in touch, primarily online. She added that her parents didn't really understand that people in her generation usually stay in touch virtually rather than in person, especially since the start of the pandemic. When asked if she was at all concerned with her current level of social interaction with people her own age, Amy paused for a long while before answering. "I know I should have more friends," she said, "but I'm not as worried about it as my mom and dad are. . . ."

Here was the crux of this family's problem: Amy wasn't taking ownership of a vital developmental task of young adulthood—forming friendships, or "becoming relational."[10] She'd been acting in a socially avoidant manner. Her stance toward her peer relationships was one of passive acceptance rather than active engagement. She was too comfortable with the status quo, partly because trying to find close friendships risked her reexperiencing the hurtful interactions she experienced in middle school as a young adolescent.

Unfortunately, because social avoidance is negatively reinforcing, it is a difficult habit to break. Negative reinforcement is at the root of most socially anxious or avoidant behavior. A person minimizes the perceived stress of interpersonal encounters by avoiding them, and the feeling of relief maintains the behavior. Steering clear of other people leads a person to feel less uncomfortable. Keeping a safe distance had become a way of life for Amy. It was so ingrained that her lack of close friends didn't bother her "that much." This qualifier statement, "that much," suggested there was more to her social avoidance than Amy was willing to admit at the moment—but it provided an opening to a future therapeutic conversation.

In our first counseling session with this family, we decided to address this impasse between Amy and her parents. As we do with all initial family visits, we wanted to recognize the positive regard Amy and her parents had for one another, and their genuine concern about Amy's long-standing reluctance to make close friends. We first turned to Julie and Brad and thanked them for encouraging their daughter to come for this initial visit. We empathized with their desire for Amy to be happy and supported their wish for her to find a way to overcome her social anxiety. We turned to Amy and acknowledged her past hardships being teased by peers and being made to feel bad about her shyness. We noted her difficulties with fitting in with the college social scene and her cautious approach to meeting new people her own age, especially when she readily enjoyed being with her family and spending time alone. We recognized that she had made some close friends and developed generally positive relationships at work. And we recommended that she consider talking with a therapist about forming new friendships at some point in the future, whenever she felt ready to learn new skills and strategies to overcome her shyness.

We offered the family a follow-up appointment in six months just to check in and see how things were going. At that visit, we learned that Amy had started working with a therapist to help her overcome her social anxiety. She pursued this path entirely on her own, without telling her parents at first. While it was still early in treatment, Amy reported she liked her therapist and that she was about to start group therapy with other young adults who have social anxiety. Julie and Brad were extremely pleased that Amy had chosen to get help for herself. When asked what they thought was the catalyst for her decision to pursue treatment, Julie replied, "I really believe our family visit with you really helped us to get unstuck. Brad and I realized that it was up to Amy to figure this out, and we understood that no amount of prodding her was going to make a difference. Once we stopped being so anxious, Amy became determined to take things into her own hands, just like you suggested she would when she was ready."

Amy smiled brightly and added, "Yup. It's like I've always told you: Stop worrying about me so much. I can figure things out for myself."

MUTUAL RESPECT FOR BETTER OUTCOMES IN FAMILY CONFLICT

We chose these two vignettes to illustrate some common developmental challenges facing young adults whose families struggle with them on the young person's journey toward independence. Underscored in both these cases is the importance of including parents in the twentysomething's developmental journey, and how a brief intervention helped lead to a favorable outcome. Amy's and John's stories, however, are not typical of the more complicated situations we most frequently encounter in our work. Many of these young people are experiencing depression, anxiety, substance abuse, learning disorders, and other challenges. Our work with them and their family members requires a more sustained intervention. We will tackle these more involved circumstances in Part II of this book. For now, we'll look at some straightforward ways parents can improve their understanding of how their young adult children are working through this stage.

The Narrative Identity

The processes of identity formation and personality development are complex, multifactorial, and multidimensional. Emerging adults must formulate a vision of the future, come up with a life plan (or blueprint), design a method for implementing it, find the means to carry it out, and engage their significant others in this journey. Psychologist Dan McAdams proposes that a prime challenge for youth is to become the author of their own life story. They must construct a narrative identity that defines both who they are and how they got to be themselves.[11] This extremely complicated task is subject to the interplay of a person's temperament or disposition, early life experiences, family relationships, character strengths and vulnerabilities, and socioeconomic and cultural influences.

How does a narrative identity emerge? To better understand the process, you could start by exploring your own journey from adolescence through young adulthood. The accompanying "Reflection" box gives you a good way to start. By asking yourself the questions posed there and reflecting on your own life story, you can begin to grasp the enormity and complexity of developing a narrative identity. As you will discover by conducting this exercise, there are few easy answers to finding one's path to adulthood. Do you see any parallels between your life story and the one your child appears to be writing? What is similar and what is different about them? Are you comfortable with how they're tackling the challenges that face them? If not, what aspects are most troubling for you? What makes you so concerned about these?

REFLECTION: YOUR JOURNEY FROM ADOLESCENCE THROUGH YOUNG ADULTHOOD

- What were the major forces influencing your decisions as a young adult to pursue the life you're currently living?
- What key events were most significant in shaping who you are today?
- What was going on in the world around you when you were an emerging adult, and how did your views of the world affect your choices?
- How did family, friends, and romantic partners influence the paths you followed toward your career, your first job (or subsequent ones), your current partner, your place of residence, and your favorite pastimes?
- How close did you keep to your original life plans, and what made you change direction?
- What mistakes did you make along the way, and how did you rectify them?
- How much do you feel you've accomplished so far compared with what you had hoped to achieve at this stage in your life?

It should be obvious that there's no one-size-fits-all solution to the puzzle of "Who am I in this complicated world, and what do I want to do with my life?" As young people transform into adults, they must learn how to balance independence with interdependence, develop greater self-reliance, master new technologies, manage their time, develop organizational skills, and find motivation and persistence. They'll also need to practice decision-making, handle risk, face uncertainty, cultivate self-awareness, and find a sense of direction or purpose. But how can parents evaluate the progress their children are making along this curvy and hilly road to relevance?

Flourishing or Floundering?

One valuable concept about emerging adulthood advanced by psychologist Larry Nelson and colleagues is the distinction between *flourishing* and *floundering*.[12] When young adults are flourishing (positive adjustment), they adapt to changes easily; have healthy attitudes, good self-esteem, and successful relationships with peers and family; and avoid serious risk behaviors. By contrast, young adults who are floundering (have less-than-positive adjustment) have lower self-esteem, may show signs of anxiety or depression, engage in risk-taking behaviors, and have more troubled relationships with friends and parents. In their 2013 studies of emerging adult college students, Nelson and his colleagues found that roughly two-thirds of subjects were flourishing, one-fourth were engaged in risky behaviors ("externalizers"), and the remainder (8 percent) exhibited "poor adjustment." These last two groups showed signs of floundering. The "risk takers" and "poorly adjusted" subjects were more likely to be male, whereas the flourishing subjects were more likely to be female.

In the decade since this study was conducted, evidence suggests that the floundering group has grown from about one-third to roughly one-half of college students. Given the complexity of today's world, along with the seismic changes in society, many young people are, not surprisingly, struggling to come up with viable strategies that will guide them toward their goals and help them resolve their most difficult challenges.

In this struggle, parents can play a profoundly important role. By appreciating your child's strengths and vulnerabilities, by listening to what is on their minds, by learning about how they see the choices before them, and by respecting their need to create their own paths, you'll find ways to promote their progress from floundering to flourishing. As John's and Amy's parents discovered, young people need their parents to step back a bit and allow them to resolve their problems. This approach may increase your anxiety and take more time and effort than you would like it to, but you don't have to remain passive or totally disengaged during this important time of identity exploration.

In the next chapter, we invite you to improve your parent and young adult relationship by checking your generational biases. You'll learn to discern what *is* true from what *feels* true. It's time to become more open-minded.

3

Truth or Truthy

Rethinking Our Biases to Improve Our Relationships

Every man takes the limits of his own field of vision for the limits of the world.

—*Arthur Schopenhauer,* Parerga and Paralipomena

WE'VE ALL LAUGHED AT THE COMICAL MEMES AND SATIRES POKING FUN AT THE foibles of young and old alike. Yet, as we observed in the prior chapters, certain tensions between parental expectations and emerging adult realities arise from generational biases, not simply amusing or annoying differences. Cognitive biases, more commonly called stereotypes, can affix labels even before the establishment of adult identities. In childhood, Gen Zers were branded as digital natives. As teens, millennials were typecast as excellent sheep, striving and grinding for stellar GPAs, then material success. Gen Xers were pigeonholed as latchkey and apathetic MTV kids, while baby boomers morphed from hippies to the OK boomer climate-change deniers. It's all good fun until no one's laughing.

"Oh, c'mon—can't you take a joke?" "What's the big deal?" "Why should we care?" After all, we each mentally categorize others to help us understand how to interact with their category. We each see, think, and believe differently. The problem arises when we hold biased thoughts about a person due to the assumption that their category accurately describes them.[1] In parent–young adult relationships, it is especially important to relate as individuals and not as categories. Because how we understand and relate to each other determines how emotionally close or disconnected we feel.

For example, Ron, a Gen X parent, is relating to his son, Jay, as a stereotypical category. He typecasts him as a lazy Gen Zer: "I'm tired of dragging my twentysomething through the next steps in his life. I did it on my own. When I was eighteen, my dad dropped me off at the corner of University and Main, and said, 'Good luck. My job is done.' I never looked back to them for help. I earned my own money, made my own decisions, settled down, worked the same job for years, and had two kids. What's wrong with this generation that they think they have it so hard today?"

Jay believes that his categorization of his dad also accurately describes him. "My dad is clueless, just like the rest of that not-woke generation. He told me I had to go to college to get a good job. Some friends dropped out because of money. I stuck it out, but I've got loans and I'm underemployed. To get by, I eat a lot of peanut butter sandwiches and live with three roommates. I thought we were supposed to inherit a better world. My generation is told to get a life already, and in our spare time, be a Greta Thunberg and save the planet."

There are multiple truths in each story, whose disparate realities amplify misunderstandings between them. Ron's linear path to adulthood was typical of his generation; yet he has a bias that his son's unexpected delays reveal a flaw of generational proportions. To Ron's point, there are mollycoddled or demanding and entitled young adults. Jay's very different experience of young adulthood is full of difficult and distressing delays. From Jay's vantage point, his dad and that entire parent generation are simply out of touch with the times. The two understand each other through stereotypes. They've fallen into a bias trap.

Biases and their stereotypes first lure us in with an underlying feeling of truth. Then they trap us in a single story that precludes any other truth, or different experience, or perspective other than our own. Without a shared story that combines individual realities, we relate from polarized positions. In today's confusing times we're particularly prone to negative stereotyping, which provokes false conflicts. Unchecked, our familial bonds are drained of trust.

This chapter applies an open mindset to detect and correct the cognitive biases of stereotyping. We begin by understanding the hold that bias has on us, followed by a quiz to learn why people fall for quick and easy answers that feel true but create distorted beliefs and stereotypes. With this boost in our self-awareness, we think fast, then think slow, and finally take an important lesson from the beginner's mind of the child that helps us simultaneously hold multiple truths and perspectives. Conversations between parents and young adults will show us the "before and after" results of rethinking our biases.

BIAS IS HUMAN

We all have biases, some of which we are aware of—our conscious biases—others that lurk unknown to us—our implicit or unconscious biases. We often reduce and simplify our complex realities through biases. Our conscious biases are most easily identified, and usually tagged with an "ism": ageism, sexism, racism, tokenism, woke- and nonwoke-ism. Confirmation bias is the worst offender. Think of it as a "search and you shall find" mission to prove your idea, regardless of its objective validity. We seek and embrace information that supports our beliefs and reject contradictory information. While confirmation bias preceded the internet, social media amplified and accelerated its viral spread and speed.

Confirmation bias has a serious design flaw in what humans pride themselves most—the ability to reason and reach sound judgments. We are all guilty of a particular variety of reasoning that drives confirmation bias, or what cognitive scientists Hugo Mercier and Dan Sperber call the "myside bias."[2] "Try to see it my way" is the human tendency to want others to validate *my* side of things, even though we flunk the golden rule of offering the same. We are better at spotting the weaknesses in another's position than in our own. Myside bias allows us to remain oblivious or resistant to modifying our own mistaken reasoning.

Since humans pride themselves on their superior reasoning ability, why don't the facts matter when it comes to myside bias? Blame it on natural selection. Mercier and Sperber make the case that the trait of reason evolved within the small band of our hunter-gatherer ancestors. Reason did not evolve to bulletproof our thinking but to serve the social function of promoting cooperation and for individual survival. For example, the small group of prehistoric hunters, using primitive weapons, depended on the cooperation of several adults to take down a large animal and supply food for all. As an individual, you were willing to join the dangerous group hunt so long as other hunters were not lounging about doing cave painting. The cave painter might have protested the important legacy of art over group hunt; however, reason did not evolve to incorporate multiple perspectives. Natural selection favored the motivated reasoning flaw of myside bias, which has not caught up to the rapid changes of the past fifty thousand years.

Today, myside bias takes our feelings and hardens them into firm convictions. The tendency to accept an assertion that sounds right but isn't is called a bias trap. This trap supports our gut feelings in a predictable sequence. First, we *feel* that something is true; then we validate our feelings by searching for shared, if inaccurate, stereotypes that supposedly prove it's true. In 2005, talk show host Stephen Colbert humorously exposed the confirmation/myside bias and supported what neuroscientists and psychologists had proven in controlled experiments. He called the trap "truthiness." In an interview, he explained, "Truthiness is 'What I say is right, and [nothing] anyone else says could possibly be true.' It's not only that I **feel** it to be true, but that **I** feel it to be true. There's not only an emotional quality, but there's a selfish quality."[3]

Ouch. To avoid the selfish trap and overcome "myside bias," we amp up our reasoning power to "hold all sides" through perspective-taking. We first evaluate our beliefs for biases, then shed inaccurate stereotypes. We invite you to evaluate some common generational biases in the accompanying "Truth or Truthy?" quiz. Remember, to spot misinterpretations, we must separate what we *feel* is true from accurate, unbiased explanations. Hint: To better evaluate the assertions in the quiz, recall from Chapter 1 the three factors that affect generational differences.

THREE FACTORS AFFECTING GENERATIONAL DIFFERENCES

- Period effects are universal experiences that affect everyone living in one point in time.
- Life-cycle effects indicate changes that occur with age.
- Cohort effects are beliefs or behaviors of a particular generation.

TRUTH OR TRUTHY? IS YOUR BIAS SHOWING?

Read each of the following assertions, and without reading ahead, ask yourself if you think the statement is accurate. Is it True (a factual answer)? Or Truthy (*feels* true, but is inaccurate)? Then read the verdict.

Assertion: Baby boomers stole the younger generations' economic future.

Verdict: *Truthy.* The oldest generations are not to blame, but they have benefited from generational trends. Both life-cycle and period effects are involved. Each successive post-WWII generation has a gloomier economic outlook than the prior generation had. Until the 1980s, all incomes rose, and incomes in the bottom fifth of U.S. socioeconomic levels rose faster than those at the top. In the 1980s incomes stalled; then after the 2008 financial crisis, they fell, creating today's uneven concentration of wealth for the few. The causes relate to economic and political policies and a growing shift toward individualism.[4]

Assertion: Millennials (born 1980–1995) are narcissists and are overindulged by their helicopter parents.

Verdict: *Truthy.* The self-absorption of many millennials is better explained by life-cycle differences, which are age-related aspects of youth. Parents began to see signs of a harsher, more competitive world for their children in the early 1990s. The competition for the best primary school was described by one urban parent as "a gladiator contest."[5] Anxious and overprotective parents correctly assessed the socioeconomic dangers ahead.

Assertion: Gen Zers (born 1996–2010) are snowflakes who require special treatment, like emotional trigger warnings for classroom material. They are raised by overinvolved parents who know little about raising a child to adulthood.

Verdict: *Truthy.* Increased parental control over childhood resulted from: (1) life-cycle effects of the role shift to parenthood, which brings with it a need to protect offspring, and (2) period effects of widespread experiences affecting everyone. Parental anxiety also increased with the growing awareness of differences and treatable problems of childhood. Consequently, as informed parents sought professional assessments, more children were diagnosed with learning differences, ADHD, autism spectrum disorders, and anxiety. The rise in prevalence of neurodevelopmental diagnoses was not an artifact of overdiagnosis but the initiative of parents who sought help earlier. Culturally, widespread school shootings became the leading cause of death for children and teens, aged one to nineteen.[6] In response, parents exerted more control over their children's physical and emotional safety.

Assertion: Millennials and Gen Zers are fickle employees who quit jobs and don't work as many hours as prior generations did.

Verdict: *Truthy.* Again, there are some differences, but these are more to do with life-cycle and period effects than with fickleness. Younger people do change jobs more often than older workers do, but that has always been true. And younger people do work fewer hours, but as several observers have noted, "Working hours of all age groups have seen a long-term decline."[7]

Assertion: Millennials and Gen Zers are obsessed with material concerns. To quote psychologist Jean Twenge, author of *iGen*, young people today "are very interested in becoming well-off and less focused on meaning than previous generations."[8]

Verdict: *Truthy.* Twenge's assertion, published in 2017, became a hard-to-shake belief. The reality? Twenge mistook life-cycle effects (age-related features of youth) for true generational trends. An in-depth and broad European Social Survey provided statistics: "Millennials attach less importance to material concerns when they get older, just as Gen X did before them."[9] And so it goes: When we have our own money to spend, we want and sometimes need to acquire a car, a house, a comfortable standard of living. Wanting material acquisitions is a function of youth, not a specific generation.

Assertion: Boomers don't care about the climate.

Verdict: *Truthy.* This assertion is an example of misinformation cited as a generational difference. Baby boomers rank alongside the younger generation for citing environmental concerns as top priorities. According to a King's College London survey, "Six out of ten Americans in all age groups say that climate change, biodiversity loss, and other environmental issues are big enough problems that they justify significant changes to people's lifestyles."[10] And baby boomers might be more idealistic than younger groups. A greater percentage of the older generation believes that their individual efforts to improve the environment will count.

Assertion: Millennials are half as likely to be homeowners as baby boomers are.

Verdict: *True.* Life-cycle and economic-period effects come into play with this issue. In the United States, millennials are about half as likely as boomers are to be homeowners.[11] According to the 2020 U.S. Census, adults under thirty-five have the nation's lowest rate of homeownership, at 37.8 percent. These millennials have rampant credit card and student loan debt, coupled with an inflated housing market and stagnant earning potential. In comparison, Gen Xers (aged forty to fifty-five) have four times the assets of those under thirty-five.[12]

Assertion: Gen X (parents to many millennials and to Gen Zers) is the smallest age cohort of the four generations highlighted in this book.

Verdict: *True.* Born between 1966 and 1979, this smaller birth cohort is what public policy expert Bobby Duffy referred to as "the overlooked middle child among the generational groups."[13]

Assertion: Teens and young adults report the highest number of mental health problems.

Verdict: *True.* Mental health problems are a period effect on younger generations. Of all generations living today, young adults report the highest levels of distress, loneliness, and lowered expectations for the future and have experienced historic rates of anxiety and depression. The pandemic has only worsened their assessment of their own developmental trajectory. "Will I be okay?" they ask themselves. "What's wrong with me? I'm not where my parents were at this age."

Assertion: The educational opportunities for young adults have worsened since the 1990s.

Verdict: *True.* The younger generations have experienced the period effects of economic scarring and Covid-related opportunity costs.[14] For example, the cost of attending a four-year college in the U.S. has increased 173 percent in the last forty years, while in the same time period, the minimum wage from forty years ago now equals $10.27. Wages have stayed flat; costs have gone up.

• • •

Our "Truth or Truthy?" quiz highlights the problem of asserting simple answers for complicated truths. The writer H. L. Mencken once said, "There is always a well-known solution to every human problem—neat, plausible, and wrong."[15] Mencken's words capture the danger of arriving too quickly at an answer and mistaking it for the truth.

Generational truthiness most often omits prevalent life-cycle and widely shared period effects. Cohort truthiness uses the commonality of the birth year of a generational age group to explain beliefs, norms, and attitudes. When cohort effects are the only factor used to explain complex societal, economic, and developmental variables, it's no wonder the conclusion is wrong. Still, these stereotypes become sticky because they take advantage of our tendency to adopt fast, easy answers.

Truthiness mixes with both popular and expert opinions to reinforce pejorative stereotypes that polarize the generations. Helicopter parents are disparaged, while twentysomethings brace themselves against the derision of some who call them out for needing safe spaces, and others who bemoan the Big Quit generation of idlers who laughably expect a work-life balance. It's a whack-a-mole game of blame the parents, then blame the young adults.

Stereotypes play off extremes. For example, some parents truly are overinvolved and overprotective, and twentysomethings may stressfully overachieve and conform on behalf of the promise of a good life. Educators may grow weary of issuing classroom trigger warnings or bind themselves to the brag sheet of which colleges accepted their students, or feel pressured to monetize the majors they teach with proof of future earnings. And some employers do value toughing it out and are annoyed by complaints about workplace conditions or the need to work overtime. But these differences, which are due to life-cycle and period effects, do not represent the glacial pace of true generational change. Yet it's easy to mistake the gut feeling of the truth in stereotypes for the objective reality. The solution requires us to think again. This time more slowly.

THINKING FAST AND SLOW, COMBINING THE BEST OF BOTH

Colbert was ahead of the curve when he called out the myside bias trap with "truthiness." Later, the scientific explanation for this all-too-human tendency to fall for the quick and easy—but wrong—conclusion earned psychologist Daniel Kahneman the Nobel Prize. Kahneman describes the basis of this problem in his book *Thinking, Fast and Slow*.[16] The idea is that before we're even consciously aware of it, we readily embrace some biases because we think fast. Thinking fast makes us fall for what Bobby Duffy refers to as "bad research and lazy thinking."[17] Yet thinking fast sounds better than thinking slow, which seems kind of dull. Your thought bias is showing: Fast is good; slow is bad. Or is it?

Thinking fast tags and guides our responses to the world emotionally, driving us to interpret reality in a self-serving manner. Our thoughts and beliefs remain in service to our feelings, which are not the best guide for sorting truth from fact. "In fact," says journalist and author Chris Mooney, "the emerging science of motivated reasoning takes this realization as its core premise in explaining the causes of human bias."[18] It's a "We think, therefore we feel, therefore we change our thinking to fit our feelings" topsy-turvy way of organizing our understanding of people and the world. Of course our feelings are important. Any mental health professional will tell you so. But to be capable of rational thought, to reason with others when we disagree, to reach resolution despite strong differences, we can't rely on feelings as our ultimate decider.

But wait! you challenge, unconvinced. *Isn't fast thinking a good thing? What about all of its "smart" connotations: quick-witted, quick on the uptake, quick with numbers, quick on your feet? Isn't quick better than slow? After all, sometimes fast thinking is literally a lifesaver.*

According to Kahneman, the adult knowledge database that often prompts fast thinking and quick answers is risk averse. This adult thinking style is what child psychologist Alison Gopnik refers to as exploitative. Adults are using—they are exploiting—their enormous base of experience in fast thinking. This thinking style is effortless, intuitive, and automatic. A deer runs across the road: Quick, hit your brakes! Risk averted. Harm avoidance is critical for the survival of the species. While fast thinking is highly efficient and sometimes crucial, it can also be a lazy shortcut. We sum up the person, group, or situation too facilely—a practice that leads to bias and group or class stereotyping.[19]

To bring the downside of fast thinking closer to home, think of a quick-tempered reaction. Now recall your last upsetting disagreement with a close family member. Two opposing views, deeply held and passionately argued, right? A back-and-forth with no resulting agreement, just hurt or angry feelings. This polarization is the downside of fast, exploitative thinking. As Kahneman's book title suggests, we need more than fast thinking alone. We also need its complement, or what he calls slow thinking.[20]

Slow thinking is effortful, analytic, and deliberate. It requires us to weigh different variables to arrive at alternative solutions to any given problem. By late adolescence, cognitive development pushes us toward the first gear of slow thinking that the twentieth-century renowned Swiss psychologist and epistemologist Jean Piaget established as formal operational thought. This slow thinking style of practical analysis forms the foundation of rules, laws, and scientific principles. In the courtroom, juries decide verdicts based on the two-sided thinking of opposing sides of accusation and defense.

Interpersonally, this higher-level thinking also allows us to integrate different perspectives—we can understand our own side and someone else's. Yet even though adults are capable of the slow thinking of reasoned thought—to make arguments to support what they think—it remains in service to motivated reasoning, where the emotional master of heart (feeling) rules over head (reason). Whether arguing impassioned topics, and even in the close relationships in family life, the adversarial display of "your side" versus "my side" of winner and loser is a power struggle where there are no winners. The clear loser is the relationship. But there's hope ahead. Children show us the way, with an important clue about how they think.

Learning from the Beginner's Mind of Childhood

It's obvious that children and adults think differently. Recall that adult thinking applies the accumulated decades of stored knowledge to problem-solving.

It draws on an enormous compilation of formal and experiential learning. Less obvious is the important lesson of what we can learn from the "beginner's mind" of a child. Gopnik explains how childhood thinking can enhance adults' exploitative thinking style to become better learners and communicators.[21]

Unlike adults, children are exploratory thinkers, inherently more curious than adults. They remain open to collecting new information far longer than adults do. Children gather more evidence to solve a problem. In new situations, this quality makes children better learners than adults. On the downside, children's solutions take longer, require the risks of trial and error, produce a greater number of wrong answers, and can sometimes deliver bad outcomes for health and well-being. That's where adult supervision can come in handy. An illustration of the pros and cons of exploitative and exploratory thinking takes us to the forest, where we forage for wild mushrooms.

Mushroom Gathering: An Example

We've agreed that learning by avoiding harm is a basic kind of intelligence. Though harm avoidance is efficient and sometimes safer, it can also be a learning trap, where learning ends prematurely. Harm avoidance, a form of fast thinking, leads adults to conclude that we should stop the learning. This exploitative thinking style is vulnerable to hidden learning traps that arise from onetime bad experiences.[22] Gopnik explains the pros and cons of exploitative and exploratory thinking with a tale of fungi foraging—a wild mushroom hunt.

Most adults in the U.S. are afraid of wild mushrooms. There's a good reason: Most of us haven't learned to tell—tasty or toxic? Eating the wrong wild mushroom can be deadly. Let's assume that on your first wild-mushroom adventure, you took a bite from one and soon felt slightly sick. That is all the evidence an adult needs to stop foraging and conclude that wild mushrooms are dangerous. You now have a bias against wild mushrooms.

As we've explained, children remain open longer than adults do to exploring additional possibilities and solutions. Returning to our mushroom adventure, even when a child's first taste of a wild mushroom results in an upset stomach, they are more likely than an adult would be to persist in their search. As an exploratory thinker, the child eludes the aversive-learning trap and goes on to discover an amazing variety of edible and delicious mushrooms. They bring home a basketful of chanterelles, morels, cèpes, and hen of the woods. Then, they sauté them in butter and onions, mix them with an omelet or into risotto or marinate them for winter (all under adult supervision, of course). Rather than wanting a quick conclusion, children as exploratory thinkers are interested in fully investigating possible solutions. The downside of this thinking style is increased risk.

The accompanying table compares the advantages and limitations of the two types of thinking.

ADULT MIND: EXPLOITATIVE THINKING		CHILD MIND: EXPLORATORY THINKING	
ADVANTAGES	LIMITATIONS	ADVANTAGES	LIMITATIONS
Fast decision-making	Learning stops prematurely	Curiosity driven	Decision takes longer
Harm avoidance	Leaves us unaware of our biases	Creative and open to unconventional solutions	Explores longer trial-and-error method
Risk reduction	Playing to win, not to find most creative solution	Knowledge gained from making mistakes	Makes more mistakes Increased risk
Feeling of expertise	Overemphasizes single perspective	Open to collaboration	

THE BEST OF BOTH WORLDS

Ideally, adults would combine exploratory and exploitative styles of thinking when facing complicated problems. The result would be a hybrid approach: an open-minded, creative, and safer thinking style that avoided the myside bias.[23]

However, adults can't mimic the beginner's mind of childhood by simply telling themselves, "Avoid that learning trap, and remember to think like a child." We can scarcely recall how we thought as adolescents, much less as five-year-olds. We can, though, learn to make the most of fast and slow thinking by using a combination hybrid gear.

A HYBRID APPROACH TO THINKING: WAYS TO DEVISE OPEN-ENDED, CREATIVE SOLUTIONS TO ENHANCE EXPLOITATIVE KNOWLEDGE

- Gather more information.
- Incorporate multiple perspectives of self and other.
- Resist playing to win.
- Model and practice this more harmonious way of relating.

THINKING AND PERSPECTIVE-TAKING: A PARENT'S BEST FRIEND

We can supercharge slow thinking when we apply the hybrid approach. Building on what we learned in Chapter 1, we are using an open mindset to explore new information and relate in a nonjudgmental and respectful manner. We avoid the quick-answer, exploitative-learning trap and lay the groundwork for exploratory perspective-taking. We move beyond the myside thinking bias. By resisting the automatic default of the quickest response, we remain open to many possibilities and increase the likelihood of an "aha moment." This thinking approach constructively incorporates the perspective of the other person with our own, despite differences. Slower, exploratory thinking allows us to better regulate our fight-or-flight response and manage our anxiety-driven reactivity when other views don't align with ours.

But remember, we need both types of thinking—fast and slow, exploitative and exploratory—to thrive. Over many years of childhood, parental fast reactivity can serve a survival function—protecting their child from danger. The earlier parental command "Get out of the street!" alerts a child to the real danger of an oncoming car. Yet this same tendency toward protective reactivity can later morph into unsolicited parental advice. By a child's young adulthood, a parent's fast-thinking conversational style has clearly outlived its survivalist function. Though well-intended, its underlying advising thrust of harm reduction and "shoulda dones" predictably garners a young adult's stony silence—or worse. A father-son story illustrates the before-and-after difference between a parent's fast myside thinking, reactive advice-giving, and then its hybrid comparison of exploratory thinking, promoting emotional regulation and perspective-taking.

Floundering in College: An Example

In the first fast-thinking version, the father rapidly and correctly analyzes his son's problem but, because of myside thinking, misses the young adult's perspective. In the second version, the father employs a slow, perspective-taking response that offers validation and understanding of his son's distress.

Version 1: Fast-Thinking Response

Sam, in his sixth year of college, begins a conversation with his dad, Paul, by complaining about an exam he bombed. Sam needed to pass the class to graduate.

"I hate this online course," Sam says. "I'm not as good when the class is all online. And then the test is monitored online. So even if you just look away from your screen, they think you're cheating. I got taken down a whole grade for that, and I didn't cheat."

"Haven't you taken that kind of online test monitoring before?" Paul asks.

"Yeah," Sam slowly replies, sensing where the questioning is headed. "What's your point?"

Paul offers his risk-averse critique: "Well, you should've known how it worked so you could've avoided that penalty."

"Thanks for your heartfelt concern," Sam retorts. "I should've remembered who I'm talking to. Won't make that mistake again."

Paul answers defensively, "Hey, what's your problem? I was only trying to help."

"Whatever," says Sam as he walks away.

Outcome: Father's fast-thinking reactivity wins points for analysis, loses points for the myside tendency to point out the flaws in another's position, and so comes across critically and costs the relationship.

Version 2: Slow-Thinking, Exploratory Response

In this version of the conversation, Sam begins his complaint as above: "I hate this online course. . . ."

This time, Paul responds empathically and with an exploratory style: "Hmmm. Yeah, I can see how taking online-only classes for a semester would be tough. And then, online tests—how does this monitoring work?"

Paul's respectful curiosity, with no implicit hint of I'm right / you're wrong bias, elicits a nondefensive explanation from Sam, who replies, "I think if you're looking down a lot or focused outside your keyboard—like you're reading CliffsNotes from your wall—they can pick that up."

"Thanks for letting me know," Paul said. "This is a tough situation. What do you see as your options?"

"Well, they do have an appeal process. But it's 'guilty' unless you can prove your innocence."

"Can I offer some unsolicited advice?" Paul asks.

"Go for it," says Sam.

"I don't know if this would work, but you could offer to do a retake, and if you get the same score or better, you get that grade. Or maybe speak to the professor, own up to anything that could have been construed as cheating, and give your explanation. Does any of that hit?"

"I'll think about it," Sam replies. "Not ideal to have to retake the test, but maybe I'll ask the prof for mercy and offer to do the retest, just to show good faith. Can't make it worse."

"There you go," says Paul. "It's important to have options. Hey, thanks for letting me know what's going on."

Sam, obviously relieved, replies, "Sure. Thanks for listening."

Outcome: Father's slower, exploratory response engaged Sam, created more open-ended conversation between them, and improved the relationship.

The accompanying table breaks down what happened and what worked.

RESPONSE	VERSION 1: FAST, EXPLOITATION	VERSION 2: SLOW, EXPLORATION
Father's responses to son's complaint	Quick answer Closed-ended, yes-or-no questions Gives unsolicited advice on what Sam should have done	Thoughtfully acknowledges Sam's distress Open-ended questions Assesses most helpful response Engages Sam in problem-solving
Son's response to father's comments	Total shutdown, disengages	Reflects on options and arrives at a collaborative action plan

THE BIG QUIT? NOT SO FAST: AN EXAMPLE

A parent's exploratory conversational approach can also boost a young adult's ability to move beyond their own reactivity toward a more thoughtful plan. In this vignette, twenty-five-year-old Alicia calls her mother, Monica, after a bad day at work. Her mother blunders into fast thinking in Version 1. But in Version 2, with consistently open-minded curiosity, she models and promotes slow thinking as her daughter arrives at a better option to solve her work problem.

Version 1: Fast-Thinking Reaction

Today, Alicia's boss informed her that she wasn't meeting her sales numbers for the month, and certainly not for the quarter. Alicia had worked as a sales associate for about half a year but didn't know if this was the right job for her. Though she cared about making the metric tied to her commission and the store bonus, she didn't know what she could do to improve. The whole day felt like getting the worst report card ever, and without any helpful feedback. Alicia's first impulse was to quit, but she finished the day, then called her mom.

"Hi, Mom," Alicia began tearfully.

"Hi, sweetie, what's going on?" Monica asked.

"I'm such a loser, and I should just quit before they fire me," Alicia said in a muffled voice, blowing her nose.

Monica immediately replied, "Honey, why don't you just make yourself a nice dinner and run a bubble bath. I'm sure it will be better tomorrow."

Alicia, now sounding even sadder, replied: "I'm not hungry. Bye."

Outcome: Monica's anxiety-driven, fast-thinking reaction derails the conversation.

Version 2: Slow-Thinking, Exploratory Response

In this version of the conversation, Alicia initiated the call as above: "I'm such a loser, and I should just quit before they fire me."

Now Monica manages her anxiety at the thought of her daughter quitting impulsively and resists bright-sided reassurance whose underlying message is:

"I can't handle this." She has learned the hard way that this is a conversation-ender. Instead, the mom begins compassionately and then asks open-ended questions. "I'm glad you're sharing this upsetting day with me. I understand how that feedback would hurt. Could you let me know more about what you understand about the first- and second-quarter numbers? What do you think is going on?"

Alicia, still discouraged, replies, "I don't know. I was trying just as hard."

Then Monica asks, "Do you think your boss cares about how you're doing, or has insight to help you improve?"

Alicia initially dismisses this possibility. "No, Mom, this was just a put-down."

Monica, sounding puzzled, continues, "I'm sure it felt just awful, but sometimes a manager's job is to help employees find their footing."

Alicia, now more thoughtful, replies, "Yeah, she seemed really rushed and nervous telling me. Like, I thought we were friends—or at least friendly. Maybe it was a hard conversation for her too."

"That sounds quite probable," Monica offers. "If you consider it that way, do you think you have more options than quitting?"

Alicia: "Yeah, I think quitting just appealed to my hurt pride. I need to have another conversation with my boss and tell her I really want to improve. After all, I did great the first quarter, so I should be able to learn from this."

Monica: "Alicia, I'm so proud of you. It took me a lot longer than it's taken you to understand that you can learn from setbacks."

With relief in her voice, Alicia says, "Thanks for being there, Mom."

Monica: "Anytime."

Outcome: The mom's open-ended responses promoted a parallel process in her daughter's ability to move from fast to slow and open-minded thinking, evaluating her feelings, incorporating other perspectives, and creating options for future learning.

RESPONSE	VERSION 1: FAST, EXPLOITATION	VERSION 2: SLOW, EXPLORATION
Mother's responses to daughter's distress	Quick answer Bright-siding with no questions Gives unsolicited advice unrelated to the problem	Thoughtfully acknowledges Alicia's distress Open-ended questions Assesses most helpful response Engages Alicia in problem-solving
Daughter's response	More discouraged, hangs up	Invites Alicia to reflect on options for learning and growth

By shifting gears into slower, exploratory thinking, we use the helpful aspects of a child's curiosity-driven process. This adds the skill of emotional regulation to a parent's repertoire. This best-of-both-worlds hybrid approach, slow plus exploratory-thinking style, allows us to resist our fight-or-flight, anxiety-ridden, fix-it, advice-prone tendencies to protect our twentysomethings from the world of mistakes. This approach is key to having conversations that build trust with our young adults because they feel heard and understood—even when we disagree with them. Chapter 4 takes this teachable cognitive superpower and uses it to decrease defensiveness and boost perspective-taking in the service of improved relationships.

We begin the next chapter with a twenty-first-century communication tune-up—a road map that shows parents how to listen so their young adults will talk, and talk so their young adults will listen and possibly share. Through family vignettes, we put the mechanics of hybrid thinking to work. We learn to resist the myside motivation behind "playing to win" in our disagreements and expand our perspectives. With a thoughtful, open-ended communication style, parents can become collaborative partners to guide their young adults.

4

Changing the Rules

How to Listen So Your Twentysomething May Talk and Talk So They May Share and Listen

PARENTS TODAY HAVE A CLOSE-UP VIEW OF THEIR TWENTYSOMETHINGS' LIVES. Their involvement is shaped by the recent shift to a prolonged period of dependence, with the possible financing of higher education, food, clothing, and shelter, then career guidance and networking. Whew! The good news is that parents know more about their young adults, who return home for months, not simply owing to harsher economic circumstances but also because the generations feel closer. Parents of today's millennials and Gen Zers express fewer gaps in cultural beliefs regarding sexuality, racial and gender equality, and environmental issues than the "never trust anyone over thirty" baby boomers and Gen Xers had with their own parents.[1]

Increasingly, young adults turn to their parents when challenging new problems arise. Though early adulthood is often portrayed as "the best years of their lives," the daily reality is more personally and professionally fraught than at midlife.[2] When twentysomethings confront novel dilemmas, they have less experience to draw on, as well as the downsides of fewer long-term job and social supports to offset their stress. Bosses and new friends are not the reflexive go-to support when you're striving to look competent, cool, and collected. Parents are.

When a young adult turns to a parent in these moments, parents are well advised to listen to understand rather than jump in to advise and convince.

You may wonder, "Why is careful listening so important?" Effective social support is more about listening than providing solutions. When we're stressed, what most of us want is for someone to care about us and "be there." Among the many definitions of parental love, a lifelong constant for a child is the experience of feeling known and understood. Feeling known begins with a sense of being truly heard. Most of us want this kind of love, even when we don't know how to give it.

Most parents want to lend help when they are needed and want their influence to count. Yet seeing the growing pains of their emerging adults leaves parents understandably uneasy. Many wonder how to provide effective support when they're witness to questionable screen-time use, lifestyle choices, substance use, or worrisome job decisions. Parents may also question how to best respond when a young adult divulges embarrassing lapses. Other parents may want to shore up a widening gulf with their young adult, with whom they once felt close. No matter the circumstances, an improved relationship between parents and emerging adults begins with the skills of better listening and thoughtful responding. We replace the earlier rule of "Parents know best" with: "Parents listen to learn so their young adult may share."

This chapter lays the groundwork for parents to become partners in respectful and meaningful collaborations, with the goal of supporting a young adult's growing competency. We build upon the open mindset and the hybrid communication style of slower, exploratory thinking introduced in Chapters 1 and 3. We recognize that the mental gymnastics required to modify and enhance our thinking and relating are easier said than done. Despite our loving intentions, when we're having a conversation with a family member, a single distressing exchange can unleash our defenses. We have at our disposal a veritable arsenal of defenses, including denial, displacement, dissociation, identification, projection, regression, repression, sublimation, and undoing. When we're on the defensive, we are likely employing one or more of these behaviors. To become a better listener and relate without defensiveness, we offer two broad guidelines: Stop Playing to Win, and Try to See It Their Way. By setting these goals into practice, you ensure that both generations may feel known and heard.

To your many years of parental sacrifices and childhood bonds of love, we offer a bridge across generational and communication gaps. On the other side is a renewed and enduring relationship with your young adult.

GUIDELINE 1: STOP PLAYING TO WIN

We all root for the home team to win. There, winning is the goal. But in family relationships, when people play to win, there are only losers. The outcome of power plays is a loss of trust that creates distance between the family members. The resolution of differences requires the goal of playing to listen, learn, and creatively resolve problems. Yet, in a discussion in which you feel misunderstood, criticized, or dismissed, it's hard to resist the urge to defend yourself, followed by a winning slam dunk. Blame your myside bias for tilting your reasoning toward winning. A mother-daughter conversation illustrates how playing to win derails their chat.

We recount an exchange reported to us between Jannie and her twenty-seven-year-old daughter, Chrissie. Their mother-daughter visit began with pleasantries. Then Chrissie told her mother about her new boyfriend, whom the mother hadn't met. Their conversation took a downturn when Jannie remarked on the young man's job history. This argument later brought them into therapy.

"Oh, he's part of the Big Quit?" the mother commented. "Third job in a year?"

Chrissie sharply replied, "No one I've ever dated is good enough for you. You're so judgmental."

"I wasn't being judgmental," Jannie said, shrugging dismissively. "Can't you take a joke? I don't know why you're so sensitive."

"I'm not being sensitive," her daughter shot back. "You are being judgmental and defensive." Chrissie then pulled the conversation-ender card: "And you get no say about who I'm dating. No say!"

As her daughter stormed away, Jannie delivered a zinger. "So next time, just let me know what script you want me to follow so I'll get it right."

Chalk up three points for criticism, denial, and dismissiveness, zero points for warm and fuzzy connection. They are playing to win. Neither owns up to their defensiveness. We'll follow the two as they unpack, then clean up the messiness of their communication misfires. We begin with the automatic default of defensiveness.

It's human nature to be defensive when we feel threatened. And although that's not exactly our fault—it's the fast-thinking brain with its lack of self-awareness—we are still responsible for better managing our reactions. Face it. We all flunk the analysis of how we come across when we argue. If asked, we could describe in detail how illogical, irritating, or ridiculous the other person sounded while remaining tone-deaf to ourselves.

When we stop playing to win, we are making a conscious effort to drop our defenses. This is a counterintuitive move, especially in parent-child and young adult relationships, where the love we give and get, and the hurts we inflict and sustain, have an uneasy coexistence. We try to forgive and forget and turn the page. Still, over time we naturally become more sensitive to and vigilant for well-known parries, which lead us to expect and protect ourselves from the worst of each other. Too often, we may not even recognize when a defensive attitude is creeping into our tone. In discussions, it's sometimes more *how* you say things than *what* you say.

Learning to relate nondefensively is a skill, quickly captured by a list of dos and don'ts. This competence is as easy to catalog as it is hard to do. Since parenting is a long game, there's time to change a pattern in how we relate, even one that's hardened over time. It's not too late, no matter how old the child—or parent.

To stop playing to win and resist the urge to be defensive, we invite you to check the list of dos and don'ts against your own responses. You might ask yourself: *How am I doing?* and *Why is this soft emotional skill so difficult to master?*

CHECKING DEFENSIVENESS 101

DO PRACTICE OPEN-MINDSET TIPS

- Listen before you talk.
- Adopt a nonjudgmental, collaborative style.
- Manage your reactive anxiety or upset.
- Show curiosity about the other person's position.
- Give the benefit of the doubt.
- Own up to and accept a share of responsibility.
- Remain open to constructive feedback.

DON'T . . .

- Play to win.

- Interrupt, talk over, or "Yes, but . . ."

- Instruct the other on their faults.

- Give a dismissive apology: "Sorry you feel that way."

- Give unsolicited advice.

- Guilt-trip.

- Bright-side.

- Condescend, dismiss, or show contempt.

- Criticize or blame the other person.

- Punish with the silent treatment.

Finally . . .

- Do make a specific plan to modify your hurtful behaviors.

CATCHING YOUR DEFENSIVENESS

Catching defensiveness begins by paying close attention to your physical level of discomfort. Defensiveness is often accompanied by palpable tension. Try to notice if your chest or throat feels tighter, or your shoulder muscles tense, your jaw clenches, or your heart beats faster. These are signs that you've stopped listening to the other person and are focused on your rebuttal. These bodily changes are sending your brain the powerful message that you're in danger. Your brain is wrong. You are not in mortal danger, just a challenging conversation. In those moments when your brain is temporarily hijacked, you lose the ability to contemplate your behavior, tone, or demeanor. The first step to override defensiveness is to calm your body, perhaps by focusing on your breath, then your brain will follow.

The next step is to manage your anxiety, which is also activated in times of perceived threat. Too often, parents express their concerns and frustrations to a young adult through edicts: "My house, my rules," or anxiety-ridden questioning: "What were you thinking?" The predictable result is a battle royale.

For example, Jannie's snide remark about the boyfriend's frequent job changes telegraphed her anxiety that Chrissie was making a bad choice.

Now, let's assume that Jannie and Chrissie have taken a break to cool down. Their first fast-thinking round illustrates a play-to-win gambit. Now calmer, do mother and daughter mend the fence through thoughtful self-awareness? Or does the calm after the storm make their situation worse? We listen in on a common post-argument mistake.

> MOM: Hey, Chrissie, peace offering. I made your favorite cookies. I'm sorry our talk got off to a rocky start. You know I didn't mean anything by my question, but I'm sorry I got caught up in the heat of the moment.
> DAUGHTER: Yeah, Mom, I know. I lost my cool, too.

Jannie and Chrissie pass the cookies and also give themselves a pass. Cookies are a tasty but poor substitute for a resolution that builds trust. Mother and daughter learn and resolve nothing. No one gains self-awareness. Each rationalizes and minimizes how badly they sounded. They ignore the fact that each did harm with judgment and defensiveness. In all likelihood, defensiveness still governs their thinking. Instead of reflective self-awareness, mother and daughter each believes they're the better person for "letting it go." Silently, each has won a relitigation of their argument.

Think about it. Haven't you ever indulged in the guilty pleasure of imagining what you could have said to prove the opposing side wrong? How you could have cleverly nailed the flaws in their position? You've remained in a defensive, fast-thinking learning trap, singularly focused on the outcome—proving you're right. In this state, we win by rigging a pass/fail "myside" system with no partial credits to the other's position. We reinforce *our* points and *their* flaws in our now-ever-more-convincing case. The problem is that we often go from the guilty indulgence of "gotcha" thoughts to actually saying them. Now there's real harm.

Instead of building a better mousetrap, try to reflect on how you came across. Your goal is to resist the temptation to tell the other person what they could have done or said better. That's cheating . . . and always far easier than looking ourselves in the mirror. With defenses down, you may recognize your demeanor was condescending, reactive, blaming, or dismissive. To use a cooling-off period most productively, keep a few open-mindset repair tips from Chapter 1, page 25 in your back pocket: Name your feelings; ask open-ended questions; give the benefit of the doubt. The decision to relate in a nondefensive manner is a goal and an exercise in self-awareness.

REPLACE DEFENSIVENESS WITH SELF-AWARENESS

- Listen to your body. When it's revving up for an argument, calm it down.
- Pay attention to how you are coming across.
- Own up to what you could have done differently.
- Before responding, reinforce your goal: "I'm trying not to be defensive."
- Listen thoughtfully and try to respond empathically.
- Acknowledge the valid points the other person makes.

Detecting Gaps in Our Self-Awareness

With defensiveness subdued, slower thinking allows us to gain insight into our motivations and behaviors. Though, as Jannie and Chrissie demonstrated, it's much easier to spot the lack of self-awareness in another person. Caution: The smarter we are, the harder we may fall for the correctness of our own conclusions. The world according to one perspective is bound to have distortions. It's as if we're in a fun house mirror at the carnival, laughing at everyone else's warped images, without seeing our own.

There's a paradox in detecting the lurking black holes in our awareness. How can we see what we don't see—the gaps that we don't even realize exist?[3] There are a few telltale clues.

CLUES TO SPOTTING GAPS IN YOUR SELF-AWARENESS

- Certainty that you're right (myside bias).
- Lack of curiosity about the other person's perspective.
- Justification because your motivations are good or based on your experience.

- Rationalization of your defensive responses.
- Unfinished business—the dismissal of how past experiences from childhood or prior relationships continue to shape how you think and relate.

To gain insight and self-awareness, we must strive to learn from another's point of view. That begins by being a better listener. A common misconception about being a good listener is that it's a go-along-to-get-along doormat role. To play the part well, we passively give in, give up, or merely parrot the other person's points. Good listening is not capitulation. Good listening is an active role. We accept the likelihood of our own incomplete understanding and listen to learn from another's perspective in order to collaboratively resolve problems.

Healthy family relationships rely on the integration of the personal stories and meanings that come from different generational experiences. When parent and young adult recognize that each brings limited perspectives to their interactions, they can remain responsive even when they disagree. As we practice this approach, we gain in understanding and misunderstandings ease. Expanding our limited perspective to learn from and incorporate different views is key to mature adult relationships.

GUIDELINE 2: TRY TO SEE IT ~~MY~~ THEIR WAY

Perspective-taking is a "do unto others" golden rule of relating by putting ourselves in the other person's shoes. Reminding us of the universal tendency to interpret the world through a blinkered view, religious, philosophical, and ethical texts all prompt us to expand our limited perspectives. Though "seeing it their way" has a moral imperative, it isn't solved by simply being a good person. Many good people, like Jannie and Chrissie, defend their positions when they feel hurt, without even trying to see it from another perspective. We return to the mother and daughter as they enter therapy. We encouraged them to stop playing to win and develop self-awareness with perspective-taking.

In the first session, defensiveness and lack of self-awareness were on full display. As they recounted their earlier conflict to us, Jannie maintained that she "hadn't meant anything," while Chrissie made a pointed critique of her mom. Chrissie expected us to agree that she was right. We disappointed her. Our therapeutic process asks family members to stop playing to win, look at how they're coming across, and consider multiple perspectives. In the therapy sessions, we modeled perspective-taking by validating the hurt feelings of each while combining their one-sided stories to arrive at a more complicated truth. This process was new to them, and you could feel the resulting strain in the room as the session ended. Jannie voiced her commitment to continue with additional sessions, but Chrissie expressed her ambivalence.

After the first session, Chrissie called to request an individual appointment. In it, she declared that our ground rules—listening without interrupting or rebutting, giving the benefit of the doubt, and considering her mother's view—were "a horrible process."

Rather than defend our expertise, we practiced what we teach—nondefensive perspective-taking. We replied, "Thanks for letting us know more about what was so hard in that first session with your mom." We then asked Chrissie to tell us about what she found most difficult about the meeting. Rather predictably, Chrissie again accused her mother of being clueless about just how awful she was.

Chrissie then reproached us: "You just don't understand. Whenever I tell her why I'm upset with her judgments on me or my friends, Mom passes off her criticisms as 'harmless' or 'just a joke.' How can you expect me to give her the benefit of the doubt when she never owns up?"

In response, we partially validated Chrissie's experience: "Sounds very tiring to expect that you won't get anywhere when you tell your mom that she's judging your choices." Yet we were careful not to side with Chrissie and throw her mother under the bus. Instead, we asked Chrissie to identify a doable change that her mother could make to meaningfully shift this pattern. We would soon ask Jannie to make a similar request of her daughter.

Chrissie felt better understood after we heard her side of things. She agreed to continue therapy with her mother. In subsequent sessions with them, Jannie (with some coaching from us in her individual appointment) was able to acknowledge her judgmental protectiveness of Chrissie. Jannie had gained the self-awareness that "wanting the best" for her daughter often translated into a put-down of some of Chrissie's choices of a friend or partner. Jannie next offered a sincere apology to Chrissie, expressing regret for her hurtful judgments. Moved by her mother's understanding, Chrissie expressed more openness to considering her mother's side of things.

"Mom, I know you've always wanted the best for me. And you have sat with me when I complained and cried about more than one disappointing relationship. But I can't tell you about my relationships if you're going to go snarky on me or judgy on them," she said.

They promised each other to make a few important changes and stated what they would do differently. Jannie agreed that she could not protect and control her daughter's adult choices, particularly through an anxiously controlling style. She promised to work to better manage her worries. Chrissie accepted that there might be times when her mother couldn't be her sounding board. Her mother could still catch her if she was falling, but young adulthood also means accepting a parent's limits. To reduce future disconnects, both agreed to pause for a calm-out when either of them needed time to regroup before continuing with a more productive conversation.

Both mother and daughter recognized the benefits of this new practice—of trying to see things from the other's perspective. Jannie gained insight into her defensive dismissiveness, while Chrissie became aware that winning the point was a recurring problem across her relationships. With the boost in self-awareness, they learned from and incorporated each other's perspectives. Jannie and Chrissie embraced the goal of relating constructively through practice, practice, practice.

With these two communication guidelines in mind (Stop Playing to Win and Try to See It Their Way), the Millers make a final appearance. They provide plenty of tips that are especially important when you are not feeling particularly loving in a moment of exasperation, hurt, anger, or exhausted worry. Scott and Elaine demonstrate the specific actions that parents can take to develop a mature parent–young adult relationship. With their effective support, Tyler grows up.

PARENT AND YOUNG ADULT RELATIONSHIPS GROW UP

You'll recall from earlier chapters that each member of the Miller family has a different take on what's gone wrong. Tyler is back in the starting blocks after a false start. He's angry and depressed that all his hard work hasn't paid off. From his vantage point, the older generations either lied about the promises of adulthood or were clueless. Blame is contagious. Next up, Elaine reproaches herself as a hovering mother, while Scott angrily dismisses the situation as Tyler's fault. The marriage is another casualty of the conflict, with the parents stuck in a Goldilocks dilemma: too hot, too cold. No parenting style gets it just right.

They need to break the old rules of parent-child relating that haven't worked for years. Tyler needs a team approach to boost his maturation.

To crack the parental polarization, we met with Scott and Elaine for a few parents' sessions. We asked them to state their long-term goals for their relationship with Tyler. They identified three goals:

1. Discuss their concerns in a constructive way.
2. Find ways to motivate Tyler to get the adult life he wants.
3. Share common interests and have some fun as a family again.

With these goals in mind, we suggested a strategy for the intermediate steps Scott and Elaine would need to take. To rewrite their old parenting styles, they would need the skills of nondefensiveness, self-awareness, and perspective-taking. Changing reactive to responsive communication would smooth their rough edges. Additionally, their biases and generational stereotypes could use a freshening up of open-minded thinking. Together, these steps would build on the open-mindset mechanics of respectful relating.

It was a tall order: Resist the urge to be right, listen without judgment but with openness to Tyler's feedback, and incorporate multiple perspectives. Their team effort would build marital harmony while also extending an emotionally safer way for Tyler to relate to them. Agreement between parent and young adult was not the goal—a more mature, closer relationship was.

These changes to their existing patterns were challenging. Common to developmental growth, there is a loss and a gain for both generations. The young adult loses a familiar dependency, which may feel both scary and exhilarating as they gain in autonomy. Parents lose a sense of control when they let go of the familiar authoritative role. Their gain is the relief in a job well done, without the need to be so responsibly in charge. Both generations gain a strengthened relationship that is sturdy enough to last a lifetime.

Scott made his resistance to change apparent by challenging us, "Why do we have to go first and do all this work? We're not the ones with a virtual life and no job." Dr. Rostain replied, "You can direct your frustration at us, but that won't improve your family's relationships." Elaine then gave Scott a look that signaled, "Zip it," as Scott shrugged his "Okay." That settled, Scott and Elaine put in the effort required for a new and better way of relating to their son. They hoped that Tyler could learn to trust them again and make room for their support and guidance.

A Deep Self-Reflection

The Miller family's journey began with self-reflection and an evaluation of their generational stereotypes. While Elaine was intrigued by the prospect of debunking their biases, Scott agreed to play along just to make sure that we weren't being too soft on Tyler and his generation. He reminded us, "You know twentysomethings are just a bunch of overentitled, materialistic whiners who expect things to be handed to them." Striving to shift his hardened bias, we respectfully asked Scott to tell us the story of his childhood and young adult experiences. This would help us understand where he was coming from.

Scott prided himself on overcoming a childhood of stark contrasts. He told us that his parents were well educated and had interesting friends, but their frequent arguments frightened him. When Scott was eight years old, they separated. That's when he began his weekly shuttle between the two households. He remarked that if there were a parenting style, it could be described as "My mother was crazy" and "My father was a hard-assed, angry, self-involved drinker." At a young age, Scott became highly independent as a way of coping with parental dysfunction. Entering young adulthood, he put himself through college and became a respected accountant. Got married, stayed married, had children. That was Scott's story.

There was a lot to admire about Scott—his early self-reliance forged his grit and tenacity—but it also fed his stereotyping of Tyler. He shared in a common parental delusion that our children will and should be like us. Author Andrew Solomon succinctly reminds us how to consider our children's differences from us: "It's production, not reproduction."[4] Our children are not us, and so it's natural for them to be different, to hold dissimilar generational views and values, and to challenge our thinking and attitudes. Scott had done so much more for Tyler than he had ever received from his parents. Scott's anger and disappointment belied his deep love for his son.

As Scott mulled over the role that adversity had played in his childhood, we asked whether he had ever gotten to a better place with his parents.

"No," he replied, sounding surprised at what he considered a preposterous question. "But I'm still a good son, looking after them when they need help."

Like Scott, many adults want to turn the page on their pasts and their parents by maintaining relationships of functional obligation that are bound by birth and history. Less often, they explore the possibility of a more emotionally connected relationship. They give plenty of reasons: *Too busy raising kids. Having our own lives. What's the point? The past is the past. They're too old now. If I told them how I felt misunderstood as a kid, it would only hurt them.* Though we can't time-travel and change the facts of our childhood lives, we may benefit from asking our parents to discuss earlier, distressing times in our relationships with them. Sometimes the older generation can surprise us with expressions of understanding, and sometimes with their regrets.

Granted, not every conversation with parents that follows the breadcrumb trail from childhood to adulthood pays off as we would hope. Still, the effort itself can lead to an increased sense of personal freedom, with gains in the emotional attunement to our children. We were asking Scott and Elaine to offer this compassionate gift to Tyler, despite the lack of that deeper connection with their own parents. Relating constructively is harder to offer if we've never received it.

Though Scott wasn't interested in looking back, he deserved credit for wanting to develop a better relationship with his son than he'd had with his parents. Scott was all too aware that the window for healing childhood wounds begins to close as young adults tackle the enormous developmental tasks ahead and orient themselves toward their futures. We assured him that the goal isn't a symmetrical, peer-like friendship, but a relationship that keeps parent and young adult meaningfully connected in this longest era of parenting.

This time, Scott didn't look at us as if we were suggesting something ridiculous. He shrugged and said, "Of course I want that. I've spent my whole life trying to be a better father. I just don't know how it works now."

To help Scott imagine that better connection, we asked him to think back on how he and his parents related when he was a young adult. Then, think about what he could change to improve his relationship with Tyler.

EMPATHY BUILDER . . . CAN YOU RECALL . . .

- The topics you couldn't share with a parent?
- Discussions with a parent that left you feeling misunderstood, hurt, or angry?
- What you told yourself you would do differently when you became a parent?

Scott's initial take was that Tyler's childhood seemed easier because he hadn't shouldered the many chores and regular jobs that Scott had from age thirteen. Instead of these early responsibilities, Tyler's "job" was to remain academically competitive, get good grades, attend a good college, find a good job, and secure a good life. Unlike Scott's mother, Elaine had shielded and guided Tyler from making too many mistakes. We asked Scott to put himself in Tyler's shoes for a moment. In this way, Scott began to unwind his biases about Tyler and his generation as he thought about his son's individual experiences rather than through the lens of a stereotypical category. He began to understand that Tyler's experiences were also hard, though different from his.

The pandemic dealt Tyler a few joker cards: job loss, a reluctant move home, and friends left across the country. He was lonely and felt like a failure. He was angry at the system and deeply disillusioned with adulthood. Like most of his generation, Tyler had never experienced the childhood autonomy that characterized his parents' generation, especially the hard-won resilience that his father had built over many years of early hardships and responsibilities.

Scott's vulnerable conversations with us about his childhood indicated his willingness to shed his bravado. He began to show curiosity and insight into Tyler's perspective. Because we often learn from our clients, we asked Scott if he could summarize how he made the shift from a fast-thinking, defensive, and angry regard for his son to a thoughtful, open-ended understanding of Tyler's troubles.

SCOTT'S TIPS FOR THINKING SLOWER AND RELATING BETTER

- "I noticed that the best communicators at work were the ones that asked questions and didn't give unsolicited advice or get in the last word. They didn't interrupt or rebut, but listened and questioned until we were all on the same page. I took that approach as my new goal."

- "I watched how Elaine got further with our son by listening and being understanding and nonconfrontational."

- "Finally, I painfully saw my biggest blind spot. I was doing to my son what my parents did to me, all in the name of love. Whatever their good intentions to correct and advise me, their criticisms drove me away. I had to stop making the same mistake with Tyler."

As Scott's perspective expanded, his biases and anger eased and he consciously slowed his conversational approach to practice responsiveness. Scott commented to us, "Now, more and more, I can calmly say things that are honest but not heated. It feels more effective than my usual fiery blast. Tyler seems to take me more seriously, too."

While Scott was making his own attitude adjustments, Elaine was dealing with the self-blame of her helicopter-mom stereotype. Mothers often both get the blame and blame themselves, as the late Stella Chess, a child psychologist, confirmed: "There are very few jobs in which one individual will be blamed for anything that goes wrong, and fewer still in which what can go wrong, and the feeling of being blamed, is so devastating."[5]

Mindful that mothers often feel at fault and develop low self-esteem when their children or young adults have problems, we asked Elaine to rethink her self-blame. We questioned whether her protective feelings for Tyler and her push for him to do well in school and get into a good college were really neurotic helicoptering or understandable responses to the abnormally harsh and competitive economic changes. Perhaps she had realistically supported his anticipated needs. We reminded her that however hard we try to do what's best for a child, there is no guaranteed outcome. Elaine breathed a bit easier and replied, "Well, it's true that my experience and worry were more complicated than just being a hovering mom. Maybe I can be a little kinder to myself."

Next up was an honest look at the gaps in her self-awareness. Elaine was surprised to realize that her intentionally kind counters to Tyler's painful recitations were a form of dismissiveness. Tyler resented her "look on the bright side" responses because he felt that his mother didn't want to face and understand his experiences. Worse, he believed that she was indirectly signaling him to stop sharing painful feelings. Elaine reflected that her difficulty in admitting that things were bad arose from her childhood role of family peacekeeper. She had always felt responsible for smoothing the waters. Though tired of being the emotional kin-keeper between Scott and Tyler, she unconsciously assumed this position whenever tensions between them flared. Elaine felt relieved when we identified this burden and encouraged her to step back from it. To facilitate that, Scott and Tyler would need to step up their efforts to relate more vulnerably and constructively.

Scott and Elaine were rewriting their old rules as they gained insights into their prior biases and the origins of their deep emotional grooves. They understood that if they wanted Tyler to open up and share, they needed to lead by example. They hoped that this new way of relating to Tyler would go well.

Owning Up

Elaine and Scott gave this approach a try in our next family session. They had decided to acknowledge their earlier missteps and tell Tyler what they had set out to change. A surprisingly lighthearted exchange ensued.

Elaine began, "Hey, Tyler, remember when you told us that we needed to see a shrink and get off your back? You were right. We've learned a lot from our parenting sessions and our family therapy. And we wanted to share some of that with you."

Tyler, looking at his mother somewhat warily, said, "Oh yeah? Like what?"

Elaine replied, "For starters, I want to thank you for telling us how mad you were at how the last year rolled out. At first I tried to be reassuring, but that's not what you needed. Since then, I've learned not to sugarcoat hard things that you tell me. I'm sure I won't get it perfectly right, but when I slip up, just say, 'Sugarcoating,' and I'll get it."

"Wow," Tyler said, taking it in. "I mean I know that you and Dad had some sessions with our docs here, but did they put something in your Kool-Aid? And can I have some?"

They both laughed.

Scott added, "And I've been a hard-ass sometimes and too hard on you."

Looking wide-eyed with surprise, Tyler replied, "Or, Dad, maybe you're smoking something, because I never thought I'd hear that from you."

Scott owned up with "Yeah. I've been doing to you what my father did to me—he used to criticize me without knowing what he was talking about. He didn't get me. I feel bad that I've been doing the same thing to you."

Tyler slowly replied, "Huh. Thanks. Didn't know it ran in the family back to Pops, but that makes sense. Yeah, you were a hard-ass sometimes. But hey, I was a smart-ass too." Tyler smiled, and his parents felt some hope.

Scott nodded as Elaine spoke for both of them. "So we hope you'll give us another chance. We'd especially like to find a way to talk with you about how to help you have the life you want. Because we know that this isn't it."

Tyler nodded in agreement, still somewhat mystified and not entirely trusting the changes in their old ways.

Finding Ways to Engage and Motivate

Midway through our course of therapy with the Millers, they felt ready to have focused, productive conversations at home. Elaine and Scott asked Tyler to help them come up with a plan for regular talks at home, with no more "surprise attacks," as Tyler called them. They agreed on a once-a-week discussion, after supper. In follow-up sessions we reviewed any talks that had gone sideways as we helped the family identify and tweak ideas to try at home.

In one of their conversations at home, and with our earlier guidance, Scott and Elaine asked Tyler if he could tell them what his goals were. They promised: "No judgment, no advice—we just need your input." At the next family therapy session, we continued the discussion, asking Tyler his ideas for activities he would enjoy now. What would he want for his future? How could his parents help?

Conversations like these are oriented toward behavioral activation—starting small by finding an activity that a disengaged young adult wants to do to replace a default activity. Tyler's pass-the-time default was online gaming. Playing video games provided a rapid, stimulating rush of dopamine-fueled excitement. His parents were worried that, taken to extremes, some of Tyler's high-dopamine behaviors, such as excessive internet usage, gaming, and substance misuse, might become compulsive.[6] These were feel-good-but-not-good-for-you examples of his poor coping.

Still, Elaine and Scott were careful not to dismiss the value of social bonding in gaming or its usefulness during the periods of pandemic isolation, when the normal, healthy stimulation ordinarily provided by an engaged personal, social, or work life was temporarily lost. Instead of an all-or-nothing approach to his screen time, they asked Tyler to consider whether there was a former activity that might appeal to him now—maybe his earlier love of skateboarding or jujitsu? Tyler remembered that there was a new skate park not far from their house. Maybe he'd try it. When he did, he felt the familiar excitement of childhood freedom. He felt like his world was opening up again. Now he looked forward to his offline time.

Whether sports or board games, or a return to art or music, the goal for a young person is to engage in an activity that mines past interests to build a healthier lifestyle. It's a low-dopamine repertoire that creates daily routines for better mood and sleep.

The talks at home between the Millers were not a slam dunk. Tyler reported that sometimes he walked away when his parents lapsed into their old ways. But as promised, they would regroup for a do-over. If, instead, Scott or Elaine bumped into Tyler's irritability, they practiced tips to resist becoming defensive. In sessions the family agreed that simply naming a feeling—"I'm feeling overwhelmed, let's pick this up later"—worked better than getting into an argument. As his parents shared more, Tyler in turn showed more vulnerability. He began one family therapy session by saying, "I don't really feel like being here. I had a crummy day. I couldn't find anyone to hang out with." Scott replied, "I'm sorry to hear that. Thanks for telling us, and thanks for coming here anyway. Join in when you feel like it." In another session, Tyler called out a communication misfire with direct feedback to his parents: "I don't want you to problem-solve. I just wanted to tell you what was happening. I didn't ask for your advice." Again, Elaine and Scott took a breath and didn't react defensively. They owned up to it: "Yep, we fell off the 'don't give advice' wagon. Sorry." Even when the progress was slow, they felt encouraged by their efforts to relate constructively.

As Scott and Elaine practiced their new parenting styles, they replaced harangues or sympathetic bright-siding with unbiased questions and conscious efforts to validate Tyler's perspective, even if only partly. In that way, when they disagreed with their son or voiced their concerns, Tyler became more open to hearing them. Tensions eased.

Slowly, Scott and Tyler came out of their corners and reengaged in earlier activities they had enjoyed—fishing, sharing funny videos, messaging rare-car sightings. Elaine was relieved to be out of the middle. She and Tyler resumed their lighter talks and engaged in mutual interests like cooking and watching films from the '40s and '50s.

The couple's at-home progress reports were encouraging. Fortunately, their worst fears—that Tyler would become another statistic in the youth mental health crisis—were unfounded. As he reengaged with his former interests, Tyler overcame the pandemic's impact and downward drag on his mood.

With renewed motivation, Tyler set goals for himself. First, he made a few important lifestyle changes. He limited his screen time and developed healthier sleep, nutrition, and exercise habits. He had just begun a job search when friends invited him to join them on a road trip. He jumped at the chance. Scott resisted his usual get-a-job lecture and told Tyler to enjoy the adventure. During the trip, Tyler and his friends found mutual encouragement in their job searches. Maybe they could all get together again. After all, they reasoned, many jobs were now remote, and employment was finally picking up. Step by step, Tyler built upon the life he had imagined—and a future he would want.

One morning, Tyler excitedly announced to his parents that he'd gotten a job interview. Then a job offer. He accepted. It meant a quick turnaround. His parents helped him pack and move. He was back with his friends, with a job, and in the life he wanted.

Some months later, each parent received a card from Tyler. In a heartfelt note, he thanked his mother for believing in him, even when he hadn't believed in himself. And his dad? He sent Scott a funny card and wrote that he appreciated all his dad's help in the online-roller-coaster apartment search, then moving a mountain of his stuff. Enclosed were two tickets to the next auto show. Scott and Tyler would both go.

Improving their parent–young adult relationship took several months. Each positive conversation reinforced the benefits of their effortful changes. Tyler's maturity jump and his ability to leap his life forward seemed almost miraculous to Scott and Elaine, until we reminded them that Tyler's changes occurred after their own transformations. They had challenged their stereotypes, dropped defensive reactions, and gained self-awareness. They had laid the groundwork for the understanding that came from putting themselves in Tyler's shoes. They had provided crucially effective support and now had an improved relationship with their son. Scott and Elaine rewrote their old rules and styles of parenting. They had undertaken many changes. Now they were all on the same team.

With the guidelines for respectful relating in our toolbox, we're ready to stretch parenting to fit the third decade of the young adult's journey. Chapter 5, Get a Job: Educational Pathways for Twenty-First-Century Careers, focuses on parental involvement in a twentysomething's educational and career choices.

5

Get a Job

Educational Pathways for Twenty-First-Century Careers

It is the most primally American thing to want our children to have better lives than we led before.
—*Xochitl Gonzalez, "The No-Pain, No-Gain Ethos of Gen X,"*
The Atlantic, *March 16, 2022*

PARENTS OFTEN ASK CHILDREN, "WHAT ARE YOU GOING TO BE WHEN YOU GROW up?" A child may know clearly what they want to be and follow their passions into a career with persistence, hard work, and available opportunities. Other children, into young adulthood, simply may not know and follow their changing interests. Still others find their way blocked by multiple factors—peer competition, flubbed exams, finances, or unexpected roadblocks. Yet, with effort, resilience, and support for their aspirations, young adults eventually arrive at careers that are often informed by their perception of good job opportunities. This quest begins in earnest when they finish their education, whether earning a high school diploma, a college degree, or an alternative credential. The recent and rapid shifts in the landscape of higher education and work make this time of life the "roiling twenties," accompanied by many unanticipated course corrections.

This chapter examines the various ways that today's young people make the transition from education to vocation. We'll explore how parental engagement guides emerging adults through the complexities of these defining decisions.

Paradoxically, parental advice based on their own experiences can inadvertently steer a young adult in the wrong direction. We'll turn to career counselors to reveal the hidden flaws in the common advising wisdom.

To explore the assortment of degrees and credentials needed for a good job, we'll follow the diverse experiences of five high school friends as they move through their twenties. Their stories illustrate the obstacles that many twentysomethings encounter. The friends want the education that Fiona Hill describes in her book *There Is Nothing for You Here*: "The right kind of education for the twenty-first century . . . is one that prepares us to weather changes—and which does so equally, without regard to where we are from or what your parents do."[1]

We'll walk both generations through the hopes, dreams, and realities that propel decisions surrounding traditional and alternative degrees that precede career employment. We'll review the tangled web of assumptions that parents and their young adults navigate. Each generation faces a new world to some extent. Our pandemic-shaped society has increased online learning, changed labor-force hiring criteria, and expanded employers' acceptance of remote work. Despite the rapid changes, we're encouraged by unanticipated and promising gains. We begin with a defining question that more and more parents and students are asking.

IS A COLLEGE DEGREE STILL THE TICKET TO A GOOD JOB AND LIFE?

The question regarding the relative importance of a college degree to employment can be simply answered: It depends. There's broad agreement that information-age jobs require education and skills training well beyond high school. However, due to very recent labor-market shifts, employers are again moving toward hiring qualifications that favor skills rather than those based only on a degree. To help you weigh this increasingly fraught subject, we consider a few variables, including historic educational and job trends, college completion rates, the appropriate fit, and alternatives to college.

Since the 1970s, and increasingly in our hourglass-shaped economy—one with a plethora of high-paying and low-paying jobs but fewer in between—a good job and life became synonymous with a college education.[2] This emphasis became supercharged in the 1980s as high levels of unemployment created "degree inflation." By the early 2000s, a significant number of employers weeded out applicants by adding college degree requirements to jobs that had not previously insisted on them.[3] The degree upgrade for the same work coincided with rising costs for a college education and a shrinking middle class.

Despite the occasional dismissal of the importance of a college degree, in today's market, a college education is often necessary for a middle-class[*] job and life.[4] Increases in U.S. college enrollment support the impression of a half-century success story, with a victory lap for young adults, their parents, and society itself. But the reality is different than its image.

Rather than becoming success stories, many college students never cross the finish line. Less than one-third of U.S. young adults ages twenty-five to twenty-nine hold a bachelor's degree.[5] Although two-thirds of students who enroll in four-year private and public U.S. colleges graduate within six years of enrollment,[6] most of the completers come from relatively well-resourced families.[7] As a totality of young adults who enroll in college, graduates represent only a sliver of twentysomethings. Consequently, the educational decisions for twentysomethings are seldom one and done but remain in flux for some years.[8] As recently as 2018, 40 percent of all college students were twenty-five or older.[9] The pandemic changed that trend, with enrollment trending younger.

How do we understand these discouraging figures? Nationally, about 25 percent of students who enroll full-time or part-time at two-year or four-year institutions do not return for their second year. The numbers are so large that the National Student Clearinghouse Research Center uses the acronym SCNC. Some College, No Credential (or degree). Most are dropouts who never return to college, while a small percentage of students are "stop-outs" who later reenroll, usually at a community college.[10] The dropout rate is highest for those enrolled in community college and associate degree programs, with first-year disenrollment at 41 percent.[11] The attitudes of twentysomethings toward adulthood often reflect their educational level and our society's growing inequalities. Ask a better-resourced college graduate in their mid- to late twenties about their life, and they might say, "You know, how can I complain? I'm doing okay. But I'm disappointed that I'm not where I should be. There's no way that I'll be better off than my parents." Ask a

---

*We're using *middle class* and *middle income* interchangeably here. According to a 2022 Pew report, the income it takes to be middle income varies by household size but ranges from $52,000 to $156,000 in 2020 dollars for a household of three. Middle class can be a self-identifier referring to profession, level of education, economic security, home ownership, or one's social and political values.

frontline service employee without a college degree, and their discouraging reply might be, "What's up with adulting—all the dead-end gig jobs, school loans, crazy politics, Covid? It all sucks."

The narrowing path to the American dream, and its powerful promise of economic opportunity and upward mobility, is littered with astronomical college costs. As the cost of living and college tuition ballooned over the past thirty years, the percentage of U.S. governmental investment in an individual's college education has not kept up proportionately. The macroeconomic forces of the past half-century, described in Chapter 1, have shifted the financial burden of a college degree. Previously, government and businesses funded college costs on behalf of the common good.[12] Now students and their parents assume those costs and are taking on "unprecedented debt burdens to do so."[13]

How much of the cost transfer you paid to attend college depends upon when you were born. If you were born in the 1960s or 1970s, federal and state need-based grants that did not require repayment were instrumental in supporting most college costs. For example, in the mid-1970s the need-based Pell Grant, requiring nonrepayment, covered two-thirds of average college costs. By comparison, in 2017 the maximum Pell Grant covered only 25 percent of average costs. If you were born toward the end of the 1990s, you inherited a "pay for your own college" bill. Students have been borrowing more since 1990, when just over half of bachelor's degree recipients borrowed. By 2016, 70 percent borrowed. The average debt burden for graduating seniors has risen to $30,000.[14]

Marginalized and first-generation millennial and Gen Z college students have even higher loan-borrowing rates and assume more debt. College enrollment for these groups has become an even greater risk calculation, with the odds stacked against them. It's a *Hunger Games* version of the odds "favoring" a longer time to degree completion, college credits with no diploma, and burdensome debt. Unsurprisingly, both parents and students now expect a greater return on their college investment through well-paying jobs.

The reasons students cite for attending college have paralleled the costs they've shouldered. In 1968, the most popular reason was "developing a meaningful philosophy of life," selected by 85 percent of first-year students. Other widespread goals included "helping others who are in difficulty" and "keeping up to date with political affairs." By 2000, with higher loan debt, the most popular motive was "being very well-off financially," selected by 74 percent of students.[15]

Returning to the question of "Is college worth it?" there are multiple answers. A college education, assuming its completion, can be a valuable financial asset. Beyond its monetization, the richness of the college experience often includes an irreplaceable period of intellectual exploration, critical thinking, reflection on and commitment to a larger sense of purpose, mentoring by professors, and lifelong bonding to a diverse community of peers. Societal benefits include a well-educated, civic-minded populace, informed consumers, and a skilled workforce. Yet education policy experts assert that until the federal government constructs stronger consumer protections, parents and young adults, especially the less financially resourced, must make painstaking decisions, weighing the value of the effort and expense of a college education alongside alternative pathways to credentialing, jobs, and careers.[16] It is important to understand that the lack of a two- or four-year college degree does not mean being doomed to a life without career prospects. As we will show, the training and education that fit a person's goals and strengths are key.

PANDEMIC SHIFTS IN EDUCATION AND JOB DISCONNECTION

The Covid-19 pandemic had some unexpected effects on young people's education and employment. Opportunities initially worsened and then, surprisingly, expanded. During the early pandemic disruptions of February through June 2020, a staggering 30 percent of people between the ages of sixteen and twenty-four were neither enrolled in school nor employed, according to a Pew Research Center analysis of U.S. Census Bureau data.[17] By comparison, in January 2020, prior to Covid's widespread onset in the U.S., the disconnection rate mirrored the previous year, at 12 percent. Covid-related job losses among young workers accounted for most of the difference.

Covid's educational impact was reflected in the 39 million SCNC dropouts—an 8.6 percent increase from 2019 prepandemic levels.[18] Even more sadly disruptive, for every four Covid-related deaths in the first fourteen months of the pandemic's outbreak, one U.S. minor in four, among them college aspirants, lost a parent or primary caregiver. Sixty-five percent of those minors came from minority families.[19] Family job loss also affected the educational and career dreams of many who dropped out. Other young people deferred enrollment because of the strains of remote learning.

The pandemic accelerated and flashed warning lights about demographic trends already in place. Overall, college enrollment dropped 9.4 percent during the 2020 and 2021 enrollment periods. By spring of 2022, an additional 4.7 percent decline had occurred since 2021.[20] By spring 2023, estimated fall enrollment had largely stabilized, but at 9 percent below prepandemic levels.[21] Higher education's enrollment drift toward younger students under eighteen signals that older students are disappearing. This despite the fact that technology and labor market changes suggest that more adults will need to return to college. With an upcoming baby bust, college enrollment is headed toward a demographic cliff.

Concurrent with enrollment declines, higher education's gender gap widened, reflecting a lower male-to-female student ratio. More men, especially students of color and first-generation students, accepted frontline jobs to provide financially for their families. Students who graduated from college into the early pandemic found scarce employment opportunities and often settled for underemployment. The life dreams of young people and their parents who supported their aspirations lie buried beneath these trends.

Kam, a recent college graduate, reflects upon this reality. "Once, I hoped to go to med school. But after my 2019 college graduation, I couldn't afford more student debt, so I took a job in luxury fashion sales. I was lucky, because I kept my job when the pandemic hit, and my commission on sales wasn't that deeply affected. After a few years, my dreams of med school faded. Instead, I sell expensive clothes to rich people who don't need them. I try not to think about it. My parents feel for me, but they still have my younger brother and sister to help put through college."

Colleges have taken notice and are upskilling their curricula to prove that their educational costs pay off. After years of frustration, colleges and governmental agencies may soon be able to quantify the value of a degree or credential through the 2023 College Transparency Act. Impressively, a detailed analysis by program, institution, and student demographics would create a public-facing online dashboard. At last, there will be accountability and transparency on all degrees on graduation, economic outcomes, and job training.[22]

Until that is available, a silver lining of Covid has emerged for twentysomethings. The entry of brand-name universities into the online-certificate and -degree marketplace, along with the pandemic's 2020–2022 labor shortage, eased employers' hiring criteria and significantly increased their acceptance of skills-training programs that were not degree-based.[23] As a result, online-degree and short-term certificate programs shed their former stigma. With the undersupply of entry-level employees, the labor market shifted to favor employees based on skills, as the barriers to remote training and work also fell.

To put a face on these trends, we turn to twentysomethings for valuable lessons from the uncertain and bumpy educational pathways that lead to middle-income jobs.

MEET THE FRIENDS AND THEIR EDUCATION TO JOB CHALLENGES

The five friends we spoke to, four men and one woman, met at an urban magnet high school specializing in science, technology, engineering, and mathematics (STEM). The school's competitive admissions policy reflected the city's demographics regarding ethnic, racial, socioeconomic, and gender distributions. Each friend aspired to the middle-class goal of earning a college degree. Their paths diverged in the two distinct worlds of traditional and nontraditional college students. Nationally, traditional students are better resourced, live in two-parent households, have at least one parent with a bachelor's degree, and graduate from a four-year residential college. A minority will also pursue graduate education. The nontraditional college student group is defined as twenty-four years or older, more often male, from a marginalized group, and the first generation in their family to attend college. Nontraditional students often attend two-year colleges intermittently because of work and family responsibilities.[24]

The five friends supported each other throughout their twenties, across their varied educational and employment tracks. Their creative solutions to many uncertainties illustrate the recently expanded education-to-job possibilities, including online learning, aptitude testing for a career redirect, and alternative certification. Their experiences varied from direct workforce entry into frontline jobs, underemployment, high-paying jobs, and career shifts. We begin by describing their families' circumstances.

Two of the friends came from families in the lowest socioeconomic quintile, two were middle income, and one was in the upper quintile. All but one belonged to an ethnic minority. Only one was a first-generation college student. Each of them experienced one or more adversities related to finances, housing, mental health, employment, or lack of parental engagement. In today's new normal, only one friend traveled a direct path from college to a high-earning career. None of the five managed without financial support, sometimes accompanied by formal career guidance. Because adequate financing is often crucial for a direct route through college and degree completion to a job, we often overlook what money cannot buy. Independent of socioeconomic status, the emotional support of familial advocacy and the encouragement to persevere positively impacts a young adult's academic achievement and college enrollment.[25] No one does it alone.

From the stories of these friends, we'll learn how parents, as well as the extended network of teachers, advisors, and peers, can help to guide young adults as they strategize to overcome barriers. We'll share practical advice that can prevent or resolve stalling before the half-life of a diploma's value expires.

The Traditional Route to a Good Job: Four (or More) Years of College

Three of the high school friends—Kahlil, Andreas, and Matt—experienced the privilege of being traditional college students, with its extended period of career and identity exploration. Kahlil and Andreas additionally shared the experience of childhood immigration. Both of their families immigrated during the mid- to late 1990s. Kahlil's parents escaped Libya during Muammar Gaddafi's rule, whereas Andreas's Panamanian parents, who were relatively well-off, immigrated to enhance their children's future livelihoods. Unlike his friends, Matt was white, from a financially secure family, and was the fourth generation in his family to attend college.

None of the three friends represent the American dream stereotype of upward mobility by virtue of rugged individualism. Rather, as is commonly true, the young men relied heavily on familial and institutional support to manage the educational-cost burden. Only Kahlil, who majored in mechanical engineering, followed a college-to-employer pipeline to an excellent-paying job—one that he soon became determined to leave. Both Andreas and Matt graduated college into years of underemployment. They based their college majors on their interests, but without a good understanding of where their strongest aptitudes lay. We'll see how each of the three closed the gap between aspiration and reality.

Kahlil: Taking Advantage of Institutional Support

Kahlil's admirably quick ascent from his family's near-poverty level to the top 10 percent income bracket belonged as much to the young man's abilities and efforts as to his parents' personal and professional sacrifices. An older uncle sponsored the parents' immigration to the U.S. when Kahlil was three and his sister was still a baby. Alarmed to discover that their impoverished neighborhood was rife with gun violence, the family soon moved to a safer, though still undesirable, industrial area. When Kahlil's college-educated father couldn't find a job in his field, he worked as a car mechanic. His mother, whose English was limited, stayed home and focused on securing her children's entrance into the best public schools. Both Kahlil and his sister gained admittance to these schools, first by lottery and then through academic competition.

During high school, Kahlil's teachers and principal encouraged him to apply to a nearby university with an adaptive curriculum that included eighteen months of paid and employer-supported cooperatives.* Kahlil was excited by the co-op model, which allowed him to earn credits toward his degree through jobs in his field of study. And to get paid for it! With this institutional support and the university's award of a generous scholarship, Kahlil secured a full-tuition ride for his five-year bachelor's in science while he lived at home to eliminate housing costs.

Upon graduation, as is the case for many emerging adults from lower socioeconomic backgrounds, it was Kahlil's turn to provide additional financial support to his family. His starting salary as an engineer in the defense industry was more than double the combined incomes of his father and uncle. Over the next three years, Kahlil paid off his parents' mortgage and their other debt, bought his uncle a car, and then drank the rest of his paycheck. Heavy drinking went against Kahlil's upbringing, his parents' values, and the extended family and community's religious tradition. His parents recognized his substance misuse as an indication of the toll his job was taking on him. Kahlil hated what he dubbed his "dogshit" job. The required minimum of 60 percent travel and long hours shrank the frame of his life to strictly work.

Both Kahlil and his parents had made sacrifices to secure better lives for one another. Now his parents made one more sacrifice—they supported Kahlil's decision to leave his high-income job for a start-up public/private partnership venture with a college friend. Like his parents before him, Kahlil would also move three thousand miles from home—this time, across the country. Since then, the start-up has been successful, and Kahlil is doing well.

---

*A growing number of universities, such as Drexel University, Northeastern University, Georgia Tech, and MIT follow this cooperative model, with jobs that earn coursework credits.

Andreas and Matt: Online Platforms and Aptitude Testing to the Rescue

"Sometimes a college degree isn't enough," Matt told his parents. It was 2017, and both he and Andreas were underemployed college grads. They complained, not unreasonably or inaccurately, that the college degree now held the equivalency of a high school diploma.

In this section, we'll examine the options available when the maxim "College is worth the investment" becomes disconnected from a student's interests and career choice. And we'll hear from an expert on the common mistakes young adults and their parents make in pairing a course of study with work goals. There's a paradox for parents. How can they wisely advise their emerging adults whose educational decisions or job experiences are so dissimilar from their own? Recent economic changes demonstrate how little we know about the future of jobs; nor can we predict the necessary credentials that our children entering young adulthood will need to obtain a good job. We cannot see what the future holds. Despite this enormous uncertainty, we ask seventeen-year-olds to decide on the training, education, and life work they want in the future.

And yet parents can impart generational wisdom that an emerging adult cannot foresee. They might review the expanding and flexible pathways from serious aspirations to a career, and how to bear the costs. Later, parents can troubleshoot specifics about how studies match workplace entry. They can reassure young adults that life is curvy, not linear—there will be starts and stumbles along the way. And parents can learn from their advising mistakes, as Andreas's and Matt's parents did.

Andreas and Matt began their college searches during junior year of high school. More than a good income, the friends sought purposeful careers. Their parents guided their searches based on their interests, best grades, and expected college majors. This approach, according to Steve Greene, New York director of the Johnson O'Connor Research Foundation,* is the most common mistake in early career guidance. People's interests are inherently unstable; they are learned, feelings-based, and changeable.[26] Although a student's best grades reflect two stable predictors—smarts (IQ) and dogged determination—even

---

*Johnson O'Connor Research Foundation is a nonprofit educational and scientific organization. https://www.jocrf.org/.

this powerful combination fails to indicate an individual's ease in, or enjoyment of, a particular field of study or work role.

Greene described how these decisive conversations between parent and college aspirant typically go: "[The parent will say,] 'Hey, you made straight A's in math.' So they try to guide their student . . . to go into business or finance. They're reflecting good grades plus interest, which isn't an aptitude. The vast majority of people I see are relatively clueless about their aptitudes. Sometimes learning their strongest aptitudes is a revelation."

Aptitudes, said Greene, are the best predictors of a successful college major and a gratifying future career: "An aptitude is the potential for learning to do something quickly or easily," he explained. "We believe it's a genetic trait and is stable over time." He then defined how aptitudes differ from skills: "A skill is a learned or acquired ability (not inherent)."

To illustrate the difference between skill and aptitude, consider the experience of learning to play a musical instrument. The yearslong challenging skills instruction includes: memorization of individual notes or chords, the mastery of scales, time signature, rhythm, sight-reading, and ear training, with variations for wind, string, or percussive instruments. Without a musical aptitude, you can diligently practice to become a passable recreational musician, but it won't be fun. However, someone with a very strong musical aptitude, such as Louis Armstrong, David Bowie, Kurt Cobain, and Prince, **can self-teach**. They turn an aptitude into a career, playing with perfect pitch, tonality, emotionality, and instrument mastery.

Asked if aptitudes are related to general intelligence (or the G factor), Greene replied, "No, the G factor of IQ is not involved in aptitude. With IQ, you end up with a number versus what aptitudes you are naturally talented at. Not having an aptitude doesn't mean you can't do a job. It's just that you'll have to work hard at it and probably won't enjoy it very much." Given a choice, most people leave ungratifying jobs.

Greene assured us that young adults can also grasp how their aptitudes align with their career choices without testing, but rather through trial-and-error experiences. Informally, individuals may do informational interviewing, internships, volunteer work, and try jobs related to their future goals. Regarding online aptitude testing, Greene cautioned that many rely on self-reporting, which is similar to asking, "What are your interests?" A formal, in-depth aptitude test, such as the individualized assessments conducted at the Johnson O'Connor Research Foundation, is better validated. The foundation's test results yield twenty-two objective aptitude scores that indicate how easily someone grasps numerical or spatial problems, visual tasks, or idea generation, among other things. The benefit of knowing your strongest aptitudes is that it links educational focus and gratifying job possibilities. In the twenty-first century, it's unlikely that you'll have the same job across your entire career. It's important to be flexible.

Neither Andreas, Matt, nor their parents had ever heard that finding one's aptitudes was a good guide to choosing a college major and career. Consequently, their decisions were based on interests and good grades. Upon graduation, both friends were disillusioned as they struggled to find jobs that led to fulfilling careers. They had expected more from their college degrees. So had their parents. We learn how Andreas and Matt overcame the obstacles that lay ahead.

Unlike Kahlil's, Andreas's immigration story was one of financial stability. Upon their arrival in the U.S., his college-educated parents secured middle-income jobs and bought a home in a safe working-class neighborhood. Like many better-resourced young adults, Andreas followed his high school interests into college, where he majored in film studies. Like Kahlil, Andreas also lived at home and attended college tuition-free, through a generous benefit from his mother's university employer. His parents advised Andreas that film majors were where dreams go to die. Their skepticism was met by Andreas's unshakable resolve.

Following his college graduation, Andreas pursued his film dreams while working part-time and still living with his parents. During this period, his life was one of serial underemployment: part-time grocery store worker, sports club attendant, substitute teacher at a public school. He casually described his "easy come, easy go" job changes as an advantage of his "partial Hispanic whiteness," explaining, "Yeah, employers give me the benefit of the doubt and don't regard me with suspicion because I can pass when I need to." In his first year after college, Andreas pitched scripts to the film and media industry. The silence of "No reply" was deafening. In year two, he wrote fewer scripts, continued working part-time, and smoked more dope as he became more discouraged.

By year three, his parents were losing patience with what appeared to be Andreas's indifference to growing up and getting out. They saw him on a meandering path to nowhere, consumed with an online after-midnight Japanese anime channel, which carried him through the early-morning hours. Unknown to his parents, however, Andreas was hatching a plan to fulfill another dream. He kept it to himself, anticipating that they'd disapprove again.

Though Andreas's interest and college major were in film, he eventually realized that his ease in learning foreign languages indicated that auditory processing was his strongest aptitude. Andreas was eight the summer his family moved to the States. Before his third grade classes began, he quickly developed English fluency through hours spent watching cartoons. Now, at twenty-five, Andreas once again turned to cartoons and free media platforms to master spoken Japanese.* He was boosting the utility of his Asian studies minor, where he became proficient reading Japanese.

Soon Andreas applied for the job of a second-language teacher—in Japan. That year, he was repeatedly rejected in favor of graduates whose major was in Asian studies. But Andreas was determined. He dealt with this second round of setbacks much better. While rejections felt bad, Andreas framed the experience neutrally, neither denying nor bright-siding his disappointment. "Managing Disappointments in a Job Search" lists some methods he used to cope with these setbacks.

MANAGING DISAPPOINTMENTS IN A JOB SEARCH

- Frame your experience objectively, and try to avoid taking it too personally.
- Validate your feelings: It's understandable that you're disappointed.
- Practice acceptance: A job rejection is tough and can be somewhat arbitrary.
- Remember, it's all in the timing. Today's rejection doesn't predict the future.
- Keep your options open. Expand upon your first choice.

Putting his disappointments aside, Andreas reinforced his Japanese language skills with a monthslong stay in Japan. While abroad, he interviewed for the teaching position. The interviewer was impressed by his determination and his self-taught conversational fluency.

Andreas's parents, who were still unaware of his plan to teach English in

* For additional free online courses, Greene referred us to this link: https://www.themuse.com/advice/45-free-online-classes-you-can-take-and-finish-by-the-end-of-this-year.

Japan, regarded his foreign travel as a frivolous indulgence. His trip was a tipping point in their frustration. They welcomed him home with two edicts: "If you have enough money to spend on a vacation, then you have enough money to pay rent." And . . . "You have a six-month deadline to move out of the house." Even under the pressure of these ultimatums, Andreas chose not to disclose his hopes. He read their lack of curiosity about his cartoon watching and his trip, along with their assumptions about his stall, as further evidence that they would be closed-minded and dismissive.

Shortly before his move-out deadline, the pandemic intervened, and Andreas finally caught a break. The number of applications to the teaching program fell, and the Japanese instructor who had interviewed Andreas offered him a job. He was overjoyed—and celebrated with his friends.

Finally, he told his parents. He was stunned by their response. Rather than posing any obstacles, his parents were thrilled. In hindsight, they regretted how much their biases about Andreas's delayed adulthood had prevented them from developing a closer relationship with him. They were sad to see him go so far from home and resolved to own up to what they hadn't understood. He left with their blessings and happiness that he had secured a job he truly wanted. His teaching term would be five years. What would follow—stay? Leave?—was unclear. But Andreas was okay—he'd had practice figuring out the uncertainties of young adulthood.

We next turn to Matt, the last of the three traditional college students. With the help of the ethnic and socioeconomic diversity of his high school friendships, Matt broadened his understanding of what it meant to be privileged. He reflected:

> I was profoundly sheltered and attended a private K–8 school. I didn't appreciate how most people live until I went to my public magnet high school. There, I saw a lot of kids that did worry about money. Twenty dollars to me was, to them, like a hundred. I got a lot of perspective from the other kids that I didn't get at my name-brand colleges. I might've become one of those guys that whined about paying taxes or health care. I learned that you can't pick yourself up by your bootstraps. I think I developed compassion for other people's lives and understood that the system isn't fair. You can work really hard, like Kahlil, and do well. And then you have smart people like our friend Z. He has worked hard too, but he hasn't gotten ahead. The myth of America is it's on you if you make it, and it's shameful if you don't. It's the great negligence of the American system.

Like many of his friends, Matt initially majored in STEM courses at college. Matt's parents supported this course of study, since Matt had excelled in the sciences in high school. Mr. Greene describes why this path is commonly misunderstood: "A lot of high school students want to go into STEM. And of course, STEM is a particular combination of aptitude scores. I try to guide them. If you love it, keep on, but it's very competitive at a college level. Students are kind of stubborn; they know what they're going to do. But in most cases, aptitudes prevail."

Greene's description dovetails with Matt's decision. "I didn't go to college to be happy," Matt said. "I went to get a good-paying job. I wanted to have the same lifestyle as my parents. To be safe, I majored in a STEM field, because I also had an interest in nutrition. Partway through, I decided I wouldn't like a clinical work life." Matt was smart enough to do the hard work in this field, but he didn't enjoy it. He had lost interest.

Matt's initial excitement at being accepted to his dream college dissipated following several hardships. Early in second semester of his freshman year, he sustained multiple-ligament knee trauma as a passenger in a car accident. Following emergency surgery, an infection required extended bed rest and delayed his recovery. Compounding the physical loss of his go-to activity of soccer, he lost his sense of belonging, as his soccer friends and social life tapered off. He continued his coursework remotely, but his academics suffered. He realized that he needed to change majors. By the end of the semester, Matt decided that he needed a fresh start to pursue another interest. He transferred to a college that specialized in postproduction sound editing. Three years later and nearing graduation, he completed an unpaid industry internship. His conclusion: "I learned that I'd be a debt serf, without a secure job or income. I mean, what was college for? So now I'm a glorified cashier, living back home while my parents are trying to help me figure out what's next. It's so depressing."

Matt's parents had a compassionate take on their son's situation. "It was painful to see our thoughtful, talented son crash and burn after graduation," they said. "We're not sure what's next, but we'll try to help him figure it out." As his floundering persisted, they sought a few sessions with us to manage their own anxieties and sadness. "Parents Have Feelings Too" acknowledges the painful emotions that parents experience when their young adult struggles through a difficult situation.

PARENTS HAVE FEELINGS TOO

- Parents may feel grief in a young adult's painful disappointments and the loss of youthful dreams.

- Anger is understandable, but it's the tip of the iceberg for many softer feelings of hurt, frustration, and sadness. Allow yourself to feel those as well.

- When you are worried about your young adult, write down your fears. Later, you may be able to listen to your adult child without feeling so responsible to solve things.

- Try to avoid gloomy forecasting. Remind yourself that feelings are not facts.

- If guilty thoughts emerge, recognize that self-reproach is the flip side of feeling helpless. We do not have as much control as we wish we did.

- You may feel embarrassed or ashamed when your friends' kids are doing great. Remind yourself that your child's situation is temporary and *not* a reflection on either them or you. Think of a compassionate narrative you may feel comfortable sharing.

We advised Matt's parents on strategies to effectively support him over the next weeks and possibly months. Being a good sounding board is important. However, parents should refer their young adults for professional counseling if they are talking in a hopeless fashion or showing signs of disengagement from everyday life and interests.

SUPPORTING YOUR YOUNG ADULT IN TIMES OF DISTRESS

Try saying this:

- "You're a worthwhile person going through a hard time. We have faith in you, and we love you."

- "I'm here for you. Call anytime."

- "I'd like to check in daily for a few minutes. Text or chat?"

Avoid saying this:

- "Don't worry, you'll be fine."
- "It was a long shot anyway."
- "Cheer up—I had crummy times too."
- "You can learn from this mistake."

Mindful that their advice on a college major had missed the mark, Matt's parents asked if he had contacted the college career office to help him regain momentum. He shrugged off their question with, "Did. Didn't seem to help."

Two experts help us understand why some students don't use college career counseling centers, which often provide valuable resources. Peter Doris was a former head of human resources at a Fortune 500 company and now volunteers as a career coach to low-income youth.[27] "Probably thirty years ago," he said, "a lot of students saw it as a badge of honor never to go into the college career center. Many of the centers had a reputation for doing little or nothing that was relevant. Over the last twenty to twenty-five years, there is now a clear distinction between college career centers that are well staffed with trained, motivated professionals and those that are overworked and understaffed."

Bill Holland, an author and business executive, is a cofounder and the board chair of United Professionals. He observed, "People who are middle-class and [higher] turn to their parents and their parents' friends for job connections."[28] Then he confirmed what Matt had learned the hard way: "Finding out what you're truly good at requires a level of maturity that eighteen-year-olds or twenty-year-olds don't have."

The experts we consulted envision higher education improving its college-to-employment connections in the future. Here are a few of their takeaways:

- Peter Doris suggests that universities, without a formal credits-for-jobs cooperative model, could equip professors to transfer knowledge through the classroom curricula to jobs that connect studies with career skills. Mr. Doris also recommends that colleges utilize aptitude testing more efficiently. Reliable tests might be administered to a large student group, then adapted to provide individualized feedback.

- Steve Greene envisions the development of high-quality aptitude testing for online use.
- Bill Holland recommends enhancing classroom education with social-media search strategies for degree-to-career opportunities.

The next game changer in education-to-career may be a full-stack higher education company,[29] which connects online programs to jobs. Steven Mintz, an educational innovator, author, and history professor, is in the vanguard of developing a full-stack educational platform at the University of Texas at Austin—a class-to-credential-to-job program.[30] The goal of a full-stack educational model is to use technologies that can make a quality education more accessible, affordable, and successful. This promising development is currently being utilized to create online educational courses and certification programs with job training in IT, coding, and technology fields.

Colleges are rethinking career prep and embracing the demands of their new role—helping students make successful transitions from their studies to a career. Career officers note that it can be discouraging for a young adult to search through job openings for the list of "need to have" skills. To understand how an individual's skills translate to other jobs or settings, they suggest broader occupational searches, such as the Occupational Outlook Handbook or the online resource center at O*NET.* By learning about job roles, wages, and occupational projections, individuals can better understand how their background aligns with relevant roles while gleaning key words to use when beginning a job search. O*NET also has a Career Changers Matrix, a great resource for making a career pivot. LinkedIn.com has a similar resource through its Career Explorer site. There are good books on the subject, including *Pivot: The Only Move That Matters Is Your Next One* and *Recalculating*. And ask around for suggestions from people you trust for articles, podcasts, videos, and webinars. Finally, career officers may suggest that before a job interview, it's okay to review a hiring manager's LinkedIn, X (formerly known as Twitter), Instagram, and Facebook profiles. Don't forget that employers will also be viewing an applicant's social media feeds—so keep it professional. Increasingly, college students and alumni have many helpful diploma-to-career resources available to them.

Matt turned to another popular career resource for students-parents.

---

*An annual publication of the U.S. Bureau of Labor Statistics, for hundreds of occupations.

Parents can provide their young adult with access to their social capital, and with connections to their friends and professional colleagues for expanded employment opportunities. Matt's parents connected him to one of their contacts, who recommended aptitude testing before Matt expanded his job search. Matt knew very little about it, but figured, *Why not?* His surprising results reflected that his strongest aptitudes aligned with careers in numerical analysis, finance, and business. In high school, he hadn't loved calculus, so he mistakenly concluded that the business world wasn't for him.

Fortified with this new information about his aptitudes, Matt learned what he could from each role at his job. As a good team player, he took on tasks that his managers valued, including doing data-driven operations reports. Over the course of the next three years, he worked his way up from his "glorified cashier" position in the luxury retail sector to corporate jobs in operations and then finance departments.

Matt later concluded, "Even though my college major didn't line up with a job I wanted, my broader education improved my soft skills, such as the ability to write and present well and to analyze text—skills that employers value. College is your foot in the door. It's an expensive ticket to help you understand a field and prepare for a career. But it's not the only way. I found my career direction based on aptitude testing, which I highly recommend. Saves a lot of struggling."

Struggle is what lay ahead for his friends Jaz and Z. We'll follow them to learn the strategies that nontraditional students use.

THE NONTRADITIONAL ROUTE TO A GOOD JOB: EXPANDED CREDENTIALING

While Andreas and Matt had degrees without the initial career impact they expected, our next two friends, Jaz and Zion (or "Z," to his friends), had college credits with little value in the job market. Both Jaz and Z withdrew from college at the end of their freshman year. Jaz flunked out, while Z lacked the finances to continue. Both left with significant student debt. The friends belong to a key demographic of Black, nontraditional students. Most of these young adults have the raw intelligence to succeed in college, but their parents may lack either the money or the experience to guide them.

Jaz is part of the small percentage of stop-out students who eventually return to complete their educational degrees. Though Jaz faced stiff academic criteria for reapplication, her divorced mother, Ava, a middle school teacher, played a key role in encouraging Jaz's degree attainment. While parental support for emerging adults often focuses on the benefits that higher-socioeconomic families can bestow, the emotional encouragement a parent can offer a child does not depend on class and may be as important to educational completion as financial support. Parental affirmation of a young adult's ability and worth helps them develop the resilience to persist in the face of challenges.[31] Z's experience reflects the discouraging news for those first-year college students who, without parental support, drop out of college and never return. Though each friend faced obstacles ahead, Z's circumstances were far more daunting.

We follow the unique experiences of Jaz and Z to gain insight into the twenty-first-century credentialing options for nontraditional students.

Jaz: Obtaining Alternative Credentials

Jaz's academic problems in college followed a breadcrumb trail of childhood learning problems that began with dyslexia. In middle school, Jaz was diagnosed with ADHD, inattentive type. Her mother helped Jaz succeed in middle and high school, with mountains of documentation to secure individualized educational plans. Behind the scenes, Ava also propped up her daughter's poor organizational skills with a spreadsheet of class assignments and due dates. Each night, she reviewed Jaz's progress. In this way, Jaz managed until college, when the academic demands increased and her mother's backup surveillance went missing. Ava's dedication to ensure that Jaz stayed on track for college acceptance had, unwittingly, contributed to Jaz's college failure.* Enabled by continued reliance on her mother's support, Jaz never developed the skills she needed to succeed in college—a situation known as overscaffolding.

A year following Jaz's withdrawal from college, Ava requested family therapy. For years, mother and daughter had experienced a fraught relationship. Ava ruled her sometimes-rowdy seventh-graders with an "I'm the boss" style, but found it a poor parenting match to support her daughter's challenges. Nor was Jaz a good match for her mother's expectations of good grades and no

---

*The underlying time and organizational problem of poor executive functioning is a chief culprit in many young adults' struggles. In the next chapter, we discuss the disorder's neurological underpinnings, along with management strategies and treatments.

excuses. Jaz had a pocketful of "I forgot" defenses that drove her mother wild. For years, Ava thought Jaz's forgetfulness was a failure of self-discipline. She repeatedly rebuked Jaz: "You aren't applying yourself like Desiree does." Her mother's shaming comparison to her older sister certainly didn't help. Ava knew that Jaz was smart, yet her poorly organized, late-on-arrival style didn't reflect it. When we first met with them, their relationship had deteriorated.

"I'm about to lose it," Ava said, shaking her head. She addressed us as if Jaz weren't present. "What's wrong with her? Is it meds, Dr. Rostain? Dr. Hibbs, is it problems with adult development? I mean, she's only working as a babysitter a couple of days a week, and I need a plan, because she can't seem to make one. And I'm tired of babysitting her life." The session had just begun, and Jaz was crying hard.

We asked Ava to hold her thoughts as we passed the tissues to Jaz and said to Ava, "Let's give Jaz a chance to catch her breath, because we want to hear from each of you."

After a few minutes, Jaz spoke. "I can't take it if Mom is just going to rail on me," she half-pleaded. We reassured Jaz, "Our first goal in family therapy is to help the two of you develop a more harmonious relationship with a constructive way of talking about hard topics."

The goal of exploratory, open-ended, and responsive communication would replace a yearslong pattern of negative interactions. Ava felt entirely justified in her harsh reprimands over Jaz's haphazard task completion. She gave examples: Jaz didn't reliably follow through on time-sensitive and important to-do items. Ava would find out too late to help. Recently, in the course of one week, Jaz lost a job opportunity because she hadn't returned calls, let her ADHD medications run out, and missed her college readmission deadline. Underlying her critiques, Ava felt anxious, responsible, and yet helpless to change her daughter's behavior. Ava could neither protect Jaz from harsh consequences nor help her make needed progress.

In response to being scolded, Jaz would push back and accuse her mother of being the problem. Name-calling would typically ensue, with Ava telling Jaz she was a lazy do-nothing and Jaz telling her mom that she was a mean teacher and a bitch for a mom. Jaz would then give her mother the cold shoulder for days or longer.

Clearly, their conversations had not followed the listen-and-talk guidelines of perspective-taking. Nor were they making conscious attempts to change what was meaningful to each other. Their now predictably painful exchanges fed a negative feedback loop.

In our early work with them, we asked mother and daughter to be good students and learn the new rules for listening and relating. (See "Checking Defensiveness 101" on pages 79 and 80 in Chapter 4.) Ava immediately challenged our assignment, admonishing us, "This is childish. I already know how to relate. That isn't the problem we're here for. We're here to help Jaz get on with it."

Gently asserting our authority, we partially validated her point, replying, "Naturally, parents and kids talk, listen, and relate. However, no one teaches us the skills to recognize and correct our commonest mistakes in relating. If you practice these skills, you can listen with new ears, and relate constructively. That builds trust and closeness. We share your goal to better support Jaz's relaunch into adulthood. And we share Jaz's goal to reduce tensions between you. These new rules will help."

With that stated, Ava dropped her protest, and they each agreed to undertake this effort. In parallel to this work, we confirmed that Jaz needed a review of her ADHD medication. Additionally, Jaz agreed to individual sessions with an ADHD coach, with the goal of improving her executive functioning.

We checked in with them regularly to hear how their homework assignment was going. Following their review of our improved communication guidelines, Jaz and her mother worked to replace criticisms and defensiveness with open-minded listening. Both mother and daughter made a list of the meaningful changes they could ask of each other. Instead of complaints, they progressed to specific requests. Ava's biggest ask of Jaz revealed how hurt she felt by Jaz's silent treatment, though she expressed it in her familiar accusatory manner: "Stop punishing me by being sullen; stop avoiding me." Jaz's request echoed a similar hurt: "Stop your bombardment about what I've screwed up and stop comparing me to my sister." Over time, with much more practice, they developed a deepened understanding of and compassion for each other's experiences.

Jaz eventually risked revealing her vulnerability. "I know you're trying to help me when I mess up," she told her mother. "I just can't take your rapid fire with a million questions. It makes me feel anxious, then angry and shut down." She asked her mother, "Give me some credit for what I get done instead of only focusing on the negatives that make me feel dumb and lazy. I feel bad enough about myself when I screw up. I'm working with the ADHD coach that our family therapists recommended to get better planning strategies in place." She added, close to tears, "I'm still a work in progress. Sorry I'm not Desiree."

Ava had seen only her daughter's anger, but now she saw her sadness and distress. In turn, Ava owned up to Jaz's feedback: "Jaz, I am so sorry that I've hurt you and brought you down. I will never compare you to Desiree again.

You have many gifts that are unique to you and that I value. I love you, though I get how it must not seem like that. I know I talk too fast with too many questions and demands. That's me being worried, because I feel responsible for solving your problems. I want to help, but I'm not helping by fussing at you. I'll do my best to catch myself. If you notice I'm doing it again, could you say something like 'Fire drill'? I'll take a breath. I guess I also have to accept that I can't control everything I wish I could, or even protect you. I can support you better, though, and I will."

Jaz responded appreciatively. "Mom, you got it. We have a plan. Just feeling better understood helps."

Ava let out a sigh with a slight smile while nodding agreement.

Gradually, over months, as their collaboration became more constructive, trust returned and their relationship improved. Now they needed to co-create a plan to support Jaz's progress. Jaz had no discernible path to finish her education or get a living-wage job. As trust built between them, Jaz became more open to her mother's supportive ideas.

They talked about how Jaz might sync her natural affinity for young children with a credential to obtain a job with benefits. With structured guidance from her ADHD coach and the use of her mother's social capital within the educational niche, Jaz came up with a solid plan. She applied for and was accepted into a state-approved associate certificate program in child development. With this credential and a twenty-hour paid program internship, Jaz could then apply credits to an associate's degree at a nearby community college. This combination would provide an impressive, skills-filled portfolio to present to prospective employers. Jaz was on her way, with an associate's degree in the near future and an independent life.

Even as valuable, Jaz and Ava were on their way to a sturdier and closer parent–young adult relationship. That one was for life.

Z: Not College but Beyond Vo-Tech

Z and Jaz remained in their hometown after Kahlil, Andreas, and Matt moved away for their jobs. Like Jaz, Z entered his twenties with some college credits but no credential. Z had been there for Jaz during her hardest times. She was one of the few friends in whom he had confided painful family events, which he called his "bad luck." Z was smart, poised beyond his years, and a hard worker.

With his many valuable qualities, it would seem that Z could count on a successful transition from adolescence through his twenties. Yet his experience of systemic racial and educational marginalization meant being excluded from many jobs. He captured it this way: "Black while applying for better-paying jobs, without a college degree." This negative stigma eliminates middle-class employment opportunities for 76 percent of Blacks and 83 percent of Latinos.[32] Initially, Z's impressive personal qualities counted, but they didn't matter enough to overcome the value employers put on a college degree.

Z's status of some coursework but no diploma is also the story of how a young adult recovers from being a college dropout. Z credits his resilience to a strong and loving childhood relationship with his parents. His childhood ended at age fourteen when his dad died from a fall. As Z grieved his father's death, he became more determined to fulfill his father's dream for him to attend college. He would be the first. His older brother had joined the military from high school and was now stationed abroad. But two more adversities were about to be added to Z's "bad luck": his mother's mental illness and poverty.

In the aftermath of his father's death, Z comforted himself with the thought that his mother would be okay, since his parents had argued much of the time. Instead, her grief became a debilitating depression that resulted in work absenteeism and job loss. She never worked again, but relied on disability income and food stamps. Her older son sent them money when he could. Z and his mother rapidly fell below the poverty line.

Three years later, Z's older brother returned stateside, and his mother moved south to join him. She asked Z to move with her, but Z wanted to finish his senior year of high school with his friends. Z's brother paid for his housing costs until after his graduation. Remarkably, throughout it all, Z maintained excellent grades.

Aware of his family's circumstances, Z's high school advisor helped him apply for a federal student loan to attend a local community college in the fall. That summer, Z worked a full-time food service job that prevented him from becoming food insecure. Z cut corners, sharing an apartment with two roommates in a sketchy neighborhood. Duct tape held up his bedroom ceiling. In September, Z enrolled full-time at the community college while he worked part-time hours. At the end of the year, he dropped out, overwhelmed by the prospect of taking on more student loan debt. He didn't know how he'd even be able to repay his existing loan with his minimum wage job. Despite Z's self-reliant, stoic presentation, his friends soon learned that he had to leave college. More bad luck followed when his computer and TV were stolen during a home break-in.

Sometimes in life, our chance relationships make a pivotal difference. For Z, that caring guidance came from Jaz's mother, who put Z in touch with a friend who ran a skills-training program for minority teens and young adults. Through this contact, Z learned of national certification programs with local affiliates that provided skills training and job connections. The groups included major nonprofit organizations with decades of experience training and finding work for underrepresented groups. A few even offered a stipend. A partial list of major nonprofits and educational and skills groups is available in the appendix.

Z was admitted to a full-time one-year coding program whose stipend allowed him to leave his food service job. Z also benefited from employers' growing acceptance of skills-based training, which expanded the earning power for youth with some college credit but no degree.[33] Finally, Z had a path forward.

As the program concluded, it taught job search optimization through the popular social media site LinkedIn.[34]

WAYS TO MAXIMIZE YOUR LINKEDIN PROFILE

- Include a profile photo, which makes you twenty-one times more likely to be viewed than you are without a photo.
- Make a brief profile video emphasizing your time management and communication skills.
- Below your name, use key words about the skills and interests that employers in your field use for searches.
- Turn on "Open to finding a new job."
- Make meaningful connections. Join LinkedIn groups to network with those with similar interests.
- Add upbeat comments to your connections when they post.

With an impressive coding certificate, Z secured a middle-income job. Z finally enjoyed the good luck that he deserved and had earned.

THE BIG QUIT?

Now that these five friends all have good jobs in their preferred careers, what can their experiences tell us about the Big Quit? This mid-pandemic period of mass resignations coincided with a hiring frenzy, in parallel with employees' pervasive dissatisfaction at work, burnout, and decades of flat wages. It was clear why older workers retired early, or why middle-aged workers, predominantly moms, quit—because they couldn't manage both jobs and online homeschooling for their kids. But why did young adults quit in such large numbers?

Some called out the younger generation as Big Quitters. Others interpreted their job changes as generational entitlement. They stereotyped the younger generation as overindulged, privileged kids who never had to work the tough no-pain-no-gain jobs of their parents' generation. They never had to wait or bus tables or work as a lifeguard or a day laborer. Think again. It's time to debunk another "truthy" generational bias.

It is true that today's better-resourced adolescents and emerging adults have often bypassed low-paying jobs for unpaid but impressive résumé fillers to better compete in high-stakes college admissions. However, no matter which generation we're talking about, individuals who are early in their careers change jobs more often than those in mid-to-late career. This is a life-cycle effect, reflecting a person's stage in life, not a character flaw of the younger generation.

The Big Quit, twenty years in the making, is more appropriately understood as the "Big Reshuffle" of 2020–2022.[35] Since only 30 percent of current employees describe their work as meaningful, the post-shutdown pandemic labor shortage yielded a long-overdue correction, where employees finally gained leverage.[36] Millions left jobs with poor work conditions, low pay, and no benefits for better jobs. For twentysomethings just starting their careers, the pandemic was a uniquely stressful period that spurred many early departures and job changes. The reason? Remote work.

If in-person work isn't particularly meaningful to most, consider the losses embedded in remote work for twentysomethings. Today's younger employees, who are not partnered or married or living at home, more exclusively rely on work to define their adult identity and provide for the social needs of belonging, understanding, and meaning. This wasn't true for prior generations, when the normal for the young adult experience of meaningful belonging could be met outside of work in a variety of ways: neighborhood social groups, pickup sports, religious groups, as well as earlier marriages and nearby and larger family groups.

Remote work frays the experience of belonging even more and has proved harder for young employees. Established employees largely prefer remote work because they know their team, their manager, and their role.[37] To the stress of not belonging, add the fretful worry for younger employees that they won't look competent if they ask for help. In each work culture, there's an invisible soft-skills curriculum for how to succeed in the workplace. Remote work makes this harder to access. Employees typically access this unwritten handbook through onboarding at a company, where they are mentored by senior coworkers. Or informally, by chance meetings at the "water cooler." Remote work deprives entry-level employees of these informal but critical experiences that help them fit in. As a result of nationwide pandemic peaks and waves, offices went online and only much later moved to a hybrid model of remote and in-person work. Humorous stories of people attending Zoom meetings in their pj's contrasted with the stressful realities reflected in the very limited availability of interpersonal resources.

Once more we turn to Matt, who confirmed this experience:

I had two jobs that began online. In the first one, I worked for a nice guy who was an awful manager. There was no onboarding, no handbook or guides that I could use to answer my questions. And who was I going to ask? The managers had never done this remotely or imagined that newbies don't want to look like they're messing up or reveal what they don't know. I felt like I was faking it most of the time. There was a small team, but no way to bond with anyone more experienced, or learn who it was safe to ask. I wanted to make this job work, but after three months of feeling like I still didn't know what I was doing, combined with fourteen-hour online days, I got recruited by another company. I learned a lot from the first super-stressful remote job experience. This time, I checked out the company culture on Glassdoor reviews. In interviews, I asked about their remote onboarding and if there were "get to know the team" meetings. The second company had adequate staffing and assigned mentors, and the manager was a good fit. Now I'm working there hybrid. It feels much better—like I belong.

FUTURE TRENDS

The tales of the five friends who were caught in a riptide of pandemic shifts foreshadow future educational and work trends. Though college has long been part of the American dream, a degree's worth often depends on the rightness of fit between aptitudes, college completion, credentialing, training or skills certification, and future career goals.

Currently, fewer than half of Gen Z high schoolers are considering a four-year college, according to four recent national surveys.[38] Nearly a third are assessing a nontraditional route. Why? Because they're scared. Three-quarters of Gen Zers are worried about not getting a job and worried about debt.[39] Even a wealthier background does little to mitigate these uncertainties. They question whether they still need a bachelor's degree, particularly in light of the gradual realization by more corporations that a college degree is a blunt instrument and not predictive of job success.[40] Because of today's increased college and living expenses, more men than women enter the workplace directly from high school or alternate skills training into well-paid trade jobs. The college enrollment and completion gender gap is widening, with women outnumbering men.

Yet there's good news for college grads. Employers still frequently prefer or require four-year college degrees, and college graduates have held on to the economic ladder, even when they weren't climbing it. Colleges have made recent changes to integrate course and degree majors to career resources and connections. In parallel, there is a growing recognition among students, parents, and employers alike that the traditional wisdom of "college for all" is neither the best nor the only way to prepare for a good job and future. The five friends we've met, both those with traditional and nontraditional educational pathways, exemplify the encouraging news that with the right kind of education, young adults can find their way to a fulfilling career and purpose-filled life.

In Part I of this book, we have described our rapidly changing times and invited you to challenge generational biases and rethink your thinking. We have offered a twenty-first-century revamp of communication guidelines for parents and young adults. We've reviewed how unanticipated educational and employment shifts have altered the landscape of higher education and expanded credentialing to meet employers' increased emphasis on skills.

Part II provides a detailed review of the stumbling blocks that mental health problems can impose on emerging adults. The onset of a mental illness can affect many aspects of a young adult's progress toward independent adulthood. Early detection, treatment, and family support are key to recovery. A certain humbling wisdom and deepening love often arises as parents and young adults compassionately confront these concerns together. In Part II, we encounter courageous parents and their adult children who generously share the lessons they have learned.

PART TWO

Young Adults' Stumbling Blocks

6

Executive Functions and Your Twentysomething's Path Toward Self-Actualization

Will power is trying hard not to do something that you really want to do.
—*Arnold Lobel*, Frog and Toad Together

IN PART II OF THIS BOOK, WE EXPLORE THE MYRIAD WAYS A YOUNG PERSON'S path to adulthood can get delayed or derailed because of psychological or mental health problems. Parents of young adults with an undiagnosed or untreated mental health problem confront challenges beyond the normative role of primary safety net described in Part I. These parents must overcome any generational bias that might confuse a mental health disorder with an unmotivated slog toward adulthood. They must cope with negative stigma and self-blame; remain open-minded and flexible in their approach; and learn specific nuances of how to relate, listen, and talk collaboratively to support their young adult, whose very recovery may depend on parental dedication to their well-being.

Effective support will have the gratifying result that the young adults will be able to invest in a future they want. This support is also needed by many of today's twentysomethings who struggle with either poor executive functioning, excessive screen time, anxiety, depression, or substance use disorders. The chapters in Part II will examine these challenges one by one.

This chapter will focus on executive functioning, or the mental skills a person needs to plan their goals and successfully accomplish them. We'll review current theories about how these skills develop as a young person matures. We'll also share several examples of executive dysfunction (or executive function deficits) and show how it is assessed clinically. We'll touch on the relevance of biological and psychological factors. You will learn about evidence-based interventions and will find resources you can use to assist young adults who are experiencing executive function deficits (EFD).

Before we delve into definitions, theories, and reviews of current clinical practices related to executive functions, let's meet Mary and her parents. She's a college student who took a leave of absence after her life-management skills proved insufficient to the demands of living away from home. Back home, she's floundering, and her parents are too. As part of our therapy with them, we educate them about the crucial building blocks of concentration, task endurance, productivity, and organization.

MARY: A FIRST-YEAR COLLEGE STUDENT WHO PRESSED "PAUSE"

Mary and her parents, Joan and Alan, sought guidance regarding her sudden, unexpected departure from college barely two months into the spring semester of her first year. Mary, the only child of older parents, sat away from them, staring at the floor and smirking. Joan and Alan were unsure of whether to begin or to let their daughter speak first. When they asked her to introduce herself, Mary angrily started into them.

"Why don't you get things going?" she testily asked her parents. "After all, it was your idea to come here." She folded her arms and turned away to look out the window.

Joan asked Mary to reconsider, but her daughter shrugged "No." Joan turned to us with an uncomfortable expression and said, "I know this is hard for Mary, but we really don't know what else to do at this point. She's been home from school for over a month and is basically doing nothing except going online to chat with friends and watch YouTube videos. We're trying to get her to find a job or to volunteer somewhere, and she says she's looking, but when we ask her how the search is going, she just blows us off and tells us it's up to her to figure things out. We need help."

Alan nodded. "We love Mary, and we know she's smart enough to figure things out. But now she just seems to be angry at the world, including us, and she isn't taking charge of the situation."

Mary suddenly jumped in. "I'm not half as mad at you as I am at myself," she said. "I could've avoided this entire mess if I'd gone for help at the learning center like I was supposed to, and if I'd stayed on top of my schoolwork. I made some stupid choices, I know, and I'm paying the price. It sucks to be home instead of at college. I hate it. I just wish the two of you could leave me alone to figure things out on my own instead of constantly badgering me to get a job. I told you a hundred times, I'm responsible for fixing this mess, not you. And I don't think anyone, including therapists, can help me until I decide how I'm going to manage my life."

At this juncture, we acknowledged that everyone seemed to be having a hard time figuring out what to do in response to this unwanted turn of events, which we referred to as a "temporary detour" on the path toward college success and adult independence. We validated the notion that Mary had the burden of figuring out what went wrong and doing something about it, but we supported the idea that her parents had a role to play in helping Mary accomplish this. We also recognized that each family member had a different set of challenges in front of them. Their first job was to figure out how to work together as a family unit to tackle this crisis. By emphasizing that everyone had something to contribute, we were establishing a framework for analyzing the situation from multiple angles and creating a dialogue through which solutions could be identified. We set the agenda for this initial session: to gather data about Mary's experiences as a first-year college student, and to learn what each family member was hoping would happen during her leave from school.

We learned that Mary had been an above-average student in elementary school but started having trouble organizing and managing her time in middle school. The executive functioning time line roughly follows the learning trope of primary education: If grades K–3 are learning to read, and grades 4–5 are reading to learn, then grades 6–8 are about managing your learning and assignments. When schoolwork demands increased, Mary's parents did what many parents in their situation do—they reviewed and helped their child keep track of her assignments. Shortly after starting high school, Mary began to require professional assistance to meet the academic demands. She was referred for a psychological assessment and diagnosed with attention deficit hyperactivity disorder (ADHD), inattentive type, along with executive functioning deficits. The psychologist recommended that Mary work on organizational and study skills. Her test results qualified her for academic modifications, including preferential seating in the front of the class and topic outlines from her teachers to help her prepare for examinations and writing assignments.

She began a medication that helped her to focus, and she met weekly with an organizational coach. With these measures in place, Mary finished high school with a B average. She was accepted at and enrolled in one of her top choices for college—a relatively small liberal arts school with a good English department (her intended major). She and her parents had the foresight to meet with the Office of Student Disability Services and submit the documentation needed for accommodations.

A student's first goal at college is to make friends and "belong." In that arena, Mary excelled. She developed a good social life and made many close friends. She joined the theater club and got involved with production management. Yet by midsemester, Mary found it hard to keep up with reading and writing assignments, especially in her two advanced English courses. Though she reliably took her medication, Mary dismissed the importance of regular study skills assistance and made only sporadic visits to the college's learning center. Her academic struggles led her to withdraw from one course and fail another.

Mary started her spring semester on academic probation, with the understanding that she would stay engaged with the learning center and keep up with her schoolwork. But despite the best of intentions, she soon fell behind academically. Her involvement with the theater club took precedence over her studying. She began to miss classes because she didn't feel prepared enough to participate. Within a few weeks, Mary became more anxious and depressed and felt incapable of continuing with her studies. She initiated a meeting with her academic advisor and chose to take a leave of absence.

Mary's return home was difficult for everyone. She felt miserable being separated from her friends and stuck at home with nothing to do. In a separate meeting with Joan and Alan, they freely disclosed their feelings to us. They expressed disappointment in their daughter, with a twinge of guilt for their oversupport of her in high school at the expense of her underperformance in college. Joan was especially worried that Mary was depressed and might not be able to "get herself together." Alan was more critical than worried. It was a year's tuition down the drain, after all. He insisted that Mary had used poor judgment in picking a college far from home and then failing to take full advantage of the services offered by the campus learning center.

All three of them were uncertain about how to proceed. Although she had the intelligence to succeed at college, Mary had not achieved the skills of independent self-management. From a family systems perspective, her expected developmental path toward separation and individuation was temporarily detoured, without a map to guide the family. Mary and her parents were confronting Mary's delayed and limited executive functioning. Part of our therapy included relevant clinical information to promote insight into the gap between Mary's intentions and her sometimes-perplexing behaviors. Later, we return to Mary and her parents to discover how they learned to pull together as a team to strategize and support Mary's relaunch to independence.

WHAT ARE EXECUTIVE FUNCTIONS?

In a nutshell, Mary and her parents were facing Mary's delayed or impaired executive functions. Although we have briefly defined executive functions as the skills needed for goal-directed actions, parents of young adults can gain better insight into their children's sometimes-perplexing behavior by deepening their knowledge about executive functions.

Executive functions include all the processes and abilities that help a person work toward a goal. The goal could be as short-term and simple as planning a date night when you have a term paper due. It could also be as complex and long-term as obtaining a degree for a satisfying career. These processes and abilities are based on neural circuits that develop over the first two decades of a person's life and reach full expression by the midtwenties, when the brain has reached full maturation.

How do all these processes and skills work together to help you achieve your goals and do what you want to do? Neuropsychologists put forth numerous models and theories, but for our purposes, we'll use the self-regulatory model, first proposed by Dr. Russell Barkley in his book *ADHD and the Nature of Self-Control*.[1] According to him, executive functions are a person's self-directed actions that are used to self-regulate. As people develop from infancy through adulthood, these capacities mature to the point where the person can control their impulses and guide their behaviors toward important goals in an efficient manner.

Barkley suggests that executive functioning usually emerges as a single factor—namely, how efficiently we do what we set out to do. According to his framework, the level of efficiency is based on five highly interrelated areas of daily functioning: time management, self-organization and problem-solving, self-restraint (inhibition), self-motivation, and emotional regulation. Barkley believes that using neuropsychological tests to assess executive functions is highly questionable since how an individual performs on a test does not typically reflect their actual daily functioning. Instead, he asks people to judge

themselves and report on their day-to-day effectiveness to determine someone's strengths and weaknesses.

Executive functions have an enormous impact on everyday life. They help
us pay attention, manage time, remember details, think creatively, plan and
organize, make thoughtful decisions, implement plans, and avoid making mistakes. People with good executive functions are more likely to have greater independence, good physical and mental health, better quality of life, success
in school and at work, and better family and intimate relationships. Impairments in executive functions are linked to several mental disorders, including
ADHD, autism spectrum disorder, and learning disabilities. They also co-occur
with head trauma, sleep disorders, obesity, smoking, and poor adherence to
treatment for chronic illnesses. Crucially, these deficits greatly interfere with
achieving key developmental tasks of emerging adulthood, such as taking
charge of, and managing, your own life. As we observed with Mary's situation,
her trouble with self-regulation and self-management, rather than her academic readiness, was the major obstacle to successful adjustment to college.

NEUROBIOLOGY OF EXECUTIVE FUNCTIONS

Executive functions have long been associated with the brain's frontal lobes. In
1848, a railroad construction worker named Phineas Gage was severely injured
in an accident while inserting explosives into a blasting hole. The tamping iron
he was holding penetrated the left side of his head and destroyed much of his
left frontal lobe. Miraculously, Gage survived the injury and lived for another
dozen years, but as someone with a markedly altered personality. Before the
accident, he was a quiet, respectful, mature, and well-tempered person. Afterward, "he was gross, profane, coarse, and vulgar, to such a degree that his
society was intolerable to decent people."[2]

The case became widely known in medical circles because it supported the
theory of cerebral localization of brain functions such as personality, intelligence, and language. While there have been controversies over the extent to
which Gage's brain damage left him with permanent changes in his personality, scientific progress over the ensuing 175 years has advanced our understanding of the human brain. For example, evidence from hundreds of cases
in which the prefrontal cortex was physically injured or damaged by neurodegenerative disease has clearly demonstrated that executive functions are
localized in the prefrontal cortex. The introduction of neuroimaging technol-

ogies over the past several decades has enabled neuroscientists to localize the circuits underlying executive function deficits. Impairments such as forgetfulness, poor concentration, impulsivity, lack of motivation, and poor organization can now be mapped directly onto specific prefrontal cortex structures and closely linked brain regions.

Recently, three parallel but interconnected circuits have been traced to the capacity of the prefrontal cortex to regulate thoughts, actions, and feelings. Disruptions in these circuits have been linked to neurodegenerative diseases (e.g., Parkinson's disease), traumatic brain injury, and developmental disorders (e.g., ADHD). For example, it has been suggested that Gage suffered the greatest damage to his affective circuit, which led to his difficulties with emotional regulation, motivation, and self-control. Beyond studying how some diseases and injuries affect the prefrontal cortex, modern neuroscience has started to map the developmental progression of executive functions in both healthy individuals and those with neurodevelopmental disorders such as ADHD, autism, Tourette disorder, specific learning disabilities, and communications disorders.

Executive Functioning in Infancy and Beyond

The building blocks of executive functioning start to develop in infancy, when basic information-processing circuits are formed. During this period, pattern recognition and sensory discrimination improve, and attention and memory start to emerge.

By the beginning of the second year of life, young children can inhibit their impulses and regulate their attention more and more effectively. By age three, children can demonstrate planning skills and cognitive flexibility, and these capabilities progress dramatically over the following years. Between six and ten years of age, children's ability to ignore task-irrelevant information shows marked improvement. The marked changes in children's self-directed behavior between kindergarten and fifth grade precedes the expansion of executive functions that enables preadolescents to tackle a host of complex daily functions on their own: getting up and getting ready for school, moving from class to class, keeping up with academic lessons, interacting with peers, doing homework, engaging in after-school and leisure activities, getting ready for bed, and starting the entire cycle anew each day.

Adolescence ushers in even more impressive improvements in executive functions, such as working memory, processing speed, selective attention, inhibitory control, and organization, as well as higher-order functions like abstraction, problem-solving, and decision-making. This developmental shift enables youth to achieve levels of self-control and self-awareness that help them to further refine their self-management skills. While the progression is by no means linear, there is growing evidence that by their midtwenties, young adults achieve the peak level of executive functioning that they will reach in their lifetimes (although their behavior may not necessarily reflect this fact).

The Perennial Nature-Versus-Nurture Debate

As with all psychological processes, there are marked individual differences in the rate and level of executive function development throughout childhood and adolescence. Studies demonstrate that both genetic and environmental factors play a major role in these differences. For example, higher socioeconomic status confers an advantage to the development of these skills in early elementary school—an advantage that persists well into adolescence.

On the genetic side of the equation, variations in critical genes that guide neurodevelopment and play a role in executive function regulation have been associated with executive functioning differences. For example, the serotonin transporter gene affects how serotonin moves in the human body. Serotonin is an important neurotransmitter with many complex functions, including mood regulation, memory, and cognition. The amount of serotonin expressed in the prefrontal cortex is directly linked to the development of executive functions such as self-restraint, cognitive flexibility, and reversal learning. Another gene, catechol-O-methyltransferase, or COMT, is responsible for maintaining the correct levels of two neurotransmitters, dopamine and norepinephrine, in the brain. Some variants of this gene code for higher dopamine levels in the prefrontal cortex; higher levels have a major influence on how a person responds to working-memory training.

Taken together, these sociological and genetic studies demonstrate the complex ways in which genes and the environment interact to regulate the development of executive functions in health and disease. Although it is too early to apply these findings to clinical practice, neuroscientific studies of executive function are being conducted using this genetics-versus-environment model.

Neuropsychologists have developed various age-appropriate and education-based tools to assess people's executive functions. Unfortunately, these standardized tests have questionable real-life validity: They may not accurately measure how any given individual will function in everyday settings.

In response to this shortcoming, clinicians introduced new, self-report scales into clinical practice. Like most self-report scales, they are well validated, easy to administer, and considerably less expensive and time-consuming than standardized tests. Both scales have two versions: a self-report and a report by someone who knows the person (see description below).

EXECUTIVE FUNCTIONING DISORDERS

As noted earlier, executive functioning disorders (EFD) are associated with a variety of conditions, most notably ADHD. The inattentive features of ADHD, for example, are highly correlated with EFD and include trouble sustaining and regulating attention, difficulty organizing tasks, easy distractibility, and forgetfulness. The hyperactive-impulsive symptoms of ADHD suggest difficulties with impulse control: fidgeting, squirming, running excessively, difficulty playing quietly, talking excessively, difficulty waiting one's turn, and interrupting or intruding on others. While most people with ADHD experience some degree of EFD, there is great variability in the impairments seen in this clinical population. Moreover, people with moderate to severe anxiety disorders and obsessive-compulsive disorder frequently have executive function impairments, as do individuals with PTSD, depression, substance use disorders, schizophrenia, and traumatic brain injury. Table 6.1 presents additional behavioral manifestations of EFD that can be seen in people with various psychiatric disorders.

Recently, a condition identified as "sluggish cognitive tempo" has been the focus of clinical research and practice and may be of interest to parents concerned about their adult child's trouble with getting things done. The hallmark symptoms of this condition are sluggishness, drowsiness, and excessive daydreaming—as distinct from the inattentiveness and poor working memory seen in ADHD. We'll return to this condition in Chapter 8 when we discuss the case of Catherine, a graduate student with anxiety and trouble concentrating and getting her work done.

Clinical evaluation of EFD should include a careful history of the individual's difficulties, their impact on daily functioning, and the completion of a standardized questionnaire or scale. In our practice, we use two instruments for taking histories. The Barkley Deficits in Executive Functioning Scale looks

TABLE 6.1 EXECUTIVE FUNCTIONING DISORDERS AND THEIR COMMON BEHAVIORAL INDICATORS

AREA OF DIFFICULTY	BEHAVIOR
Working memory	Forgetting what's just been said or someone's phone number; not remembering appointments
Attention regulation	Easy distractibility; short attention span; extraneous information recalled instead of salient information; overfocusing
Inhibitory control	Trouble inhibiting impulses: frequently interrupting others, talking excessively; trouble controlling emotions
Cognitive flexibility	Difficulty switching to an alternate strategy when current approach fails
Self-monitoring	Failure to notice errors while completing tasks; trouble being aware of one's internal state of mind
Planning, organization	Underestimating time; inability to plan events; disorganized approach to tasks; messy desk
Problem-solving	Difficulty analyzing or processing information; trouble making decisions

at the previously mentioned five areas of executive functioning: time management, self-organization and problem-solving, self-restraint (inhibition), self-motivation, and emotional regulation.[3] The scale has eighty-eight items. For example, the time management domain includes items such as "poor sense of time, waste or mismanage my time, late for work or scheduled appointments, trouble motivating myself to start work, and lack of self-discipline." As with most standardized scales, the scores are totaled and compared to a normative table to determine whether the individual is in the clinical range of symptomatology.

The Behavior Rating Inventory of Executive Functioning—Adult Version (BRIEF-A) is another widely used scale.[4] It includes seventy-five items in two broad dimensions (behavioral regulation and metacognition) and nine clinical scales. For example, the behavioral regulation section includes three subscales: inhibition (ability to control impulses and stop behavior), shifting (capacity to move freely from one activity or situation to another, to make transitions, to problem-solve flexibly), and emotional control (ability to modulate emotional responses appropriately).

Both of these tools enable clinicians and individuals with executive function deficits to pinpoint which aspects of everyday life are giving the person difficulty and therefore warrant some intervention. We will review examples of such interventions after we revisit Mary and her parents.

A WORKABLE TREATMENT PLAN FOR MARY AND HER PARENTS

At the end of our initial evaluation of Mary and her family, we offered the following observations. Mary met the criteria for ADHD (inattentive presentation), executive functioning deficits, and adjustment disorder with anxiety and depression stemming from her college adjustment difficulties. She was struggling to adapt to being home and finding meaningful activities during her leave of absence from school. It seemed to us that neither her ADHD nor her executive function deficits were adequately managed before she started college. She had certainly received a great deal of support from her parents and her high school teachers and had benefited from academic accommodations and organizational skills coaching. But neither Mary nor her parents had anticipated the degree of difficulty she would face at college without the scaffolding her home and school had provided.

On the Barkley Deficits in Executive Functioning Scale, Mary showed ongoing problems with time management, self-organization, and self-restraint. On the ADHD rating scale, she continued to have significant symptoms of inattention and working-memory issues on her current dose of stimulant medication. We recommended that her regimen be adjusted to give her longer symptom-free periods throughout the day. We further suggested that she enroll in an organizational skills class run by an ADHD coach with extensive experience working with college students. Just as important, we offered to work with Mary, Joan, and Alan to help them devise a set of goals for the coming months and formulate a plan for achieving them. This work would involve family sessions and separate sessions with Mary and her parents to create a plan for facilitating change and fostering independence. We were careful to emphasize the importance of each family member's role in this process.

In the initial family session, Mary and her parents struggled to find common ground on their expectations for her time away from school. While she had agreed to adjust her medication, Mary was not ready to commit to joining the organizational skills class because she believed that she already knew what it was going to teach her. Her resistance to this idea prompted an angry response from Alan.

"Oh, come on, Mary!" Alan said. "What do we have to do to get you to realize that you *do* need this help?! You've had it so good your whole life, and you just don't appreciate how hard your mother and I have worked to get you ready to succeed in college. It was your choice to go to this school despite our reservations, and you promised us you would work with the folks at the learning center there. You *knew* how important it was to stay on top of your work, and instead, you did things your own way and you completely ignored the reality of the situation. Even worse, when we asked you about how you were doing in school, you told us everything was fine, *which was clearly not true*! What more do I have to do to make you own up to the fact that you have to get your act together and stop pretending you've got it all under control?"

At this point, Joan turned to her husband and quietly asked him to lower his voice and give Mary a chance to respond. "We already know your position on all this, Alan. You've made it perfectly clear that you're upset with Mary. But yelling and criticizing isn't going to get her to listen. It's just going to make her feel worse about herself."

Alan retorted, "Sure, Joan. Go ahead and take her side for a change. I'm the bad guy, right? I'm just a hard-assed father who really enjoys putting his daughter in her place when she messes up and can't admit she's wrong. Give me a little credit, please. Can't you see how protecting her only makes things worse? She's not taking charge of her life the way she needs to succeed. And you're just making excuses for her."

During this heated exchange, we noticed Mary gazing sadly out the window. We offered her a chance to weigh in on the conversation.

In a reprise of her initial visit with us, Mary softly began to speak: "Dad, I'm sorry. I really am. I know you want what's best for me. I know you want me to do better. I get why you're so angry at me. I guess I would be too if I were you. But your being angry isn't helping me figure things out. It just makes me even more upset with myself. I'm even angrier than you are that I blew it this semester. It's nobody's fault but my own. I get it. But I'm not ready to go back to an organizational skills coach now, especially since I'm not in school or anything. I'd rather take some time off to figure out what my game plan is going to be while I'm out of school. I know it's not enough for me to wish for something to happen. I've got to get my act together. Give me a couple of weeks, and I'll come up with something."

We ended the session with a recommendation that we hold separate sessions with Mary and with her parents in the coming week, to be followed by another family session in two weeks to discuss everyone's expectations for her leave of absence from college.

During the subsequent individual session with Mary, we focused on helping her process her sadness about being away from school and deal with her parents' emotional reactions. She was able to reframe her time away from school as a chance to learn to manage life on her own, and to practice the executive function skills of self-discipline and self-organization. She recognized she needed to find activities that would help her with these goals, and she expressed hope that by the time she and her parents met with us in the family session, she would be prepared to discuss concrete steps she was ready to take.

In the parents' session, we learned more about Alan's background and the sources of his excessive frustration with Mary. As it turned out, he had difficulties similar to hers when he was younger, including dropping out of college twice because of poor grades and being fired from his first few jobs because of lateness (poor time management), disorganization, and lack of motivation. Watching his daughter struggle had activated a strong sense of protectiveness in him.

"I never want her to go through what I went through. It was awful. I felt so ashamed of myself. I thought I was dumb and lazy. I didn't understand why I kept making the same mistakes over and over again. I was miserable for a long time, until I met Joan. She understood and accepted me, and she helped me get my act together."

To this, Joan added, "I know you want what's best for Mary. It's natural to want to protect her. But it's not your fault you have ADHD. And it's not your fault she has it. You've learned to deal with it, and so will she."

The rest of this session was devoted to helping Joan and Alan learn about and manage their anxiety about Mary. Alan's impatient critical outburst reflected his distress and was an example of "talking at" Mary. That went nowhere, as both Joan and Mary pointed out. He and Joan had become polarized in a too hot / too soothing style, while both wanted to help their daughter. We emphasized the importance of resetting their expectations within a more realistic framework and appreciating the generational differences that were at play here. Mary was not alone in taking time off from college. Many of her peers were finding it hard to adjust to the demands of being on their own away from home. And perhaps this unexpected setback could serve a bigger purpose: to help her gain new self-management skills, which she still lacked.

Joan and Alan were able to see that their pattern of overly supporting their daughter during high school had been well intended but ultimately unhelpful. It was time for her to learn to manage herself better on her own, and for them to learn how to give her the space to do this. This meant refraining from their pattern of micromanaging her daily activities and monitoring her task performance. We introduced the notion of "less-is-more parenting," encouraging them to step away from the situation rather than try to micromanage her, along with some suggestions for redirecting their energies, from observing Mary to taking care of themselves and each other.

In a family session the following week, Mary led the discussion and immediately offered up a set of proposed goals and objectives for the coming months. She planned to take a theater course at the local community college and to volunteer at a community theater in their town. She agreed to help her parents out with family chores (shopping, cooking, and cleaning the shared living space) and to enroll in the ADHD coaching class we had recommended. Her main request of her parents was that they agree to make efforts to let her manage things on her own rather than watch her every move. Joan and Alan were duly impressed with Mary's positive take-charge attitude and her strong motivation to address her challenges directly.

For their part, the parents were open-minded and accepted the challenge of "less-is-more" parenting, as well as Mary's request. The couple agreed to refrain from micromanaging Mary and, instead, shift their energies to taking better care of themselves. Joan was happy to accept Mary's help with family chores and hoped to use the newly freed-up time to take a pottery class. Alan readily admitted he had been avoiding going to the gym on a regular basis and that he was ready to return. They agreed to check in with us every two weeks to keep us informed on how these plans were working out and to problem-solve as the need arose.

Before discussing how Mary made use of her time away from college, we will review the growing field of interventions for EFD. Parts of the following discussion may provide more technical information than many parents are used to reading. But a deeper understanding of the treatments for EFD can help you see your adult child's problems in a more objective way and can help you decide sensibly on the best course of action. Moreover, by learning about professionals' time-tested and evidence-based interventions, you will become familiar with the approaches that experts have used with much success. You can be a better-informed part of a team that has your twentysomething's best interests at heart.

INTERVENTIONS FOR EFD

Fortunately, people with EFD can consider several options to help them cope with their condition. Among these are self-education, environmental modifications, lifestyle changes, executive skills coaching, cognitive behavioral therapy (CBT), computer-based cognitive training, and, especially for young adults, family-based interventions.

Self-Education

The appendix offers a wide variety of books, articles, online videos, and social media sites describing the basics of EFD (especially in the context of ADHD) and demonstrating the tools and strategies with the greatest promise for remediating the most common impairments. Patient advocacy groups like Children and Adults with ADHD (CHADD), the Attention Deficit Disorder Association (ADDA), and the Learning Disabilities Association of America (LDA) have links to important articles and videos about EFD.[5] The bottom line is that it's up to your young adult, and you, to become familiar with the broad range of options that are available for people with EFD so that they, and you, can make informed choices about the ones that are most likely to benefit them.

Environmental Modifications

There are myriad strategies and practices to reduce distractions such as noise and messiness and to increase structure and organization. Basic steps include keeping rooms tidy and organized, creating calm and supportive environments, creating low-distraction work areas, and using timers to signal the beginning and ending of activities. Consider adapting classroom modifications that can be applied to any workplace, including preferential seating, posting tasks or assignments, and frequent breaks. Among other practices, parents can provide quiet spaces, avoid unnecessary distractions, build in regular opportunities for weekly desk cleanup, schedule breaks, consider books and manuals in audio format, and post visual reminders of daily schedules, tasks, and project time lines. You can adapt similar strategies for the home, which during the pandemic became the workplace for a large percentage of the population. Interestingly, the shift to working from home has enabled people with EFD to customize their workspaces to suit their needs and priorities.

Lifestyle Changes

Lifestyle changes that enhance executive functioning include proper nutrition, sleep, exercise, mindfulness and stress-reduction practices, avoidance of harmful substances (nicotine, excessive alcohol, and addictive substances), and limiting distractions from digital devices.[6, 7] The diet should include fresh, unprocessed foods (no sugar and artificial additives) and fish and nuts that are high in omega-3 fatty acids. Be mindful to eat a variety of foods to absorb sufficient zinc, minerals, and vitamin D. Limit your daily caffeine intake.

Sleep hygiene is also critical for optimal brain functioning. To ensure good sleep habits, develop predictable sleep routines that give you seven or more hours of continuous sleep. Reduce your exposure to screens in the late evening and take melatonin if you have problems with falling sleep.

Daily moderate to vigorous exercise of one hour per day, along with sufficient time spent outdoors, is also important for brain health. Mindfulness-based stress reduction has also been shown to reduce stress-induced anxiety and to improve one's attention span and working memory.

Reducing or eliminating exposure to nicotine, alcohol, and recreational drugs promotes physical and mental health. Young adults often minimize the damage of binge drinking and cannabis use, but an abundance of research demonstrates that chronic drug and alcohol usage reduces academic, occupational, and driving performance.

Finally, placing limits on digital technology usage, especially smartphones, is a major health challenge for everyone. As media reports continuously remind us, internet addiction is a growing problem for young people. It is linked to disrupted or insufficient sleep, excessive stress, anxiety, and even depression. We will focus more on this issue in Chapter 7, Shiny Screens Everywhere.

Taken together, these lifestyle changes have been shown to have health-promoting effects on cognitive functioning for everyone, especially for people with EFD. Besides encouraging your young adult to adopt these lifestyle changes, you can model them yourself for your own mental and physical health.

Coaching

Since the early 1990s, ADHD coaching has been available to help people mitigate the negative effects of the disorder on their daily lives and to improve their self-management skills. These coaches act as process facilitators to help clients achieve their desired goals, *not* as therapists or counselors.[8] When meeting with clients, they tend to use Socratic questioning and invite them to reflect on strengths, challenges, and options for action steps. Coaches help clients define and prioritize goals, anticipate roadblocks to their goals, develop strategies to address the roadblocks, create reminder systems to promote self-monitoring and follow-through, and provide external accountability and evaluate progress toward valued goals. The emphasis of coaching is on performance, which is a key problem for people with EFD.

A growing body of scientific literature documents the effectiveness of coaching for college students with ADHD.[9, 10, 11] Such coaching is now considered a standard offering at college and university learning centers. A smaller set of studies validates the benefits of coaching for other adults with ADHD. Recently, coaches have incorporated principles of cognitive behavioral therapy into their practice. The therapy helps clients become more engaged in challenging tasks, allows them to identify their own unproductive patterns of behavior, and try strategies that could help them perform and successfully complete a task.

Cognitive Behavioral Therapy for ADHD

Over the past twenty-plus years, several clinical research groups in the United States, the United Kingdom, and Europe have adapted cognitive behavioral therapy for adults with ADHD.[12] These treatment approaches share many common goals:

- Providing psychological education about ADHD
- Helping patients accept the diagnosis and commit to change
- Modifying the environment to reduce distractibility

- Describing the cognitive model of psychopathology (especially the role of distortions and negative beliefs)
- Providing executive function skills (time management, organization, and planning)
- Dealing with procrastination
- Handling stress
- Promoting adaptive thinking
- Managing impulses and risk-taking (thinking before acting)
- Adhering to medication treatment
- Maintaining physical and mental health

J. Russell Ramsay, Ph.D., and Dr. Rostain have published two manuals delineating the principles of ADHD-focused cognitive behavioral therapy.[13, 14] Dr. Ramsay has also written a book that expands on these concepts.[15] The Penn model for ADHD-focused cognitive behavioral therapy views ADHD through the lens of self-regulation, with an emphasis on the difficulties people have in implementing the necessary skills and strategies to effectively manage a task, role, or situation. People with ADHD don't lack the knowledge of what needs to be done. Nor do they lack the skills to get things done. But they do have trouble turning their intentions into actions. These implementation problems arise from chronic developmental difficulties related to impaired self-regulation. Without self-regulation, young adults—or any other person—don't believe they can carry out daily tasks successfully.

Taken together, self-regulation problems make it difficult for a person to organize, initiate, and sustain actions over time to achieve something that they know will be important to them in the future. Trouble with initiating and sustaining behaviors are linked to problems like procrastination, low motivation, and poor task endurance. Difficulty with future-oriented actions is tied to the tendency to favor immediate rewards over delayed ones. The tendency to opt for short-term over long-term rewards results in temporal discounting. Deficits in self-regulation are also associated with disorganization and emotional dysregulation, which further interfere with effectiveness. These magnify and are magnified by coexisting psychiatric and learning disorders that, in turn, lead the affected individual to disengage from feasible and personally important tasks, duties, goals, and objectives.

The Penn cognitive behavioral therapy approach consists of four types of intervention: cognitive modification; behavioral modification and coping skills; acceptance, mindfulness, and persistence; and implementation strategies.

Procrastination is another challenge that lends itself to cognitive behavioral therapy. Our work with adults with ADHD for three decades has underscored the centrality of excessive procrastination in the lives of our patients. Despite the negative consequences they frequently encounter with delaying the start or completion of important tasks, adults with ADHD readily admit that this is a difficult habit for them to break. Repeatedly, they wait until the last moment to get started on important projects, only to discover that they don't have enough time to complete them. More recently, thanks to insights provided by our patients, Dr. Ramsay has coined the term *procrastivity* to describe the self-defeating behavior whereby "an individual makes a good-faith plan to engage in a priority task, but when it comes time to perform the task, engages in a lower priority (but still productive) endeavor."[16]

Dr. Ramsay continues: "Procrastivity is not unique to ADHD but illustrates the distrust cognitive theme of poor self-regulatory efficacy. Adults with ADHD become dispirited (i.e., lose motivation) at the point of performance because of doubts of their capacity to carry out the steps of an otherwise logical and feasible plan. This thought and related feeling of discomfort result in procrastivity—jumping to a task for which they view themselves as more able to manage." Cognitive behavioral therapy for ADHD helps adults identify their own patterns of dysfunctional procrastination and come up with alternative strategies for addressing these behaviors. In this way, people learn to correct themselves before wasting too much time. This is one example of the many cognitive interventions that cognitive behavioral therapy for ADHD employs.

Computer-Based Cognitive Training

Computer-based cognitive training approaches for EFD (including ADHD) are rapidly gaining traction as the research base documenting the effectiveness of these interventions is growing. These "digital therapeutics" are typically delivered in the form of a computer game that requires processing speed, inhibition, and the repetition of such mental tasks as inductive reasoning, spatial orientation, and executive functioning, in combination with attention span and working memory.[17] The idea behind this kind of training is that higher-order thinking can improve with repetitive practice or direct instruction delivered by digital platforms. Although initial small studies show promising results, there is still a need for large, randomly controlled clinical trials to determine the efficacy of this computer-based training. Recently, the Software

Treatment for Actively Reducing Severity of ADHD was approved by the U.S. Food and Drug Administration for use in children with ADHD after registry trials demonstrated substantive improvement in test subjects' performance on a computerized test of attention and vigilance as compared to controls.[18] This work has been extended to children on medication for ADHD and is currently being tested in adolescents and adults.[19] Undoubtedly, in the coming years, tools like these will continue to be developed and tested in adults with ADHD and EFD.

Family-Based Interventions

EFD can present multiple challenges to young adults and their families. Among these are the impact of delays in achieving self-management skills, young adults' greater-than-expected reliance on their parents for support in daily demands, setbacks in the process of separation-individuation, and inevitable detours on the path toward self-reliance and independence. Parents wonder how much support and direct supervision is appropriate. It's hard to know what to do when whatever level of support is being provided doesn't seem to be helping the young person manage their lives or move forward on their path toward self-sufficiency. Most advice books encourage parents to facilitate independence by stepping back and giving their twentysomethings enough space to figure things out for themselves. This "less is more" advice only goes so far, especially when the setbacks the young person encounters are imposing great mental hardship, or when they don't seem to have a handle on how to address their EFD. Most parents in this situation know that there are no simple answers or quick fixes to the functional impairments that are both hardwired, or brain-based, and software-based, or learned over time. If your young person is exhibiting persistent moderate to severe deficits of executive functioning, it's important to get outside help, as self-help approaches are hard for them to initiate and sustain.

A planned, family-based approach is the most effective way to help young people find their way through the rough waters of growing up with ADHD, or any other disorder that affects executive function. It also assists parents in defining their roles in facilitating positive change. The family members will need to face some fundamental truths, such as the reality of EFD and its impact on personal development. The family should also discuss and have a common understanding of the consequences of EFD. They should explore their expectations for each family member's role in bringing about change and should clarify and respect the basic ground rules for living together. All of this takes time and patience, as well as a willingness to negotiate solutions and seek help when all else fails.

In family-based treatment, there is clearly no one-size-fits-all approach. Each family's story is different, each person's perspective is unique, and each family member's efforts—no matter how ineffective—must be understood and respected.[20] The initial phase of treatment (engagement) requires that the therapist create a safe space for people to come together, discuss goals and objectives, raise concerns, identify strongly held values, validate strengths and vulnerabilities, and address questions or fears about treatment.

The intermediate phase (working through) involves an assessment of family dynamics that are causing problems in daily life. The therapist determines which factors are perpetuating these dynamics, learns how the family has dealt with problems in the past, and examines how each family member contributes to the situation. A major objective of this phase is helping family members renegotiate their expectations by introducing new approaches to communication, problem-solving, and conflict resolution.

The final phase of treatment (maintenance and termination) is signaled when the family's dynamics shift toward greater harmony, better communication, and improved problem-solving. As the family handles stresses and challenges on its own, the frequency of sessions can be decreased until everyone in the family feels that their treatment goals have been achieved. Toward the conclusion of treatment, the professional often plans for a future follow-up session or two to make sure that the gains achieved in treatment are being maintained.

A FOLLOW-UP WITH MARY AND HER FAMILY

Mary's participation and engagement in individual cognitive behavioral therapy and executive function coaching were extremely helpful in her ability to turn things around. Her individual therapy was focused on identifying her self-defeating thoughts and patterns of escape and avoidance of difficult tasks. She began to see that her self-distrust led her to become anxious whenever she had to complete a writing assignment, and that this anxiety, in turn, led her toward procrastivity. She learned that her pursuit of social activities at the cost of her academic preparation was another form of procrastination. Soon, after she began to formulate strategies for challenging her negative thoughts, she found that she could engage more fully in her studies. Her increased engagement then helped her feel more confident about her ability to succeed in school. At the same time, her coaching sessions helped her learn to keep track of her daily chores by creating a to-do list that she kept with her at all times. She practiced setting priorities to avoid getting overly involved in less important tasks. She improved her time-management skills by learning how to use the timer on her cell phone to estimate how long certain tasks would take her and to set reminders for when she had reached the end of a planned period of work.

After three months of meeting every two weeks with Mary and her parents, we noted steady gains on all fronts. Mary was actively engaged in managing her life demands in a consistent and relatively efficient fashion. She did well in her theater class and decided to take additional courses the following semester at the community college. After volunteering for several months at the local theater company, she was offered a paid part-time position in ticket sales and promotional work. She chose to remain at home for the following year instead of returning to her original college and eventually transferred to a local four-year college. Her success on multiple fronts enabled her to move out of her parents' home and live off campus with friends from her new school. Meanwhile, Mary's parents shifted their focus from worrying about Mary to improving their relationship and enhancing their own quality of life. Joan retired from her position as an administrator at an insurance company and began a second career as a potter and craftsperson. Alan continued working but gradually reduced his hours so that he could devote more time to his favorite pastimes—boating, fishing, and working out at the gym.

As we have shown throughout this chapter, executive functioning disorders not only affect the young person but also create challenges for their families. Parents struggle to know whether outside help is needed and, if so, what they can expect from professional counseling. Mary's case study shows that a family-based approach has the best chance of helping the emerging adult and their family work their way toward the young person's ultimate independence and self-actualization.

7

Shiny Screens Everywhere

We are living through a crisis of attention. . . . As our mental lives become more fragmented, what is at stake often seems to be nothing less than the question of whether one can maintain a coherent self.
                                        —*Matthew B. Crawford,* The World Beyond Your Head

WHEN WE ASK PARENTS AND YOUNG ADULTS TO DESCRIBE THE MOST STRIKING differences between their respective coming-of-age experiences, digital technology and social media are invariably mentioned.* Parents often have a hard time imagining what it's like to grow up in a world dominated by digital devices. They understand the centrality of digital media in their youths' educational, professional, and social lives, but they are often uncomfortable with just how much time young people spend on online relationships and activities. As one young adult recently told us, "You just have to understand one basic fact: We're the beehive generation. We all live in this big hive, and we need to know where everyone is all the time because it helps us know what's going on and where the action is."

Youth view parents as overly anxious about the dangers of digital media

---

*We will use the term *digital media* to capture the array of types and sources of computer and smartphone communication technology applications, including education, science, art, commercial enterprises, social communication, and recreation. This media ecology, or cultural context, is what emerges as technology and humans interact, and as the latest phase of the information age, it represents a profoundly new social environment.

usage, and hopelessly naive or even ignorant about how online life operates for their generation. Twentysomethings were in their early teens when smartphones appeared on the scene in 2014. They experienced their adolescence in the midst of the rapid evolution of digital media—an evolution that is now continuing in their young adulthood and has created a unique divide between them and their parents.

New technologies have long caused intergenerational conflict. In the mid-twentieth century, the advent of radio, and then television, lessened people's reliance on family or friends for entertainment. At the end of the century, the introduction of personal computers, home video games, and the internet transformed family life as well. Now the dissemination of portable digital media technology during the first two decades of the twenty-first century has created yet another brave new world in which access to information is instantaneous and continuous. Only this time, it is completely transportable and incessant.

Smartphones have dramatically increased access to the internet and enabled us to remain constantly connected to digital media. They have also catalyzed the rapid creation and dissemination of social media platforms, which are ubiquitous and dominate every aspect of our lives. In today's world, access to smartphones is a necessity and a burden. The immense increase in connectivity and productivity that these devices have introduced has come at a cost. Whether the source of digital communications is at school, work, or from family, peers, or social networks, we all feel an urgent need to be available, and to notice messages and respond immediately.

In this chapter, we'll consider how the lure of shiny screens everywhere is changing patterns of living, learning, working, and socializing for twentysomethings and their families. We'll also explore digital media's advantages and disadvantages, including its impact on the brain, our identities, personhood, and social relationships. We'll define problematic usage of digital media and review promising ideas for combating technology addiction or overuse. As digital immigrants rather than natives, we parents accept the presence and centrality of digital media in our daily lives, even as we struggle to adapt to its multifaceted influences on us. Simultaneously, as practicing clinicians, we are all too familiar with cases in which insufficient mastery of digital media has contributed to significant difficulties for our clients. And as observers of our culture, we are concerned about the far-reaching effects of this technology on our mental health and our interpersonal relationships.

DIGITAL MEDIA: TOO MUCH OF
A GOOD THING?

According to a 2021 study, roughly 84 percent of Americans eighteen to twenty-nine years old use social media, especially Instagram, Snapchat, Facebook, and TikTok. Ninety-five percent say they use YouTube.[1] The vast majority of twenty-somethings report visiting these sites daily, and almost half report "near constant" internet use. What's the draw of social media? In a 2020 survey, young adults cited three primary reasons for their social media usage. First, alleviating boredom, followed by information-seeking and social connection.[2] The good news? There was no significant relationship between general use of social networking sites and later onset of depression. So, you might think, no worries, right? Not quite. Survey participants who sought out social media to relieve loneliness were more likely to experience problems like greater anxiety, internet addiction, and depression. It is not clear whether this is a causal relationship or a circular effect. Regardless, as we will discuss shortly, there is good reason for concern.

Social media usage has many perceived benefits, including wider and deeper networks of friends and stress and anxiety relief, which was especially important during the Covid-19 lockdown. Through social media, people can also share important information, participate in affinity groups and communities, and enjoy greater civic engagement and activism. And for young people who are at risk for mental illness, social connection via digital media tends to improve their sense of belonging and of well-being and buffers them against depression. Social media use in young adults is associated with greater awareness of mental health information and resources.[3] Additional benefits of digital media usage include access to important information for academic or job performance, personal and/or career development, self-help, and cultural activities.

On the flip side, the social isolation that many people experience when using social media can increase the severity of depression. The risks of digital media usage by young people have been widely debated in scientific, clinical, and popular arenas over the past decade. The most commonly cited risks are shown in the accompanying box.

COMMONLY CITED RISKS OF DIGITAL MEDIA USE AMONG YOUTH

- Increased distortions in body image (e.g., extreme thinness as body ideal)[a]
- Exposure to discrimination, bullying, and harassment
- Promotion of maladaptive behaviors (e.g., self-harm, restricted eating, substance abuse)[a]
- Reduction of adaptive behaviors (e.g., sleep, exercise, studying)
- Increased loneliness, anxiety, and depression
- Excessive or problematic internet use and video gaming (addiction)[b]
- Approval anxiety (e.g., excessive concern with "likes" or other signs of approval on social media)
- Connection overload (e.g., brain overstimulation)
- Excessive distraction
- Fear of missing out (FOMO): the sense of being excluded from what others are doing
- Nomophobia (no mobile phone phobia): the need to be in constant contact with phone

[a] More common among females than among males.

[b] More common among males than among females.

See Twenge and Martin (2020) for details on gender differences in social media use and their impact on psychological well-being.[4]

Most research has focused on the impact of digital media on the mental health of adolescents. While the jury is still out, the vast majority of young people can apparently manage these risks with few problems. Highly reliable long-term studies of young people between ten and twenty years old support this conclusion. By their own report, most youth cope well enough with the potential stressors of digital media usage.[5,6]

Despite this reassuring news, many young people are at risk for developing the problems cited above. Studies indicate that excessive digital media use is associated with myriad mental health concerns. Those at the highest risk include youth who are from marginalized, under-resourced families and communities, youth who have been exposed to trauma, LGBTQ+ youth, neurodiverse youth, and youth with mental health and/or substance use disorders.

On May 23, 2023, the U.S. Surgeon General issued an advisory on social media and Youth Mental Health. The advisory noted that

> recent research shows that adolescents who spend more than three hours per day on social media face double the risk of experiencing poor mental health outcomes, such as symptoms of depression and anxiety; yet one 2021 survey of teenagers found that, on average, they spend 3.5 hours a day on social media. Social media may also perpetuate body dissatisfaction, disordered eating behaviors, social comparison, and low self-esteem, especially among adolescent girls. One-third or more of girls aged eleven to fifteen say they feel "addicted" to certain social media platforms and over half of teenagers report that it would be hard to give up social media. When asked about the impact of social media on their body image, 46 percent of adolescents aged thirteen to seventeen said social media makes them feel worse, 40 percent said it makes them feel neither better nor worse, and only 14 percent said it makes them feel better. Additionally, 64 percent of adolescents are "often" or "sometimes" exposed to hate-based content through social media. Studies have also shown a relationship between social media use and poor sleep quality, reduced sleep duration, sleep difficulties, and depression among youth.[7]

Parents want to know if their twentysomething's frequent use of digital media is harmful or nonpathological. After all, most of us feel compelled to check our phones, emails, and social media sites frequently, despite our better judgment. How many times during the day do you notice yourself checking your device when you should be doing something else? And when you catch yourself, what do you do? Do you make a conscious effort to resist it, or do you just ignore your observation and keep going? At what point does this repetitive behavior become a disorder? Before considering these questions separating normal from pathological digital media use, let's explore what makes all of us susceptible to this siren call.

WE'RE ALL DISTRACTED BY TECHNOLOGY

In a landmark 2016 book, *The Distracted Mind,* Adam Gazzaley, a renowned neuroscientist, and Larry D. Rosen, a distinguished social psychologist, explain the cognitive science of how our ancient brains manage attention, problem-solving, and information-seeking in the digital age.[8] They posit that we are "information foragers" who are constantly seeking data from the environment to help us formulate goals and devise ways to achieve them. Our ability to selectively direct our attention to novel and salient stimuli, to suppress nonessential information, and to maintain our focus over long periods depends on our evolved frontal lobes. These neural networks in the brain underpin our working memory, our response inhibition, and our capacity for delayed gratification. As we discussed in Chapter 6, these capabilities form the building blocks of executive control of behavior. Naturally, there are limits to our ability to focus and sustain attention. When we focus, we must suppress irrelevant stimuli ("noise") while holding ideas in our working memory to prioritize actions to reach highly valued goals.

What could possibly go awry? For starters, aging, fatigue, sleep deprivation, hunger, and clinical conditions such as ADHD, depression, or dementia, to name a few. Add to these conditions the ubiquitous and readily available sources of highly reinforcing, but not necessarily relevant, information that is incessantly offered by digital devices, and you've got the prime conditions for mental disruption. The clinical literature confirms what we intuitively know—that modern devices can disturb our consciousness, perceptions, language, decision-making, and concentration. We're all exposed to near-constant, multiple distractions that affect our mental functioning and psychic well-being.[9] And we make it worse by multitasking.

MULTITASKING MAKES YOU STUPIDER

Just as we may pride ourselves on being able to get by on too little sleep, we can feel a similarly perverse satisfaction in flexing our mental agility with the disruption of multitasking. This task-switching behavior leaves us in a state of continuous partial attention rather than full attention to whatever we are trying to accomplish. Multitasking takes its toll on cognition. When we try to do more than one thing at a time, we become inattentive, distracted, impulsive, and less efficient. Yet people tend to mistakenly believe that they can multitask without any adverse effects. This misdirected confidence promotes continued multitasking. In effect, we are conditioning ourselves to be incapable of attending to a single task at one time.

The signs of people's devotion to multitasking are all around us. The average length of time that college students can focus on any single task is three to five minutes! Over three-fourths of youth report sleeping with their phones nearby with the notifications on, and it's likely similar rates can be found among adults. People have a growing impatience with delays in getting information from their preferred device—a delay as short as two seconds leads them to look elsewhere. This impatience with information seeking is accompanied by the unreasonable expectation that messages we send should be answered within minutes, if not seconds! This constant pressure to be socially engaged competes with other tasks that require attention. And one task that requires the greatest focus—driving—is becoming more dangerous because of people's frequent attempts to multitask by texting while behind the wheel.

THE SEDUCTION OF DIGITAL DISTRACTION

Given the growing catalog of risks involved in the overuse of technology, why do we allow ourselves to get so distracted by digital media? The answers are far from simple. From a global historical perspective, some argue that our preoccupation is the inevitable by-product of an evolving social-economic order that is increasingly dependent on information technology. We all live in an internet-based social context. Businesses large and small, news and cultural media, scientific and health-care entities, educational institutions, government agencies, and political organizations all use digital platforms to engage in communication, commerce, and political action. In effect, we are inextricably bound to digital media since we rely on this technology for our collective existence. We cannot conceive of the modern world without the pervasive presence of the internet as a prime mediator of social interaction. But the more the internet has come to define our social environment, the more we struggle to discern its impact on our individual and collective consciousness. As in the parable of the two young fish meeting up with an old fish, we just don't know what water is (see David Foster Wallace's 2005 Kenyon College commencement speech).[10] We fail to fully grasp the psychological consequences of constantly connecting to everyone everywhere.

Many experts attribute the rise in anxiety among today's youth to the need to be intimately linked to their devices. In our counseling sessions, our conversations with young adults convince us they are well aware of these challenges and resigned to them. While most people want to have more control over their digital media usage, especially when they feel stressed by it, many feel powerless to change their behavior. This mindset can easily lead to greater anxiety, guilt for wasting time or for neglecting important activities, and a sense of loss of control.

To better understand how to take control of digital devices and push back against the flood of continuous engagement with digital media, we should first look at a common concern that parents have about their adult children and technology. In the following vignette, a parent is worried about a twentysomething's potential technology addiction. The questions we had when consulting with this mother and daughter can help you with your own assessments of your twentysomething's state of well-being.

THE UNBEARABLE LIGHTNESS OF STREAMING

Twenty-six-year-old Casey and her mother, Rachel, consulted us for guidance. Rachel was concerned about Casey's near-incessant YouTube watching.

"From the time she awakens until long into the night," Rachel told us, "Casey is immersed in viewing YouTube videos, TV series, and movies, especially fantasy and science fiction. I mean, is this normal now?"

Casey, thin and soft-spoken, avoided making eye contact with any of us. Gazing out the window, she offered a mild defense against her mother's characterization. "It's not all the time," she said. "I mean, I work twenty hours per week as a barista at a nearby Starbucks. I know I'm an underemployed college graduate who still lives at home, but I've been there for four years, and it's good enough for me to stick with it." She continues, "It's not terrible. I like the people I work with, and the pay and benefits are good enough for me. Best of all, it's not too stressful. I listen to podcasts while I make drinks for customers, and everyone is pretty chill. I'm fine as long as they don't make me work double shifts."

Casey looked quite a bit younger than her age. She wore no makeup and had wire-rimmed glasses and long, wavy hair. Dressed casually in a blouse and slacks, she projected an air of indifference when replying to our questions.

When we asked her to describe how she spends her free time, Casey smiled. "Like everyone else in my generation," she said. "I watch YouTube videos and send Instagram messages to my friends. I don't see the big deal in that, do you? It's not like I'm using crack or opiates or even weed. I just like to relax when I'm not at work. For some reason, my mom thinks I have some kind of addiction and need therapy. I don't agree, but that's beside the point, isn't it? My mom can tell you why she thinks I need help. As far as I'm concerned, she's just a worrier and needs to deal with her stress level being too high."

We then asked Rachel to share her thoughts. She was thin and dressed in the business attire of jacket, silk blouse, long skirt, and low heels. Consistent with the office look, Rachel wore makeup and jewelry, with her hair styled in a tight bun. The mirror image of her daughter's casualness, Rachel appeared quite serious, and after glancing at Casey, she spoke to us loudly and rapidly.

"Casey wants you to think that everything is fine and there's no real point in coming here to see you," she said. "But the truth is, I'm convinced that's not the case. She's a bright girl with lots of potential who's just sitting around and wasting the best years of her life. What can I say to convince you? It's just not normal. She goes to work, true—but it's hardly a suitable job for a college grad, and it's certainly not going to lead her to a fulfilling career. Anyway, she goes off every day, then comes home and spends the entire rest of the day and night alone in her room, looking at her laptop nonstop. It's hard to have a conversation with her because she prefers to be left alone to watch her precious YouTube. You'd think there was nothing else to do with your life but work at Starbucks and come home to escape into the world of constant entertainment. Is that normal? I don't think so. She's not meeting her full potential in life. It's as if the internet has taken away her drive to achieve anything more. That's why we're here. To figure out if she needs help or not."

As with any initial visit, we spent time listening to each side of the story to learn as much as possible about how each person saw the current situation and what was motivating them to seek change. We also sought to validate each person's viewpoint as we searched for some common ground on which to define the central issues that needed to be addressed.

According to Casey, life was going well for her. She was working at a job that met her modest needs, and she spent most of her free time pursuing her favorite pastime: streaming fantasy and science fiction movies and TV series on YouTube (about eight to ten hours daily). She had a few friends from college she would stay in touch with mostly via Instagram, and she went out to local venues with friends from work about once or twice a month. She was not especially interested in finding a romantic partner, although this was a topic that she didn't feel comfortable discussing with us.

When it came to her relationship with her mother, Casey said they had gotten along well for the most part. "My mom and I are chill most of the time. Like, we were fine throughout the lockdown—each of us did our own thing and we respected each other's needs. It's not like we fight all the time or anything. She's a worrywart about me, and it's too bad she doesn't appreciate that I'm basically okay. The only times we argue are when she bugs me about looking for a better job or cutting back on my YouTube watching. I understand she wants the best for me. I just wish she could see that I'm basically fine with the way things are going for now."

From our perspective, Casey was not showing signs of depression, anxiety, or any other serious mental disorder. She may have been somewhat overly involved with her streaming pastime, but she was not especially interested in changing this behavior at the moment. The main consequence of this hobby was that their chronic discord, and Rachel's distress, led to great friction between them.

Rachel was facing a dilemma many parents of twentysomethings cope with: what to make of their young adults' online habits. It's a new-age parent-child version of "Not under my roof" combined with "I'm okay—it's your problem."

In our sessions with mother and daughter, we had to assess who or what needed to change. First, we reflected on these questions: Is streaming YouTube for eight to ten hours daily a sign of a disorder? Is it any different from an adult who binge-streams TV shows after work? How do we assess if a habitual behavior is the sign of digital media use disorder—that is, an internet addiction?

Beyond examining the pattern of behavior itself, our job was to evaluate its impact on Casey's life. Was it a form of escapism that was keeping her from facing the developmental task of finding a career and moving out on her own? If Casey did meet the criteria for a disorder, what could be done about it? Or did Rachel's perception of her daughter's behavior need a generational adjustment? What was interfering with the mother's ability to see Casey as a well-adjusted young adult? How could we help Rachel learn to accept her daughter's choices even if she didn't agree with them? And how would we support her wish to help her daughter move on with her life?

Before answering these questions, we needed to educate mother and daughter about the difference between habits and disorders. Different social media platforms attract media users of all ages, but their pull varies by age. Adults Rachel's age are more likely to use FaceTime and YouTube. Casey's generation gravitate toward Instagram, TikTok, Snapchat, and YouTube.[11]

The extent of daily use also varies by generation, with Gen Zers spending the most time on the platforms, then, in descending order, millennials, Gen Xers, and baby boomers. Rachel considered her own internet use normal. And characteristic of her age cohort, she spent much less time online than her daughter did. Each woman had a habit, but did either have a disorder? And with the different access points—viewing, posting, gaming—how do clinicians define the criteria for disorder? Let's break down the types of problematic use before returning to Rachel's concern about Casey's potential social media addiction.

OVERUSE OF INTERNET AND SOCIAL MEDIA: A DIAGNOSABLE ADDICTION?

This section will discuss new diagnostic categories for describing problematic digital media use: internet addiction disorder and internet gaming disorder. Each condition has a specific profile and a recommended treatment. What exactly is internet addiction disorder, and how is it diagnosed? Excessive, harmful use of digital media has not yet been codified into a mental disorder by the World Health Organization (WHO) in its International Classification of Diseases (ICD) or by the American Psychiatric Association in its *Diagnostic and Statistical Manual of Mental Disorders* (DSM-5). However, in May 2019 the WHO added gaming disorder to its classification system. A critical feature of the disorder is that it should be "of sufficient severity to result in significant impairment in personal, family, social, educational, occupational or other important areas of functioning" and would "normally have been evident for at least twelve months."[12] The new classification was based on "reviews of available evidence and reflects a consensus of experts from different disciplines and geographical regions that were involved in the process of technical consultations undertaken by WHO in the process of ICD-11 development."

This decision sparked a great deal of controversy both in the video game industry and in the mental health community. Many clinical researchers call this classification premature because the evidence is insufficient to justify the diagnosis. Pathologizing gaming without better scientific studies risks stigmatizing individuals who engage in digital play but without harmful consequences. Additionally, no treatment studies to date have demonstrated effective treatments for a gaming disorder. Instead, the American Psychiatric Association has listed internet gaming disorder in the DSM-5 research appendix as a proposed diagnosis requiring further investigation before being officially accepted into the manual. However these concerns are codified and diagnosed in the future, many people with internet-related problems need to be treated, even when formal diagnostic criteria are not fully met. We will explore other serious but not formally DSM-5-listed conditions in greater detail in Chapter 9.

Unlike gaming disorder, there is no diagnostic category for social media addiction, the condition that Casey's mother was worried about. The proposed criteria for this type of addiction (sometimes referred to as problematic internet use disorder) have used dimensions similar to those for internet gaming disorder, namely, problematic and compulsive use of social media platforms that significantly impairs an individual's functioning over an extended period.[13] A major challenge of this proposed diagnosis has to do with delineating the terms "problematic," "compulsive," and "impairment." For example, at what point does frequent social media use, which has become normative for most youth, become problematic? And what if a person, such as Casey, does not regard their usage as problematic? Then how would this criterion be met? What defines *problematic*? Is it in the eye of the beholder—the witness to it, calling out the glaring gaps in another's self-awareness?

A similar issue arises with the notion of "compulsion." How can we distinguish the nearly incessant, habitual use of social media by young people from a compulsion? A casual observation of people riding the bus or sitting in a waiting room would immediately reveal the extent to which we are thoroughly engaged with our preferred social media platforms. Does checking your TikTok or Instagram account several times an hour to look for messages from "friends" constitute a compulsion, or are these check-ins merely an unconscious habit? Does the term *compulsion* refer to the intense urge to seek social contact (which is fostered by the structure of social media platforms), or is it delineated by how much this habitual behavior resists our self-control? An analogy could be made to ingesting snack foods that are scientifically designed to induce an intense desire for consumption. Does eating a large bag of potato chips in one sitting constitute compulsive behavior, or is it a matter of diminished impulse control in the face of a pleasurable habit? In other words, where do we draw the line between reward-driven pleasure-seeking behaviors and compulsive ones? Assuming these boundaries are fuzzy, how might clinically useful distinctions be applied to these very frequent phenomena? After all, for many of us, Instagram's short, snappy videos are like mental potato chips: so easy to watch and so hard to stop at just one. When does consumption of videos become hazardous to our health?

Turning to the third diagnostic criterion, how do we measure impairment from social media use? According to social researchers, the *amount* of social media use is unrelated to most common measures of impairment like diminished educational, occupational, or interpersonal functioning. In fact, frequent social media users are often extremely competent in these domains. Moreover, if the majority of self-reported social media usage occurs during people's discretionary time (free time), it is difficult to define what makes such usage excessive. Rather than the total amount of time, a better measure of impairment is the *timing* and impact of social media usage. Is it late at night, during classes or work? Does it negatively affect sleep duration, exercise, or subjective mental health?[14] At present, tools to measure social media usage, like the Social Media Disorder Scale, are largely inaccurate because people grossly underestimate the total amount, the timing, and the impact of their usage.[15] Further complicating the issue, clinical self-report scales generally emphasize the negative aspects of usage rather than the positive ones. If social media use is the primary means by which people stay in touch with friends and acquaintances, attitudes toward the practice will tend to be positive. In most surveys, the general population's attitude toward social media skews positive; most people view these digital tools as desirable, rewarding, and compatible with their goals and values.

Despite these limitations and controversies, mental health professionals are reaching consensus about social media addiction. They believe that a significant minority of adolescents and young adults are especially susceptible to the harmful effects of excessive, problematic, and compulsive use. Preliminary research suggests that some conditions increase the risk of a youth's developing a social media addiction. Those conditions include co-occurring mental disorders, such as anxiety, depression, OCD, and ADHD. Additionally, youth whose disorder impacts friendly sociability, such as with an autism spectrum or personality disorder, are vulnerable to being marginalized by peers and may cope via virtual life. The risk of social media addiction also rises for those living in highly stressful environments, or with families with high rates of emotional conflict. What remains unclear is how this addiction arises and evolves and what can be done to prevent or treat it.

HELPING CASEY AND RACHEL FIGURE THINGS OUT

After talking with Casey and her mother and deliberating, we concluded that Casey's YouTube streaming activities did not meet the criteria for a treatable mental disorder. We shared our findings with mother and daughter. While we empathized with Rachel's concerns that her daughter was indeed engaging in a lot of online video watching, we pointed out that she was able to hold down a job, to maintain healthy friendships, and to keep to a reasonable sleep-wake cycle. We also acknowledged that Casey seemed to be underachieving in her career development. We recommended that she pursue an assessment of her vocational aptitudes to find a suitable alternate occupational path that would engage her more fully than her job at Starbucks did. Following up on goals Casey had shared with us, we also supported her idea to pursue psychotherapy to explore her inner motivations concerning long-term plans such as living on her own and being in a committed relationship. Casey seemed pleased with these suggestions and accepted our offer to meet again to dive deeper into these issues.

We supported Rachel's caring concern about her daughter's well-being and reassured her that Casey was neither depressed nor impaired by her frequent internet activities. Some of the mother's discomfort might have stemmed from Casey's contentment with underemployment or from Rachel's not knowing how to facilitate her daughter's movement toward independent adulthood. That could be a suitable therapeutic goal for Casey if she chose to pursue it. Regarding the digital media generational divide, we asked Rachel to watch some of Casey's fantasy and science fiction shows with her daughter so that she could learn more about their appeal. Our intuition was that by joining her daughter in the YouTube world, Rachel would become more comfortable with her daughter's form of recreation.

WHAT FEELS NORMAL
TO DIFFERENT GENERATIONS?

The rapid development and dissemination of information technology since the onset of the information age has produced a veritable revolution in the way we humans live. The entire landscape of human endeavor has been rapidly transformed, and we are still trying to adapt to the myriad ways we use digital technology, the internet, and social media and to understand their impact on our daily lives. As digital immigrants, parents of young adults are often perturbed by the dramatic shifts in social mores that their digital-native offspring seem to take for granted. Being continuously connected to digital media may not feel normal to older people, but it is a fact of life for those who have come of age since the turn of the twenty-first century. The generational divide mentioned at the beginning of the chapter is most clearly revealed during discussions between parents and their young adults regarding the appropriate use of digital technology, with respect to both its total amount and its timing throughout the day.

Young people think nothing of interacting with their smartphones while carrying on conversations with people in their immediate environment, while parents often feel upset at the disrespect they think this behavior reflects. Requests to put away the smartphone during face-to-face conversations are often met with disbelief or dismissal by their young adults. Expressions of concern that total immersion in the digital world might be harmful to their physical or mental health are similarly disregarded. To some extent, these differences in worldview are not particularly surprising. Think of how upset your own parents may have gotten with you for spending too many hours on the phone with friends, watching television, or playing video games on your Atari or Nintendo system. If you reflect on those conversations, you'd probably admit that although you may have fended off your parents' objections, there was some truth to their arguments. Since the invention of movies, radio, and television, mass media have offered rapid information sharing, social connection, education, and entertainment—all of which are powerful motivators for intensive consumption.

Social scientists in the mid-twentieth century, most notably Marshall McLuhan, studied problems with the overconsumption of mass media and their influence on human behavior.[16] Their potential for manipulating public opinion and consumer behavior was noted by authors like Vance Packard, who reported on the ways advertisers used motivational research to design overt campaigns and subliminal tactics to stimulate desires for products in American consumers.[17] He listed eight "compelling needs" advertisers promised these products would fulfill: "emotional security, reassurance of worth, ego gratification, creative outlets, love objects, sense of power, roots and immortality." The popular TV series *Mad Men* similarly depicts how a Madison Avenue advertising agency designed its campaigns to persuade people to buy a host of consumer products by appealing to these needs.

The advent of the internet and its dominance by privately owned companies has created a digital landscape rife with advertisements and other inducements to engage in commercial transactions. Search platforms like Google; networking and messaging platforms like Facebook, X (formerly known as Twitter), and Snapchat; media platforms like YouTube, Netflix, and Apple TV; purchasing platforms like Amazon and eBay; and service platforms like Uber, Lyft, Airbnb, and Expedia all share common features. Among other things, these platforms embed advertisements throughout their web pages and collect users' personal and private information. This information is used to target marketing messages based on the person's platform usage and their psychological profiles. The platforms collect this data and store it in vast databases either for sale to companies that buy the information or for direct use by the platform itself to keep the user engaged. Applying sophisticated artificial intelligence algorithms, these corporations adjust the shape and content of their platform to the individual's preferences, as measured by their online behavior. From the user's standpoint, this increases the likability and subsequent time spent on the website. For the platform owners, website users provide invaluable data that enable the company to gain substantial revenues from advertisers and endorsers.

In effect, the methods of hidden persuasion first noted by Packard and others in the mid-1950s have evolved to be so compelling that they drive most of us toward compulsive or addictive consumption of digital media. These frightening developments are depicted in the documentary *The Social Dilemma* (2020), which examines how social media platforms have been purposely designed to foster addictive behaviors in their users.[18] Interviews with experts from Silicon Valley formerly employed by companies like Google, Facebook, and Firefox shed light on corporate strategies to guide people's behavior to maximize engagement. These strategies include psychological profiling and AI-informed targeting of content to increase time spent on the platform. The film encourages viewers to consider ways to reduce overuse of digital media and invites them to participate in efforts to regulate these companies' practices through political action.

The take-home message is simple: Digital media platforms are not simply neutral purveyors of information, social connection, and entertainment. They are powerful, profit-driven influencers of human behavior on a global scale, and their strategies to drive us toward overuse need to be countered by some type of governmental regulation. We believe these external causes of digital media overuse must be addressed from a public health perspective, much as society and government have worked to regulate and reduce tobacco smoking and to promote wearing seat belts in cars. While we can educate and encourage individuals to exercise self-control to avoid cigarette addiction or motor-vehicle-related injuries, government policies that provide incentives to quit smoking or to wear a seat belt are far more effective. Unfortunately, such policies lie far off on the horizon. People must vote for leaders to take up these issues. Until we reach such a massive change in public policy, we need to examine the *internal* causes of digital media usage to reduce overuse at the individual level.

PRACTICAL WAYS TO LIMIT DIGITAL MEDIA HABITS

Looking at your own social media usage can have two benefits. By learning how difficult breaking a digital habit can be, you'll have more empathy for your young adults and the challenges they face in this digital world. And if you share with your twentysomething your own attempts to limit your device habits, you'll be modeling positive behavior rather than acting as a nagging parent. Given the preponderance of shiny screens in our world and the overwhelming impact they exert on our daily lives, how can you effectively cut back on your own digital media usage? The first step involves becoming aware of how digital media is affecting you. Ask yourself some thought-provoking questions such as these:

- Is my smartphone use a problem for me? If so, in what ways?
- Am I spending more time on my smartphone or computer than I want to spend?
- Am I too distracted by notifications on my smartphone or computer?
- Am I compulsively looking at my smartphone when I don't really need to be?
- Do I worry too much about what I'm missing if I'm not checking my smartphone?
- Is it hard for me to resist looking at my smartphone when I'm doing other things like working, studying, spending time with people, walking, or driving?
- Am I unhappy with my social media presence?

If you answer yes to many of these questions, you're probably dissatisfied with your approach to digital media use. Next, dig deeper into the sources of this discontent—in particular, your motivations. If the primary reason you overuse digital media is boredom, you might want to find suitable alternative means to address that. If the primary reason has more to do with anxiety, you'll want to confront this issue straight on and develop approaches for resisting these hard-to-control habits and for countering the anxiety-ridden thoughts and mindsets that reinforce them.

Next, develop a broader framework for thinking about your habitual behaviors and for recognizing your most common rationalizations for them.

"Metacognition," or thinking about thinking, enables you to observe your own thoughts and pinpoint how certain thoughts lead to unpleasant feelings and unproductive actions designed to mitigate these feelings. By understanding the thoughts and feelings that drive you to your preferred digital devices and apps, you can better formulate alternative actions. Instead of reflexively checking your messages or allowing notifications to interrupt your flow, you can practice an alternative response to interrupt the habit or the action cycle. With greater awareness comes the ability to alter the reflex action cycle.

Metacognition enables people to gain greater cognitive control over their habitual or reflexive behaviors. The most cited evidence-based strategies for reducing excessive habitual digital media use include education; meditation/ mindfulness training; cognitive training exercises or brain games; computer-based video games; neurofeedback; physical exercise; spending time in nature, whether taking a walk or "forest bathing"; medications; and the neuromodulation of brain stimulation. A detailed description of these interventions lies beyond the scope of this book, but resources are provided in the appendix for readers wishing to explore them.

Beyond using cognitive enhancing strategies, an important approach to reducing digital media overuse is limiting access, also referred to as stimulus control. Whether it is simply turning off your devices or programming them to shut down after a certain amount of time, limiting your contact with digital technology goes a long way to help reduce excessive usage.

We're all too familiar with the instructions to turn off all digital devices during theater productions or other shows so as not to disturb the performance or other audience members. And we've all attended events where someone failed to heed these directives and suddenly their phone started ringing, much to the chagrin of everyone in earshot of the device. While a ringing phone may be a sign of carelessness, it also reflects the lack of awareness people have about their habitual behaviors. Instead of turning our cell phones to silent mode (which still allows them to vibrate), it is much more effective to put them on airplane mode or to power them down.

Another access-limiting tactic is to take an inventory of the time you actually spend on various websites and apps and to decide which of these should be eliminated or curtailed. Eliminating an app is equivalent to abstinence— "No more TikTok!"—whereas curtailing one is similar to a harm-reduction strategy: "Only an hour a day playing Words with Friends." But setting time restrictions on these activities is not sufficient. You need to decide what you plan to do with the time you've freed up when you limit your digital media access. Maybe it's time to resume hobbies you once enjoyed (e.g., playing music, drawing, cooking) or to take up new activities that can help you avoid the boredom or anxiety that will inevitably arise with these changes.

Limiting access includes setting technology-free spaces and time zones in your daily schedule. Creating tech-free times and places is especially important at bedtime for two reasons: It reduces the chances that you will stay up too late, and with no devices in your hands, you will avoid the sleep-onset delays that result from staring at shiny screens at night. During the day, creating tech-free spaces and times can break the cycle of stress and anxiety that often accompanies excessive digital technology usage. Surprisingly, taking a regular break in the action gives people a greater sense of well-being.

Beyond limiting your access to devices, you can shut off routine notifications to reduce the frequency of unwanted interruptions. You can also battle boredom-induced tech use by finding alternatives to the downtime default of smartphones. Try a return to the former world of print via books, newspapers, or crossword puzzles instead. You can reduce your FOMO by notifying significant others that you're cutting down your digital media use and are limiting access during certain hours. Automated messages to this effect go a long way toward keeping others informed that you're not ignoring them. And you can moderate your nomophobia by deliberately putting your phone out of reach for increasing periods. Psychologists refer to this gradual practice as a *systematic desensitization*. Eventually, you won't feel upset when your smartphone is not in your immediate vicinity.

To summarize, there are myriad ways to gain better control over habitual digital media use that is excessive or compulsive. The most promising methods include limiting access, increasing intentional self-control, and reducing boredom and anxiety. Naturally, all these strategies are easier said than done. Given the multiple external and internal forces that keep us plugged into our devices 24/7, each of us has to make conscious efforts to interrupt our bad habits. Like all behavioral change, it requires daily commitment to maintaining self-awareness, exerting self-control, and challenging negative thoughts that reduce our sense of well-being. Much like attempts at cutting back on eating junk food or compulsive shopping, the effort requires dedication and hard work.

HOW TO CHANGE DIGITAL MEDIA USE

Getting your young adults to change their underlying beliefs and attitudes and to tackle their compulsive behaviors in relation to shiny screens is a bit more complicated. There are no shortcuts here. If they're willing to begin examining their assumptions, feelings, and patterns of behavior, then the steps we've outlined for you should be a good starting point for them. The resources in the appendix should also be helpful. If your young adult is unwilling to make any changes, then your entreaties will probably be ineffective unless they're linked to incentives. In other words, unless the young person expects that changing their behavior will offer tangible benefits that are rewarding and sustaining for them, your twentysomething is likely to carry on as usual. Unfortunately, even if their behaviors meet the criteria for a diagnosable mental disorder, such as anxiety disorder, depression, or digital media addiction, you will probably struggle to convince them to pursue treatment unless they are convinced they need it.

Getting them to accept this reality requires a great deal of patience, understanding, good humor, and ongoing dialogue. The most that parents and other family members can provide as motivators for change are practical constructive messages, tangible rewards or inducements, and concrete examples of positive change in their own lives. After all, the reason digital media usage is so reinforcing is that it fulfills profound needs for social connection, access to information, technical mastery, and the temporary amelioration of boredom and anxiety.

In later chapters, we will explore how various anxiety disorders can co-occur with excessive internet use and gaming disorders. Since anxiety has risen to even higher levels since the pandemic, it is important to understand how anxiety affects young adults and what parents can do to address these mental health issues.

8

When Distress Becomes a Way of Life

Nobody realizes that some people expend tremendous energy merely to be normal.

—*Albert Camus*, Notebooks *(1965)*

AS WE'VE NOTED FROM THE OUTSET, THE CHALLENGES OF GROWING UP IN THIS age of tremendous change and uncertainty have given rise to high levels of stress and apprehension among twentysomethings and their parents. Indeed, chronic anxiety is the new normal for most young people. Ask them how they're doing, and chances are they'll answer, "Stressed out" rather than "Fine." But what do we make of this situation? Is *everyone* suffering from some form of anxiety disorder, or is this just an idiom of distress for our times? This chapter will discuss what we know about anxiety and anxiety disorders in young adults and their parents. We will distinguish between stress and anxiety, and describe features of anxiety disorders, including common thought and behavior patterns, and emotional states. We'll review the underlying mechanisms of anxiety disorders and the conditions that often accompany them. Because anxiety disorders affect not only the individual but also the family, managing these disorders can improve the quality of life for all members of the family. We conclude with practical approaches to handling anxiety and stress.

NOT A PRETTY PICTURE

By all accounts, Gen Zers are extremely stressed out and highly prone to psychological disorders.[1] So are the youngest millennials, born in the early 1990s. In our 2019 book, *The Stressed Years of Their Lives*, we discussed the far-reaching implications of this observation, especially in college-bound youths. Since the onset of the Covid-19 pandemic, things have gotten worse for everyone, especially twentysomethings. By way of comparison, in 2019 the average share of adults reporting symptoms of anxiety disorder or depressive disorder was 11 percent. By 2021, this rate had jumped to 41 percent. Among young adults, the figure had skyrocketed to over 56 percent (see the table below)![2]

The pandemic accelerated preexisting concerns about unemployment, job security, student debt, climate change, technology, and gun violence, all of which have contributed to the worsening state of mental health for youth. In 2021, U.S. Surgeon General Dr. Vivek Murthy officially declared a "youth mental health crisis" that needed to be addressed urgently: "We can and must

Share of Adults Reporting Symptoms of Anxiety and/or Depressive Disorder During the Covid-19 Pandemic, by Age

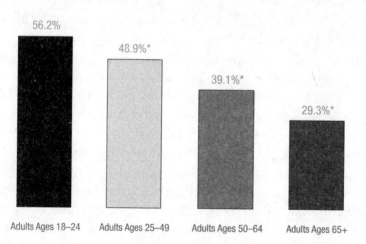

NOTES: *Indicates a statistically significant difference between adults ages 18–24.
Data shown includes adults, ages 18+, with symptoms of anxiety and/or depressive disorder that generally occur more than half the days or nearly every day. Data shown is for December 9–21, 2020.
Source: U.S. Census Bureau, Household Pulse Survey, 2020.

protect and promote youth mental health. Mental health is an essential part of overall health, affecting how children, adolescents, and young adults feel about themselves and the world."[3]

Parents of twentysomethings are also experiencing a great deal of stress. A recent survey of mothers of Gen Zers found that 79 percent reported anxiety symptoms, with 45 percent of the sample indicating moderate to severe anxiety.[4] While family finances and inflation were major contributors to this anxiety, the mothers' desire to be a perfect parent was also prevalent. Additionally, smaller social support networks were highly correlated with levels of parental anxiety. The bottom line: Unrealistic expectations and lack of social support are major sources of anxiety for young adults and their parents.

A 2022 Pew Research Center survey found that 70 percent of middle-aged adults under fifty believe that today's young adults will have more trouble than their generation did in saving for the future, paying for college, and buying a home.[5] The majority of both parents and young adult generations agree on the increasing generational hardships. To the extent that these attitudes reflect the hourglass economic squeeze on the middle class, it is not surprising that both twentysomethings and their parents are reporting historically high levels of anxiety.

STRESS AND SURVIVAL

Stress is the way we adapt to increased demands. Life events, even positive ones, challenge us to respond physiologically and psychologically. The stress response is an evolutionary accommodation to prepare, act, and survive. For instance, the well-studied fight-or-flight response is a vital mechanism for coping with danger. When threatened, our bodies release stress hormones (adrenaline and cortisol) and our minds become hyper-focused on the danger confronting us. At times, we seek escape—we literally run away to safety. At other times, we stand our ground and confront the crisis head-on. Our response depends on the situation we are facing, the resources at hand, our predispositions, and our preferred patterns of problem-solving—different strokes for different folks. There is no one best way to adapt to change or to face danger. The circumstances at hand and personal factors play key roles in our stress response.

In general, anxiety is a subjective response to stress. It is the feeling of fear, dread, apprehensiveness, or uneasiness we experience when confronting unfamiliar, unpleasant, or potentially threatening situations. These feelings are inevitably accompanied by physical changes like increased heart rate, blood pressure, and respiratory rate. For some, even minor stresses can produce intense discomfort and an overwhelming physiological response. For others, anxious feelings are less easy to provoke. Again, individual differences in genetics; physical and emotional constitution; learned responses; and other environmental influences are at play in determining both how people manage their stress and how much anxiety they experience.

THREE LEVELS OF STRESS RESPONSES

Stress is a natural part of our lives and can be roughly categorized as positive, tolerable, or toxic. Our responses to stress can determine which effect the stress will have on us. In most situations, when the source of stress is removed or managed successfully, we return to baseline and our anxiety subsides. If the stress is persistent, our anxiety is likely to continue. In some cases, such as when we learn to drive, we habituate to the stress and our stress response subsides. Think back to that time when you first sat in the driver's seat, stressed by the task of figuring out how to simultaneously move the pedals and turn the steering wheel. Didn't you experience moments of anxiety? Yet as you mastered the challenge of learning to drive, your stress and anxiety level decreased. There may still be times when you feel anxious driving—perhaps in inclement weather or when you're overly fatigued. In these instances, your anxiety is a natural and typical response to the implicit dangers of the stressful situation. But when people successfully manage stressful situations, they learn that they can master challenges and, in so doing, conquer their anxiety. This type of stress—which is present when a person is learning something new and which diminishes with familiarity and increases again in situations requiring attention—is referred to as "positive stress."

Not all stress is positive. There is also "tolerable stress" and "toxic stress." In situations of tolerable stress, the stress response is triggered for a longer period and generates greater levels of anxiety than that generated by positive stress. Tolerable stress may be elicited by experiences such as injury, serious illness, loss of a loved one, natural disasters, or significant financial losses. These adverse events intensively activate physiological and psychological defenses, leading to more prolonged anxiety. If the situation is time-limited and a person has sufficient resources available, their anxiety will eventually subside. Of course, some people are more sensitive to the impact of tolerable stress because of their genetic makeup and their environment. These people require additional support to cope with these more stressful experiences. They are more likely to develop an anxiety disorder or some related mental health issue.

Toxic stress is the most severe type of stress. It results from exposure to extreme threats to physical and mental well-being. Sources of this stress include physical or emotional abuse, intimate-partner violence, neighborhood violence, political violence, military conflict and war, and severe natural disasters like famine, earthquakes, floods, and fires. These adverse events cause heightened, excessive activation of the stress response, which is extremely difficult to tolerate, especially over prolonged periods. Although we may be able to cope with such hardships, they exact a toll on our physical and mental health. When exposure to toxic stress occurs early in life, it can lead to intellectual impairment, emotional blunting, social deficits, and high risk for stress-related disease and mental illness. In adolescents and adults, a variety of traumatic stress patterns such as acute or post-traumatic stress disorder, anxiety disorder, depressive disorder, substance use disorder, and even psychosis can emerge.

COVID-19 ANXIETY

The Covid-19 pandemic introduced historically unprecedented stress throughout the world. In the initial lockdown phase, most people experienced toxic stress reactions with varying degrees of anxiety. Common symptoms included nervousness, restlessness, or tension; a sense of impending danger or doom; worry about the future; trouble sleeping; trouble concentrating or thinking about anything other than the virus; weakness or tiredness; and the inability to relax. People with Covid-19 anxiety also showed signs of overarousal, such as hyperventilation, rapid heart rate and palpitations, sweating, trembling, headaches, muscle tension, and chest tightness. After this initial phase, many people found ways to reduce their anxiety, whereas others fell prey to chronic worrying and signs of generalized anxiety disorder. The accompanying box invites you to reflect on how you and your family reacted to the pandemic.

COVID-19 ANXIETY AND YOU

Think about your and your family's reactions to the pandemic. How anxious did you feel in the early phases? How did you express this anxiety, and how did you cope with it? Did you notice anxious reactions in your twentysomethings? How did they manage their feelings? Could you discuss your worries with one another? What enabled you and your young adult to get a handle on your anxieties and support each other? Did your anxiety and your ability to cope improve over time? Once the initial health threats of the virus waned, what other stresses caused you and your family the most anxiety? When the pandemic reemerged during its second and third waves, how did you all readjust to masking and additional vaccinations?

The term *Covid-19 anxiety* was introduced to describe ongoing symptoms specifically related to concerns about catching or spreading the virus. People at greatest risk of catching the virus and developing a life-threatening version of the disease were most vulnerable to Covid-19 anxiety, as were their close family members. People whose loved ones became sick and either died or came close to dying from the virus experienced a spectrum of traumatic grief reactions.

People with limited economic resources or social contacts, prior physical or mental health problems, reduced access to health care, or some combination of these challenges fared the worst during the crisis. Children, adolescents, and young adults were particularly vulnerable to Covid-19 because of the first mentioned reason: Their access to education and social networks were profoundly disrupted. This anxiety was especially prevalent for young people from working-class families. These young adults were often forced to drop out of school to take care of family members, take on family maintenance duties, or earn money to support the family's income. Those from families with greater material resources were less likely to interrupt their education or other pursuits, a status referred to as "privileged dependence."[6]

The pandemic radically altered family dynamics for young adults, the majority of whom lived at home in the early phases of the outbreak. This sudden disruption of the developmental separation-individuation process obliged parents and young adults to revise plans, adjust expectations, and renegotiate relationships. While most appear to have adapted, a substantial minority found it very hard to deal with the chronic stress and anxiety symptoms engendered by the crisis. Most experts agree that the long-term effects of the pandemic on this generation of youth remain to be determined. What is clear, however, is that the aftereffects of Covid-19 both revealed and amplified a decades-long trend of increased anxiety among youth.

WHEN WORRYING BECOMES AN ANXIETY DISORDER

To better understand the various types of stress and stress reactions, we need to distinguish between people's common phrases for nonpathological worry (e.g., "Ty is stressing about his exams"; "Cara is a nervous Nelly") and the truly pathological forms of anxiety. While the continuum from one to the other is gradual and difficult to discern, there are clear criteria for determining when worrying becomes an anxiety disorder. As we stated in *The Stressed Years of Their Lives*, "Whereas momentary anxiety is a normal reaction to a real or perceived danger, an anxiety disorder creates a chronic experience of perceived threat. Anxiety disorder is an umbrella term covering several different manifestations: panic attacks, obsessive thoughts, social anxiety, specific phobias such as agoraphobia or claustrophobia, and the broadest category, generalized anxiety disorder (GAD)."[7]

People with anxiety disorders feel powerless to manage their negative thoughts, feelings, and patterns of behavior. They may be aware that their distress level is out of proportion to the situation they are facing, but they often feel overwhelmed and helpless to control their overly aroused physical and psychological states.

There are four core features of anxiety disorders:

1. the presence of *excessive* fear or worry in situations that are not threatening or not overwhelming for most people
2. intense subjective *distress*
3. the *persistence* of symptoms over time
4. *impairments* in the individual's functioning

The emotional symptoms of anxiety disorders range from uneasiness or apprehension to more profound states of panic and terror. Behavioral expressions of anxiety include avoidance, escape, and safety-seeking. Because these highly reinforcing behavior patterns reduce a person's exposure to a perceived threat, they remove the triggers of negative emotions or thoughts. For example, if you feel anxious about meeting new people, you might avoid parties. By avoiding them, you are relieved of the anxiety you might have felt had you attended. The perceived safety of avoidance encourages you to further sidestep social situations. This pattern of "negative reinforcement" is a powerful means of behavioral conditioning.

The cognitive manifestations of anxiety disorders include worrying, over-focusing on negative thoughts, and overriding preoccupations with emotional, bodily, or social threats.

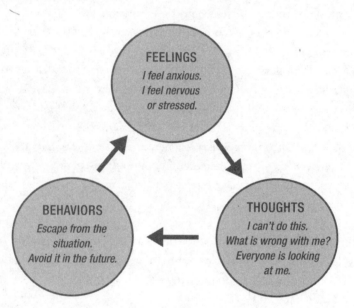

Cognitive triad of feelings, thoughts, and behaviors of anxiety disorders.

Source: Adapted from Aaron T. Beck, *Cognitive Therapy and the Emotional Disorders* (New York: International Universities Press, 1976).

According to the cognitive theory of anxiety proposed by Dr. Aaron Beck, "cognitive triad" of thoughts, feelings, and behaviors underlies most anxiety disorders (see image above).[8]

People with anxiety disorders are prone to view themselves, the world, and the future through a negative lens. When they encounter a stressful situation or imagine themselves in one, negative feelings like anxiety, nervousness, and worrisome physical sensations are triggered. They interpret these feelings as confirming their negative thoughts, such as a belief that they cannot handle the stress successfully. The belief prompts them to respond with avoidance, escape, or safety-seeking behavior. These behaviors temporarily reduce their anxiety and in turn keep the negative thoughts and escape patterns intact. Beck's cognitive theory identifies several typical patterns of negative automatic thoughts, or "cognitive distortions," which are common to people with anxiety disorders (see table below).

ANXIETY'S CONTROLLING COGNITIVE DISTORTIONS

Catastrophizing	Exaggerating the importance or negative aspects of things or situations—focusing on worst-case scenarios
Emotional reasoning	Negative emotions are seen as reflecting reality and hence overwhelm rational reasoning
Overgeneralizing	Viewing one negative event as a never-ending defeat and as an indicator of one's inabilities to succeed
Mental filtering	Picking out one single negative detail of a situation and obsessing over it
Labeling	Viewing self or others in simplistic, negative terms: "stupid," "worthless," "hopeless," etc.
Fortune telling	Assuming a bad outcome when there's little or no evidence to support this conclusion

To summarize, someone with an anxiety disorder assumes that bad things will happen. This negative bias spawns a continual and exhausting vigilance for possibly threatening words and criticism. With this downhearted bias, people interpret neutral but ambiguous situations as menacing. They increase the frequency of their negative self-talk, underestimate their own strengths, and believe that they cannot handle stressful situations. They anticipate worst-case scenarios and outcomes. The impact of anxiety disorders extends well beyond the individual to include those closest to them. To illustrate this dynamic interplay, let's meet the Roberts family.

THE ROBERTS FAMILY:
WHEN A PANDEMIC PROMOTES COPING

Catherine Roberts, a twenty-five-year-old Ph.D. student in American studies, met with us through telehealth with complaints of worsening anxiety and concentration difficulties leading to significant problems with coursework and relationships. Thanks to the financial support of her parents and a university teaching stipend, she'd been living on her own for three years.

Soon after the start of the pandemic, however, Catherine moved back to her family's home while she continued her studies remotely. Within a few weeks, she noticed her stress level was so high that it was hard for her to engage in her usual daily activities. Her constant worries ranged from the personal threat of the coronavirus to her own and her family's health, to her ability to complete her dissertation, to professional success. She was also concerned about universal threats, including the impact of global climate change and the future of American democracy. She reported feeling constantly on edge, restless, tired, and easily fatigued. Catherine also described having trouble concentrating and completing her graduate school reading assignments to prepare for her oral examinations. Whenever she tried to study, her mind wandered. Despite a college assessment in which ADHD was ruled out, she couldn't shake her conviction that she had it. She told us that her forgetfulness had gotten noticeably worse and that she had recently been having trouble organizing her work, managing her time, and setting priorities. These difficulties had worsened over the past six months. That's when she considered taking a leave from grad school. When asked about how things were going for her at home, Catherine broke down in tears.

"Living back at home full-time has been really, really hard for me," she said. "Honestly, I don't know how I am going to get through this pandemic. I just don't know how any of us are going to make it. I mean, I know my parents love me and they support me to the best of their abilities. I'm luckier than many people my age who don't have the financial support or the resources that I'm privileged to have. But even with their help, I'm just too overwhelmed to keep up my studies. I'm just a hot mess, and I really don't know what to do."

We also learned that Catherine's parents, John and Julia, were concerned about their own parents' health and safety. Since the start of the pandemic, John's parents had been quarantined with his younger sister in a nearby town. Though limited in their social contacts, they seemed to be faring reasonably well. Julia's widowed and extremely frail mother was living in a senior living facility about a six-hour drive away. Julia was devastated that the institution prohibited in-person visits from family members. Catherine's older brother, James, who was stationed with the military in South Korea, was available for Zoom calls, but it fell to her to cope with her parents' understandable fears for the family's health.

Being the dutiful daughter was a lifetime role for Catherine, who always did her best to please her parents. She had been a hardworking, above-average student in high school, although it took her longer than it took her friends to get through assignments. In college, she found it hard to keep up with all her assignments but managed to get a 3.6 GPA by dint of hard work and extra time in the library.

Catherine described being stymied by time management and organizational challenges throughout college, and these challenges led her to seek an evaluation. Instead of ADHD, the report pointed to academic performance anxiety. A brief course of cognitive therapy helped her manage these difficulties. But she still believed that something was wrong with her.

Catherine found graduate school to be even more challenging than college. There was considerably more intensive reading and writing than in college, and she was chronically late turning in her work. Because of the workload, she avoided socializing with other classmates. Despite her best efforts, Catherine received mediocre grades in her classes and below-average evaluations by the undergraduate students whom she taught. Her anxiety level was chronically high, but she was determined to plow through school and achieve her dream of earning a doctorate degree. By the time she moved back home, however, she'd realized that her usual coping mechanisms just weren't cutting it, and she was seriously considering taking time off from school.

We asked Catherine to describe how her parents felt about her struggles with anxiety in graduate school. She immediately began to cry, and in a muffled voice said, "They just don't understand what it's been like for me. I'm trying the best I can, but they think I'm just undisciplined and I waste too much time on things that aren't important. I know they're worried about me, but I'm worried about them too. And every time we try to talk about things, someone ends up in tears. . . . Mostly it's me."

We suggested to Catherine that we ask her parents to join us for the next telehealth session so that we could hear their perspectives on how the family was handling the stress of the pandemic. We also thought we could enlist their assistance in helping Catherine gain a better handle on her anxiety. She hesitated at first, thinking that their participation would place an additional strain on her already overburdened parents. But she eventually came around when we reassured her that a family session could provide them with support during the Covid-19 crisis.

John, a mechanical engineer, and Julia, a fourth-grade teacher, greatly appreciated the invitation to attend the next visit. Julia was friendly and engaging, with a warm smile and a steady gaze. John was a bit shy and uncomfortable at first, deferring to his wife when we asked them to tell us a little about how things were going for them during the pandemic.

"It's been terrible for everyone," Julia replied, "but I'm really worried about my mother. She's not used to being alone, and they're not letting anyone visit her at her senior care living center. We're able to Zoom with her, thank God, but it's just not the same. And we're scared to death about her catching the virus. It's been exhausting, really. Plus, my job is really stressing me out. Virtual education is wearing me down. It's just so hard to get the students engaged, and by the end of the day, I'm just exhausted. It is nice to have Catherine at home, though. I just wish she was doing better. . . ." Her voice trailed off.

We asked Julia to share her thoughts about how her daughter was holding up.

"You know, it's been very hard on her," Julia said. "I'm sure she'd rather be living in her own place again, but we just didn't think it made sense, given that her university is completely in remote learning mode. And we're not sure what to make of what's going on with her lately. We think Catherine is very intelligent and highly motivated. We've always admired her diligence when it came to doing well in school. But she seems too upset to get her work done, and that's making her doubt herself to the point where she's unable to function. We don't know what we can do to help her. Every time we ask how things are going, she starts crying and saying that she doesn't think she's cut out for graduate school. And given how much it's costing us, we're starting to wonder about it as well."

We asked John and Julia to describe how they felt about Catherine's career choice. They admitted they weren't sure about the value of getting a Ph.D. in American studies. They wondered what she'd be able to do with her degree, and they were very clear that they could not afford to fully support her financially. John and Julia had said they'd provide her with financial aid if she agreed to take out some student loans, sign up to be a teaching assistant, and live within her means. In exchange for their support, Catherine assented to their requests and lived up to her end of the bargain.

Over the ensuing months, when they saw how much Catherine was struggling with graduate school, her parents raised questions about the wisdom of her continuing with it, especially because of the high cost. They were worried about their daughter's academic struggles and the poor job prospects for college professors in her chosen field. But despite their reservations, John and Julia didn't want their daughter to give up on herself. "We know it's been hard for her to deal with being back home while she's trying to study for a Ph.D.," Julia said. "And we really want her to succeed on this path. But we aren't sure how to help her."

For the rest of the session, we encouraged Catherine to tell her parents what was making it so hard for her to stay on top of her schoolwork. She spoke eloquently about her guilt for being financially dependent on them and about her recent mediocre academic performance. She explained that her problems with time management, getting things done efficiently, and staying motivated to study were interfering with her schoolwork. And she described how her worsening anxiety about her grades was leading her to question her career choice and to consider leaving graduate school altogether.

John and Julia were quiet and attentive as their daughter spoke. They acknowledged that they, too, were very worried about her stress level and were unsure about how to be helpful. They wanted her to take better care of herself and learn how to deal with her anxiety. Most of all, they wanted her to stop feeling guilty for needing their financial assistance. "You've always been a wonderful daughter," they told her. "We know you are struggling to get through this. Everyone is having a hard time with life since the pandemic started. But don't beat yourself up. We're here for you. We'll do whatever it takes to support you through this crisis. Just tell us what you need from us, and we'll do the best we can. That's how families get through hard times."

At the conclusion of the session, we recommended that Catherine get evaluated further for her executive-functioning difficulties, which were being made worse by her chronic anxiety and the current crisis she was facing. We offered to write a letter asking her program leaders to grant a brief leave of absence. And we suggested that John and Julia remind their daughter as often as needed that they would lend support no matter what she decided to do about grad school. We will return to Catherine and her parents after we explore how stress and anxiety manifest themselves in the lives of young adults and their parents.

IT'S A FAMILY AFFAIR

In our work with young adults and families, we take a life-span perspective on family systems. With this approach, we consider mental health problems in light of the person's developmental stage and overall circumstances. Earlier psychological approaches blamed the parents for the mental illness of an adolescent or a young adult. But a family systems approach acknowledges that problems like anxiety, depression, and substance abuse are not necessarily caused by family interactions but instead cause profound effects on family relationships.

When we apply this family perspective over a person's life span, we find common patterns. Families often become most stressed and seek our help during significant life-span changes. Psychologist Monica McGoldrick calls these times "transition points from one life cycle phase to another." She says that during these times, "families must rebalance, redefine, and re-align their relationships."[9] Change is hard for everyone, but it's more challenging for families when anxiety disorders frame the *risks* rather than the benefits of change.

The transition of leaving home to attend college often precipitates anxiety symptoms in young people and their parents. Unconscious messaging between parent and student frequently emphasizes the stress and uncertainty of being away from home. Caught in this negatively reinforcing feedback loop, the young person, when they encounter a setback, feels lonely or insecure being away from home and signals to their parents that they need help. The parents then leap in and try to rescue their child from the stressful situation. The message is "You aren't prepared; you can't handle this. We'll jump in to help." This approach unintentionally thwarts the young person's ability to solve these problems on their own. When triggered, this vicious cycle gets reactivated and reinforces the young adult's belief that they can't cope effectively with stress. The image above illustrates the sequence of actions and reactions that leads to overprotective behavior, usually on the part of one parent, and to polarization between parents.[10]

Family systems treatments for anxiety disorders have been shown to improve symptoms better than individual therapy does.[11] By changing their dysfunctional problem-solving approaches, anxious parents and anxious young adults become more competent at handling stressful situations and reducing their levels of distress. We'll return to the Roberts family to share the strategies to reduce anxiety's hold on each of them.

Family Stress / Anxiety Cycle

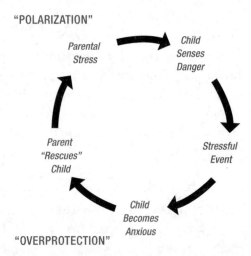

"POLARIZATION"

Parental Stress

Child Senses Danger

Stressful Event

Child Becomes Anxious

Parent "Rescues" Child

"OVERPROTECTION"

Family Systems Model of Anxiety

FINDING A WAY OUT OF THE ANXIETY TRAP

The onset of the pandemic triggered an anxiety reaction in everyone in the Roberts family. Once she moved home, Catherine's underlying anxiety about succeeding in graduate school was heightened by her changed living and learning situations. She was distressed by being forced to leave the school campus and give up independent living. She was very worried about the risks of the coronavirus to her parents' and grandparents' survival. And she was overwhelmed by the demands of distance learning, finding it increasingly harder to remain engaged in her academic work. Not only were Julia and John worried about their parents' and their own health, but they also became increasingly alarmed by their daughter's unsuccessful struggles to cope with the crisis she was facing. This perfect storm of excessive stress and insufficient coping resources became a family anxiety disorder.

As recommended, Catherine took a leave of absence from school and was evaluated for her concentration and academic difficulties. Clinical assessment and psychological testing revealed that she met the criteria for a generalized anxiety disorder[12] (see the accompanying box below) and for a proposed new diagnosis referred to as "sluggish cognitive tempo" (SCT). This new diagnosis is much less common than ADHD but is closely associated with high levels of social anxiety and other types of anxiety. Because of the lack of precision and the pejorative connotations of the term "sluggish cognitive tempo," a working group of experts in this field has proposed replacing it with the term "cognitive disengagement syndrome" (CDS).[13] The accompanying box presents the symptoms of this syndrome. The hallmark symptoms are sluggishness, drowsiness, and excessive daydreaming—as distinct from the inattentiveness and poor working memory seen in ADHD.

DSM-5 CRITERIA FOR GENERALIZED ANXIETY DISORDER

a. There is excessive anxiety and worry (apprehensive expectation), occurring more days than not for at least six months, about a number of events or activities (such as work or school performance).

b. The individual finds it difficult to control the worry.

c. The anxiety and worry are associated with three (or more) of the following six symptoms (with at least some symptoms having been present for more days than not for the past six months). Note: Only one item required in children.

   1. Restlessness, feeling keyed up or on edge

   2. Being easily fatigued

   3. Difficulty concentrating or mind going blank

   4. Irritability

   5. Muscle tension

   6. Sleep disturbance (difficulty falling or staying asleep or restless, unsatisfying sleep)

d. The anxiety, worry, or physical symptoms cause clinically significant distress or impairment in social, occupational, or other important areas of functioning.

e. The disturbance is not attributable to the physiological effects of a substance (e.g., abuse of drugs or medications) or another medical condition (e.g., hyperthyroidism).

f. The disturbance is not better explained by another medical disorder (e.g., anxiety or worry about having panic attacks in panic disorder, negative evaluation in social anxiety disorder [social phobia], contamination fears or other obsessions in obsessive-compulsive disorder, separation from attachment figures in separation anxiety disorder, reminders of traumatic events in post-traumatic stress disorder, gaining weight in anorexia nervosa, physical complaints in somatic symptom disorder, perceived appearance flaws in body dysmorphic disorder, having a serious illness in illness anxiety disorder, or delusional beliefs in schizophrenia or delusional disorder).

Source: American Psychiatric Association, *The Diagnostic and Statistical Manual of Mental Disorders,* 5th ed. (Washington, D.C.: AMA Publishing, 2013).

SYMPTOMS OF COGNITIVE DISENGAGEMENT SYNDROME / SLUGGISH COGNITIVE TEMPO

- Prone to daydreaming
- Easily confused or mentally foggy
- Spacey or inattentive to surroundings
- Mind seems to be elsewhere
- Stares blankly into space
- Underactive, slow moving, or sluggish
- Lethargic or less energetic
- Trouble staying awake or alert
- Has drowsy or sleepy appearance
- Gets lost in own thoughts
- Apathetic or withdrawn, less engaged in activities

- Loses train of thought or cognitive set
- Processes information less quickly or accurately

Source: Stephen P. Becker et al., "The Internal, External, and Diagnostic Validity of Sluggish Cognitive Tempo: A Meta-Analysis and Critical Review," *Journal of the American Academy of Child and Adolescent Psychiatry* 55, no. 3 (March 2016): 163–78, doi: 10.1016/j.jaac.2015.12.006.

People with SCT/CDS have problems with self-organization, problem-solving, and time management. They are also more likely to demonstrate anxiety, rumination, depression, and social withdrawal. The condition is associated with impairments in overall functioning, poor quality of life, and poor social functioning (with greater shyness, social withdrawal, and loneliness). People with this syndrome also have lower academic and occupational functioning and greater difficulty managing household chores and finances. They often struggle with driving and have significant impairment in health-related behaviors and aspects of social adulthood such as marital relationships and parenting.

While there are only a few published studies of SCT/CDS treatments, the condition appears to be more resistant to interventions than ADHD is. Stimulant medications are not as effective for SCT/CDS as they are for ADHD. Nonstimulant medications show promise but lack adequate research. Psychosocial treatments have not yet been developed or tested, although strategies like behavioral activation, cognitive behavioral therapy, sleep hygiene, and assistive technologies are all being investigated.

For Catherine, getting diagnosed with general anxiety disorder and SCT/CDS was a game changer. She finally had an explanation for her difficulties with concentration and self-organization. Now she understood why she needed more time than her peers did to get things done and why she had to work so hard to meet the academic demands of her rigorous graduate school program. Her testing results made her eligible to receive extended time on examinations and enabled her to consider options for continuing in her program. After meeting with her graduate advisor to discuss the possibility of extending her course of study by reducing her class load, she was pleased to learn that she qualified for accommodations. This flexibility helped her formulate a plan for completing her doctorate by redesigning her coursework to suit her learning profile.

Next, Catherine began acceptance and commitment therapy (ACT).[14] This therapy is designed to help people who have anxiety and other disorders learn to manage their symptoms with techniques derived from mindfulness and other principles of positive psychology. The goal is to promote psychological flexibility and openness to experience so that people can live rich, meaningful lives. Rather than challenging or neutralizing your painful feelings, you instead notice these feelings, understand where they are coming from, and learn to respond rather than overreact to them.

This form of therapy posits that life is difficult, that all humans must face hardship and suffering, and that we all share a natural tendency to amplify our suffering and thus develop unhealthy reactions to these challenging experiences. The core of many our psychological problems can be found in the acronym FEAR:[15]

- **F**usion with your thoughts (identifying yourself with your thoughts)
- **E**valuation of experience (judging everything as good or bad)
- **A**voidance of your experience (cutting yourself off from what's going on)
- **R**eason-giving for your behavior (rationalization)

Dr. Russ Harris, a therapist and world-renowned trainer in ACT, has simplified the six important skills a person can develop through this therapy.[16]

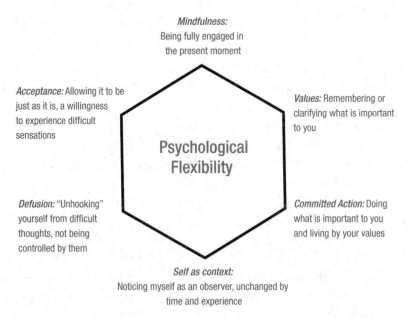

The framework of acceptance and commitment therapy.
Source: https://www.researchgate.net/figure/The-framework-of-Acceptance-and-Commitment -Therapy_fig1_353665422

As he explains, to improve our psychological flexibility, which is the key to resiliency, we must (1) be in the present moment, (2) define our values, (3) commit to act on those values, (4) see ourselves in context, (5) defuse our negative self-labels, and (6) accept our imperfect selves (see image on previous page).[17]

Catherine quickly became engaged in her therapy. She began by learning the mindfulness and acceptance techniques: noticing the process of her thoughts, practicing nonjudgmental awareness, and developing an "observing self" that enabled her to better tolerate the self-doubting, anxiety-inducing thought patterns that had dominated her life. She grew increasingly comfortable staying in the present moment rather than jumping ahead into fearful scenarios of the future (failure, embarrassment, rejection). She also identified her core values by considering the things she wanted to do in her life and the principles by which she wanted to live. From this vantage point, she could choose how she wanted to act. She committed herself to physical and mental actions that included taking better care of herself and giving herself the benefit of the doubt when she encountered situations that appeared difficult to master.

Within a few months, Catherine had grasped the basic mantras of ACT: Be present. Open up. Do what matters. Without becoming governed by her anxious thoughts, she noticed them, allowed herself to be present and accept them as thoughts rather than facts, and then took action to achieve her immediate goals. She discovered the multitude of choices she had when approaching challenging tasks like organizing her daily schedule, sitting down to read, or taking notes during a lecture. Instead of avoiding these tasks or succumbing to self-criticism, she learned to lean in to them and move toward her goals. As expected, Catherine became more comfortable with herself and better able to engage in her graduate studies. Now, instead of berating herself for having to use accommodations or needing extra time to finish an assignment, she could acknowledge her abilities and her unique needs. In so doing, she grew more . assertive and became a better self-advocate.

We kept the door open for Julia and John to join in Catherine's treatment sessions on an as-needed basis. Not long after she received the SCT/CDS diagnosis, Catherine invited them to come in to discuss the results. The session offered her parents the opportunity to learn more about how her condition had been affecting her path toward adulthood. Early on, as sometimes happens, an adult child's diagnosis generates a parent's reassessment of similar struggles. Julia confessed that she could see signs of SCT/CDS in herself. She also struggled to get things done efficiently and to keep focused on things that were not particularly engaging for her. She acknowledged that she had once dreamed of going to graduate school to study British literature but that her mediocre grades in college had led her to give up these plans. Julia told her daughter how much she respected her efforts to overcome her learning challenges, and expressed her hopes that Catherine would pursue her dreams to finish school.

A few months after Catherine began working on her anxiety issues, she felt it would be helpful to hold another family session to discuss her plans for returning to grad school in the fall with a modified schedule. She was increasingly confident in her ability to manage both her coursework and her teaching assistant role. She was ready to do what mattered to her. This family session gave Julia and John a chance to both reaffirm their faith in their daughter's ability to complete her education and to allay any residual guilt about the economic cost. They shared their admiration for how earnestly and diligently Catherine had applied the lessons learned from therapy. They were impressed with the positive changes they were witnessing in her attitude and mood and were hopeful that the skills she was learning would prepare her for any tough times in the future. Catherine and her parents were finally able to look to the future with confidence and optimism.

POSITIVE STEPS TO REDUCE ANXIETY IN YOUR LIFE

Of all the lessons we've learned since the onset of the coronavirus pandemic, perhaps the most salient ones pertain to finding ways to reduce anxiety in our daily lives.

In the early days of the pandemic, Dr. Harris came up with the acronym FACE COVID to help people cope better with the anxiety they were experiencing.[18] You might recognize some of the basic principles of ACT in his recommendations, which we have slightly adapted here:

- Focus on what's in your control
- Acknowledge your thoughts and feelings
- Come back into, and connect with, your body
- Engage in what you're doing
- Commit to positive action
- Open up to accepting your difficult feelings and being kind to yourself

- Value what matters, and act on those values
- Identify resources that can help you
- Disinfect your physical environment (e.g., wash your hands frequently) and practice social distancing when necessary and where you can

Although most of us are no longer strangers to the threat of the coronavirus, these tips are still relevant. They can help us manage the challenges we all face living in this age of uncertainty.

Techniques like living in the moment and practicing mindfulness have become necessary survival tools for our overwhelmed psyches. Through mindfulness, people learn to be open to their experiences and to accept their thoughts and feelings, even unpleasant or painful ones. Mindfulness enables us to slow down and focus on the things we can control or modify, like our breath or our attention, and helps us move away from threatening, anxiety-provoking thoughts. Breathing exercises help us focus on our basic bodily processes so that we can let go of muscle tension and reduce our physiological overarousal. Mindful eating helps us slow down our food intake and enjoy our meals more fully. Mindful walking offers us an opportunity to observe the world around us with greater openness and engagement. All of these forms of mindful practice help us to be present as fully as possible in the moment rather than rushing ahead with apprehension about a future state we are trying to achieve.

However, if you're reading these suggestions and thinking, *That doesn't work for me, I can't sit still,* then let's expand on what mindfulness means. Yes, it is a practice, and take it from the two of us, who were never naturally inclined to sit still and chill: mindfulness can encompass knowing yourself well enough to recognize when you need to get out of your head and into your body. It can take the form of body-scan relaxation (where you mentally assess each part of your body and deliberately try to relax it) and breathing, but it can also take the form of going for a jog, working out, or quickly running up a few flights of stairs. Our bodies and our minds become calmer after even a few minutes of intense exertion. There are many ways to destress and take care of ourselves. We'll continue to explore these ways in Chapter 10.

In Chapter 9, we'll consider the plight of young adults with complex mood disorders and their families. We'll review what we know about the incidence of mood disorders, their causes, and their effects on individual functioning and family relationships. We'll also review clinical approaches to assessing and treating these disorders from a family perspective.

9

Solutions for Complex Disorders

Internet Gaming, Mood, and Substance Use

The complexity of things—the things within things—just seems to be endless. I mean nothing is easy, nothing is simple.
—*Alice Munro*, The New York Times *(Oct. 10, 2013)*

UP TO THIS POINT IN THE BOOK, WE HAVE LOOKED AT MORE STRAIGHTFORWARD problems that many emerging adults face in their transition into adulthood. We've shown how family therapy can enable both adult children and their parents to reframe their outlooks to better understand one another. Through familial support and therapeutic guidance, twentysomethings can successfully get past the roadblocks that have prevented them from outgrowing an adolescent mindset.

Sometimes, however, young people face more intransigent challenges, like substance abuse or chronic mental disorders. These complex problems require more complex solutions.

In the following example, we describe a young man with several problematic syndromes: depression, internet gaming disorder, and alcohol misuse. By examining his and his parents' point of view, and by understanding how we as therapists addressed this family situation, you can learn about appropriate pathways for your young person's struggles.

KEVIN: GAMING AND SLEEPING A LIFE AWAY?

Meet Kevin, a twenty-three-year-old living at home with his mother, Jenny, and stepfather, Adam Chapman. His younger twin sisters, Zoe and Emma, are nineteen and away at college. Jenny is a dental hygienist, and Adam is a certified public accountant. Kevin's birth father is not in the picture, having left his mother while she was pregnant with him. The family has been in treatment with us before, beginning when Kevin was in fifth grade and was first diagnosed with ADHD and dysthymic disorder, a mild form of ongoing depression. A serious and brooding adolescent who was prone to rumination and procrastination, he had always disliked school because it was both boring and difficult for him, academically and socially. Getting up in the morning and getting ready for school was always a chore that often led to battles with his parents. Instead of doing his homework after school, he surreptitiously played his favorite games long past the dinner hour. Often, he would delay getting ready for bed to indulge in his gaming activities, with the predictable result of his morning struggles, which fueled the family's conflicts over his ineffective wake-up routines.

A series of family sessions took place during Kevin's senior year in high school, when his excessive lateness, numerous missed assignments, and poor performance on midterm exams threatened his graduating on time. In response to his stubbornness and his refusal to limit his video-gaming, Jenny and Adam shut off their home internet service from Sunday through Thursday at dinner time and from 9 p.m. until 7 a.m., though they offered him the option of keeping the internet on until 10 p.m. if he had completed his homework assignments. Although he was initially furious at them, Kevin eventually relented and learned to live within these limits. He was able to catch up on his work, went to sleep at a decent time, began getting up in the morning without distress or conflict, and graduated from high school on time. Following graduation, he started working as a nurse's aide in a special care facility for older people while living at home. Once things settled down and he was performing reasonably well at his new job, the Chapmans decided to take a break from treatment.

Four years after our last contact with them, Kevin and his family returned for help. Right from the start of the session, the tension in the room was palpable. Kevin sat opposite his parents with his arms folded across his chest; Adam sat glaring at the floor. Jenny turned to us and started the conversation.

"My husband and I are out of ideas about how to help Kevin deal with his video-game addiction," she said.

At this point, Kevin shrugged and shook his head as if to say he'd been through this argument before and didn't care to listen to his parents' concerns.

Jenny continued: "He's really become dysfunctional, to the point where he stays up all night playing, then sleeps through most of the morning and early afternoon. He works the evening shift at the nursing home, but he's often late and they're threatening to fire him. He's gotten several warnings and is now on probation for lateness. Mind you, he's a good worker and they really like him there. But he just keeps oversleeping and getting up too late to make it to work on time. We're really concerned that he's going to lose this job, just like he lost the previous two jobs he's had as a nursing tech. It's really a serious problem, but whenever we try to talk to him about it, he just shuts down and tells us to mind our own business. We just don't know what else to do. That's why we're here."

We asked Kevin if he's ready to share his thoughts about what's going on. He paused for a moment, glancing over at his stepfather, who'd been avoiding his gaze. He then shrugged and said, "What's the point? They think I'm like a drug addict because I like to play video games. They keep yelling at me that I'm screwing up my life and everything, especially him." He gestured at Adam.

At this point, Adam looked directly at his stepson and said, "Well, am I wrong? Aren't you screwing things up again like you did during high school, when we had to shut the damn internet off so you would get to sleep at a reasonable hour? You almost didn't graduate! And now you're on the way to losing another good job *again*! It's not the first time or the second time. This is the third job you're going to get fired from because you can't get your act together and manage to get to work on time. When are you going to grow up and take responsibility for your life? It's not like you're a kid anymore, but you sure act like one!"

Kevin glared back at his stepfather and then turned to us. "You see?" he said. "All I get is criticism and insults. I'm a loser. I'm a screwup. I'm irresponsible. I'm never going to keep a job. And it's all because I like playing video games. You'd think I was smoking crack or something. They forget that I'm twenty-three years old now and I've got a good job and they like me there. Besides, *CrossFire* is my thing. Just because they don't like it doesn't mean it's bad for me. I work all my shifts, I come home, have something to eat, then relax and play it with my friends. What's the big deal if I stay up late? Is it so terrible? I'm not the only one who's playing late at night."

Kevin continued, "I get that they don't want me to lose my job, but they make it sound like I don't care about it. I do. I want to stay at this place as long as possible. I just wish they'd stop calling me a video-game addict. It's very insulting. Besides, I'm paying my share of the rent and the food I eat. I'm pretty independent when it comes to making my own meals. I'm saving up to get my own place eventually, and I'm making progress. But they never acknowledge how far I've come since high school."

At this point, we addressed the family with the following observation: "You're back for help with an old problem that has resurfaced. Kevin, you have a history of being 'hooked' on video games, but you don't really see it as a problem. You see it as a lifestyle choice rather than an addiction. Adam and Jenny, you're having a déjà vu experience. The past is not past; you're fighting the same battle with your son going on ten-plus years. Only now you can't use the same strategies you did when he was an adolescent.

"The first step in figuring all this out is for the three of you to understand what internet addiction disorder is (and isn't), how it affects people and families, and what can be done about it. That's going to take further inquiry into the specifics of Kevin's internet behaviors and their impact on his health and functioning."

NOT JUST A BAD HABIT BUT A MENTAL DISORDER

As we discussed in Chapter 7, the American Psychological Association has proposed a new diagnosis, internet gaming disorder (IGD), in the research appendix of its diagnostics manual (DSM-5).[1] As proposed for the manual, the disorder is defined as the repetitive use of internet-based games, often with other players, that leads to significant issues with functioning. Five of the following criteria must be met within *one year*:

- The person has a preoccupation or obsession with internet games.
- The person experiences withdrawal symptoms when not playing internet games.
- The person has had a buildup of tolerance—more time is needed to be spent playing the games.
- The person has tried to stop or curb playing internet games but has failed to do so.

- The person has had a loss of interest in other life activities, such as hobbies.
- The person has had continued overuse of internet games even with the knowledge of how much they impact one's life.
- The person has lied to others about their internet game usage.
- The person uses internet games to relieve negative moods (e.g., anxiety or guilt).
- The person has lost or put at risk an opportunity or a relationship because of internet games.

What do we know about the prevalence of IGD? A study of adults in the United States, the United Kingdom, Canada, and Germany found that more than 86 percent of young adults between the ages of eighteen and twenty-four had recently played online games, but no more than 1 percent of them met criteria for IGD.[2] By contrast, in certain Asian countries, the prevalence may be as high as nearly 6 percent.[3] A 2021 international study of self-described adult internet gamers found a prevalence of IGD of around 4 percent in this sample (roughly 5 percent among players between eighteen and thirty), with a rate of around 3 percent in the United States. The average amount of game-playing time reported was a remarkable thirty-six and a half hours per week, and the most common symptoms reported were escapism (from negative feelings), preoccupation, tolerance, and continuation despite psychosocial problems.[4] Several psychiatric disorders have been found to be highly associated with IGD. They include depressive disorders, anxiety disorders, social anxiety disorder, and ADHD.[5]

At present, there are no widely accepted, replicated, evidence-based treatments for IGD, though some promising behavioral interventions have been proposed in the clinical literature. Family-based approaches are the most widely utilized, because they help patients, parents, and other loved ones learn about the difference between acceptable video-game playing and IGD. Family therapy emphasizes improving the communication among family members via active listening, establishing time limits for the affected person, and strengthening family bonds to promote positive affiliation and reduce isolation and conflict.[6] Boot-camp programs and coercive techniques have been found to be ineffective for treating IGD.

Cognitive behavioral therapy for internet addiction combines CBT and motivational interviewing techniques to help patients gain better skills at resisting cravings for gaming and at finding alternate ways to spend free time.[7]

This harm-reduction approach includes behavior modification in the form of rewards for time spent away from games and cognitive restructuring or the intentional evaluation of the role internet gaming is playing in the patient's life. In the cognitive restructuring steps, patients are asked to consider how internet gaming has improved their lives, what they've given up to enjoy internet games, and what trouble the games may have caused in their lives. By reconsidering the impact that internet gaming is having on their lives, young adults can begin developing strategies for reducing their game playing.

With respect to pharmacotherapy for IGD, the best-studied medications are bupropion, atomoxetine, and opiate antagonists like naltrexone. While these medications show promising results, with modest improvements in IGD symptoms, the limited findings make it difficult to promote specific treatment recommendations. Until large-scale, scientifically validated studies are available, we advise parents to seek the expertise of practitioners to guide the behavior- and medication-related treatments of this disorder.

TREATING KEVIN'S INTERNET GAMING DISORDER

Despite his minimization of his symptoms, Kevin met six of the nine criteria for IGD. Among the warning signs, he had withdrawal symptoms when he was not playing internet games, and he had lost interest in other life activities. He continued to overuse internet games even when he knew how much they were affecting his life, and he lied to others about his usage. He was also using gaming to relieve anxiety, and he was putting his job and his family relationships at risk because of that.

Initially Kevin resisted this diagnosis. Like most addicts, he was in denial about the extent of his problem. To break through that denial, we presented the symptoms in an objective fashion and asked Kevin and his parents to review the IGD criteria. Kevin eventually acknowledged that he needed to curb his gaming to avoid risking his job and ruining his family relationships. In educating everyone about IGD, we helped steer them away from the blame-shame game that had taken over the family dynamics.

We also explained that there were clear differences between IGD and disorders involving chemical dependency. Deficits in the dopamine-rich reward pathways of the brain make certain people susceptible to behavioral and chemical addictions. In Kevin's case, his ADHD and dysthymic disorder primed him for developing IGD. He became more easily "hooked" than players without these disorders.

After Kevin stopped denying that he had a problem, we emphasized harm reduction rather than abstinence as a treatment goal. We told him that there were ways he could reduce his internet gaming behaviors without having to give up playing his favorite games. We proposed a combination of individual cognitive behavioral therapy for him and family systems therapy for him and his parents. Each family member would benefit from adopting an open mindset and skills to reduce the negative consequences of his addictive behaviors. In particular, Adam would have to learn to adopt a different stance toward Kevin's gaming. Rather than being reactive, Adam could learn to be more responsive and avoid playing the role of the rule enforcer. We suggested to Kevin that we adjust his medication regimen by increasing his dose of fluoxetine to enhance his motivation and his capacity to change his entrenched behavior patterns. He agreed.

Kevin's individual therapist encouraged him to describe how much his internet gaming was a positive force in his life, what skills he had learned and applied during gaming, and how much it contributed to his happiness, including as a source of important friendships. The therapist then asked Kevin to consider how gaming impaired his ability to reach his life goals. Kevin reflected on the harmful consequences to his job and his family and saw how his excessive game playing robbed him of time—for example, time to play basketball like he'd always enjoyed and time to hang out with friends who weren't into internet gaming.

By considering the pros and cons of his current approach to internet gaming, Kevin was able to formulate the following statement to himself: "As much as I love gaming, and as much as it contributes to my happiness, there are times when I overdo it, and that's not a good thing for me. I need to find ways to limit my game time so I can do other things with my life, including sports, and so I can make sure I don't get fired from this job I have now." With this attitude adjustment, Kevin took ownership of the harm reduction part of this change. He felt empowered to start setting limits on his gaming activities and to experiment with ways to resist the temptation.

Kevin and his parents also undertook a brief course of family therapy in support of his goal of harm reduction. Jenny and Adam were eager to look at their own enabling behaviors, including nagging, waking him up rather than letting him do it on his own, and offering him money to wake up on time. They also wanted to learn to minimize their negative emotions of anger, criticism, sadness, and anxiety when Kevin stayed up too late and had trouble with morning routines. Adam committed to stop putting Kevin down when his stepson failed to meet his and Jenny's expectations. Jenny was surprised to learn that her sad and anxious facial expressions were causing problems for Kevin; she had always thought they conveyed love and caring. Each parent accepted this new information and focused on ways they could change their mindsets and behaviors.

After several sessions, we saw a noticeable shift taking place during family meetings. Kevin and his parents were genuinely more positive in their interactions, and the mood in the family shifted from negatively reactive to more neutral and responsive. Kevin was able to share his gaming achievements with his parents, instead of hiding them, and as he did so, his parents began to appreciate how accomplished their son had become in *CrossFire*'s player hierarchy. Eventually, Kevin cut back on his playing time from fifty to thirty hours per week, which left him enough time to return to basketball and hang out with friends.

After four months of weekly therapy, the frequency of sessions was reduced to twice a month and eventually to monthly. By the time the treatment was completed, Kevin's self-management skills were noticeably improved in all life domains. He was no longer in trouble for tardiness at work, and his family interactions were the best they had been in many years. At our final session, Kevin admitted to us that at first he wasn't convinced he had IGD, but as the treatment unfolded, he realized he was addicted and needed to change his relationship to gaming. He was appreciative of our help and was especially happy with how he had gained greater awareness and self-control in the process of reducing his excessive internet use. He and his parents were pleased at the progress they'd seen during therapy and were hopeful for the future. Unfortunately, things got much more complicated for Kevin and his family in the ensuing months.

BACKSLIDING: WHEN THINGS JUST AREN'T QUITE RIGHT

Roughly eighteen months after our last visit with the Chapmans, Jenny called to inform us that she and Adam were worried about Kevin. Over the previous six months, they'd seen considerable backsliding in his mood and behavior. Instead of keeping to the agreed-on gaming limits, he had slipped. He was staying up until the wee hours and was sleeping beyond his usual wake-up time the next morning. Unfortunately, there was little interaction between Kevin and his parents during the workweek. Typically, he was asleep when they left for work and was gone when they returned. By the time he came home from his evening shift, they were asleep.

"Adam and I aren't sure what to do," Jenny told us. "On the one hand, he's keeping up with his work schedule and he isn't going in late anymore. He has managed to keep his job through all the craziness of the pandemic. On the other hand, we hardly get to see him at all, and we're really concerned that he's spending much more than thirty hours per week on his video games. He's stopped going to the gym, and he's not doing much in the way of socializing with friends. He's holed up in his room when he isn't going to work.

Jenny continued, "We keep inviting him to join us for dinner and he flatly refuses. Claims he's busy hanging out with his friends online and they're all having a good time gaming together. Every time we bring up the agreement we had with you, he just blows us off. Says he's fine and we should mind our own business. We just don't know what we can do about this situation."

"What's his mood like when you do interact with him?" we asked.

"He's quite short-tempered and very impatient with us," Jenny said. "Answers with short sentences if at all and seems to be intent on avoiding any substantive conversations. It's like he doesn't really want to have anything to do with us, which just isn't like him."

"Is his primary care doctor still refilling his medication?" we asked.

"Yes. As far as I can tell."

"Do you have any idea if he's taking his medication?" we asked.

"Yes. He seems to be. But that's entirely in his court, so we don't really know."

We brought up the idea of another visit. "Have you suggested that we all get together for a follow-up appointment?"

"Yes," she said. "He refuses. He's insistent that it isn't necessary and that we're trying to run his life instead of letting him run it for himself."

"You're in a tough spot, Jenny, that's for sure," we told her. "Perhaps you can let him know you're seeing some worrisome signs: social isolation, lack of exercise, and irritable mood. Tell him you're worried that he might be depressed. Explain the evidence you have for your concerns. Emphasize that it's fully up to him to decide how he's going to take the feedback you're giving him, but remind him that you're doing what anyone would do in your situation—trying to communicate your views honestly and openly. Your goal is help him to see the situation differently rather than getting him to do something about it."

We continued, "The problem is, if he doesn't change his mindset, he isn't going to take your advice. That's why asking him to come in for a follow-up session now isn't going to work. He needs more time and evidence to figure things out. We're always here for him whenever he decides he wants to see us. If things get more worrisome and he still isn't willing to get in touch with us, we can set up a session for you and Adam to discuss things further."

Jenny thanked us for our advice and said she'd be back in touch if things got noticeably worse. We understood her concerns about Kevin, and we supported her efforts to get him back into treatment. It's very common for young adults with mental health issues to rebuff their parents' concerns. Typically, the young adult may view parental expressions of concern as meddlesome. If pressed, they may get angry and accuse their parents of being overprotective or insensitive to their needs. This response places parents in a difficult spot. On the one hand, parents want to support their young persons' efforts to manage their lives, including any mental health issues, on their own. Yet, when there's backsliding, as in Kevin's case, parents often feel the need to problem-solve with suggestions, guidance, or direct instructions. Our advice to Jenny was counterintuitive, perhaps, but highly collaborative and the most effective strategy, according to what experts in psychology and behavioral science call the "transtheoretical model of behavior change." Let's now look at this important model.

A PRACTICAL MODEL OF CHANGE FOR PARENTS AND THERAPISTS

For over four decades, psychologists James Prochaska, Carlo DiClemente, and John Norcross have studied how people with medical conditions, mental health disorders, or addictive behaviors become invested in modifying their behaviors.[8] Their model, the "transtheoretical model of behavior change," is so named because it incorporates several psychological theories of behavioral transformation. It is one of the most powerful paradigms in psychology for understanding how people intentionally change their behavior.

As the table on page 201 illustrates, people seeking to change their health-related behaviors move through five stages of change.[9] In the *precontemplation* stage, sometimes referred to as the denial stage, the person does not recognize the need for or express an interest in change. In the *contemplation* stage, the person is beginning to think about changing but is not yet committed to it. During the *preparation* phase, the person is determined to act and starts planning how they

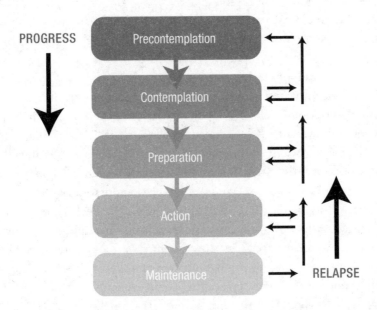

Five Progressive Steps of the Transtheoretical Model of Behavior Change
Source: https://meganjmartin.wordpress.com/2012/10/03/transtheoretical-model/

are going to go about making the changes they desire. In the *action* phase, they are adopting new habits, either reducing problem behavior or acquiring new healthy behaviors. In the *maintenance* phase, they are sustaining healthy behaviors and avoiding problem behaviors successfully.

People in the precontemplation stage of change are not ready to engage in change-oriented behaviors, since they are neither aware of having a problem nor interested in modifying their behaviors. Attempts to convince them to change are unlikely to work, because they aren't motivated to do so. The most effective thing to do with people at this stage is to raise their awareness that there is a problem that needs to be recognized and addressed. Both parents and therapists can do this by offering the person information or evidence that a problem exists and that they might consider learning more about it. Exploring what the person would define as a "problem" could also help stimulate their curiosity or pique their interest.

For Kevin and his parents, it would make sense for Jenny and Adam to present their concerns in a factual manner. They might say, "We see that you're spending more time than usual in your room" or "We've noticed that you're not spending any time at all with us, which isn't like you," and see how he responds. They might also express a hope that Kevin will view their concerns as authentic, not as a guilt trip or infantilizing. In this way, Kevin could assess the validity of their observations. Over time, by exercising patience and showing genuine empathy—rather than confronting an adult child—parents in situations like the Chapmans' may well convince their young adult to reconsider their stance and adopt a more open mindset.

As we have indicated, both health practitioners and parents can use the transtheoretical model of behavior change to guide their interventions. Another counseling technique developed from this model is "motivational interviewing." This technique has reportedly been effective in decreasing alcohol and drug use in adults and adolescents; reducing sexual risk behaviors and addressing problem gambling and smoking cessation; improving adherence to treatment and medication; and promoting positive health behaviors such as exercise, healthy eating, and good sleep hygiene.[10] An underlying principle of this type of interviewing is respect for the person's autonomy and for their intrinsic capacity to change—it is a collaborative approach.

Motivational interviewing takes advantage of the natural ambivalence all human beings have about change. Clinicians note that ambivalence "is particularly evident in situations where there is a conflict between an immediate reward and longer-term adverse consequences."[11] In motivational interviews, the therapist encourages the client to explore how much they are willing, able, and ready to change and to examine the pros and cons of acting versus not acting. Clients in the precontemplation phase are either unready or unwilling to change. The primary task of the therapist is to raise doubts and increase clients' perceptions of the risk and problems with their current behavior. Therapists also provide harm reduction strategies for clients to consider should they be interested in making a change. With some adaptations, parents can learn and adopt some of these tactics in conversations with young adults (see text box on the following page).

The basic skills of this interview include asking open-ended questions, affirming the person's best intentions, and using reflection and summarizing statements. These are implemented with a nonjudgmental, respectful approach that emphasizes the client's active engagement in problem-solving. Asking open-ended questions enables the client to do most of the talking, enabling the practitioner to gain a better sense about what the person cares about (the person's values and goals). Making affirmations helps to build rapport by noticing and emphasizing the client's strengths, positive behaviors, and efforts at self-care. Reflecting involves rephrasing the client's words in a manner that helps them more fully explore their motivations. And summarizing statements help ensure that the client and the clinician are on the same page when it comes to the central themes of their conversation. As we will describe next, we used all these techniques when Kevin and his parents returned to our office several months after his mother reached out for help a second time.

TALKING WITH YOUNG ADULTS WHO ARE STRUGGLING WITH SUBSTANCE USE AND RELATED ISSUES

- I'm noticing you seem to be using ___ more. Are you willing to talk to me about it? I promise I won't lecture. I just want to understand what's going on with you.
- Can you tell me a little about your use of ___? How do you go about deciding when to use and how much to use?
- What are the things you like most about ___? What does it do for you? Does it make life more fun or less miserable? Does it boost your mood? Does it relieve your anxiety?
- Do you see any downsides to using ___? If so, what are they?
- Do you think you might consider reducing your use of ___? If so, how would you go about doing it? If not, what would need to happen for you to be willing to consider that idea?
- I'd like to share some observations about your use of ___, but only if you want to hear what I have to say. I promise this isn't unsolicited advice or a scold. It's just feedback.
- I hope you understand I'm always here for you.

"STUCK IN THE MUCK"— WHEN DEPRESSION COMES CALLING

Kevin and his parents entered the office with serious expressions on their faces. A week earlier, Jenny had told us that Kevin was in crisis and needed help but that he was unwilling to come in. We offered to meet with Jenny and Adam alone and were expecting to hold a parents' session. Instead, the three of them arrived. We ushered them in and invited them to update us on what was going on.

Kevin immediately began: "I'm here because I don't want my parents talking about me behind my back. I know they've been in touch with you over the past few months. And I know they're really worried about me and think I'm depressed. Maybe I am, who knows? I didn't really want to come, but when they told me they were planning to see you whether I came along or not, I decided to join. After all, if this is about me, then I should be here, right?"

"If you're okay with your folks sitting in on this conversation, please go on," we replied.

"Yeah, it's fine they're here," the young man said. "I don't have any objection to them hearing what I have to say. To start with, I'm really stuck in a rut. I mean, I'm twenty-six, almost twenty-seven years old, I still live with my folks, I'm still at the same job for the past three years, and I'm going nowhere fast. My friends from high school are much better off than me. A few of them went to college and have pretty cushy desk jobs earning fifty thousand a year. One buddy is in the military and is moving around the country—he's doing okay for himself. And a couple of friends have started their own landscaping business and are making out okay.

Kevin went on, "Me, I'm just a dumb nursing assistant making fifteen dollars an hour. And right now, I don't really give much of a damn about anything, really. I used to like my job, but ever since the pandemic, I pretty much hate it. It sucks, really. Most of the people I started with have left the place, and the new folks aren't especially friendly. I'm checked out, really."

"Sounds like you're feeling disappointed in how your life is going," we responded.

"Yeah, well, wouldn't you feel the same way?"

We nodded.

"So, what I'm saying," he said, "is that I'm not especially feeling very good about my life now, and it's not my fault that I don't really want to hang out with my parents or do much of anything besides play *Fortnite Battle Royale*. That's my latest hobby; *CrossFire* got too boring—we'll see how long *Fortnite* keeps me entertained. It's about the only thing I look forward to lately. I don't care about going out with friends or to the gym. It's too much effort."

We reflected back what we had just heard from Kevin: "It sounds like you've tried to make the best of things, but despite that, you're losing your motivation to go to work or to do things that once gave you some pleasure."

"Affirmative. It's like one day just blends into the next and I'm stuck in the muck. . . ."

"Have you thought about what you might want to do about it?" we asked.

Kevin gazed at us for a moment, then looked over at his parents. "I know they want me to start back in therapy with you," he said. "How can talking about my stupid-assed job and my boring life help me feel better? I already did that cognitive behavioral therapy, so that would be a rehash. What I really need is a new life. But where do I find that? And that's why I get mad at my parents. It's like they're always trying to get me to feel better. They want me to try harder to do things for myself—go to the gym, get together with friends, go back to school, and maybe find a better job. It's easy for them to say all those things, but they don't really understand how hard it is for me to just get through each day without them pushing me to try harder. It really gets on my nerves, you know? I'm so tired of it. . . ." Kevin's voice trailed off as he started to tear up. "There's not much for me to look forward to, because the situation I'm in is completely messed up. And nobody really understands what it's like to walk in my shoes."

We waited for a moment before affirming. "Kevin, you're right," we said. "The situation you're in is very difficult indeed. Things look bleak now, for understandable reasons. And hearing your parents' words of advice or encouragement isn't doing much to help, despite their best intentions. But despite how down you're feeling, you're still getting up every day and going to work. That shows you have grit. You haven't given up entirely, and that's a sign of hope."

"Yeah, I suppose," he said. "But what if I'm really not up to doing all the things people are telling me to do? It's not like I can just wake up tomorrow and pretend it's a brand-new day and everything's going to be coming up roses. That's what my mom seems to think."

Again, we affirmed Kevin's comments, then summarized what we'd learned: "It's true that it takes more than wishful thinking to make things better in life. It takes figuring out what's wrong and then coming up with a feasible plan to deal with it. For now, what we've learned today is that you're 'stuck in the muck' and haven't figured out how to get out. We believe you're quite depressed and that's why you feel so helpless. Your situation is difficult. But when people get depressed, they start to think that it's impossible to change things for the better. We call that 'learned helplessness'—and we want to help you find a way to get out of that awful state of mind as quickly as possible. Are you willing to give it a try?"

Kevin nodded and looked over at his parents. "I know they want what's best for me," he said. "But I want them to stop trying to take care of me so much. It just makes me feel worse. I already feel guilty for feeling down all the time. They need to get some help too. They're just wearing me down with all their worrying, nagging, and arguing."

At this point, Jenny started to cry, and Adam reached his arm around her shoulder to comfort her. We sat in silence for a few moments and then acknowledged this truth: Depression is a family affair.

The fact that Kevin decided to join his parents for this family session signaled that he had shifted out of the precontemplation stage into the contemplation stage of change. He was ready to explore the possibility that things could get better despite his depressed state of mind. Our strategy at this point was to help him see that change was possible and that there were steps he could take to improve his situation despite his feelings of helplessness and hopelessness. We will return to Kevin and his family's journey after we briefly review some important facts about mood disorders and their treatment.

MOOD DISORDERS IN YOUNG ADULTS

As we discussed in the book's introduction, the prevalence of mood disorders in young people has been rising steadily over the past two decades and has worsened even more rapidly in the past several years. Data from the National Survey on Drug Use and Health from 2015 to 2020 shows continuing surges in

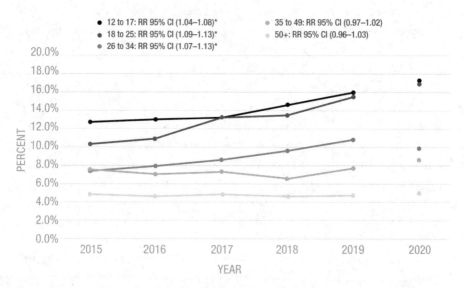

Percentage of U.S. Survey Respondents Saying They Had Depression in the Past Year, 2015–2020.

Source: Renee D. Goodwin et al., "Trends in U.S. Depression Prevalence from 2015 to 2020: The Widening Treatment Gap," *American Journal of Preventative Medicine* 63, no. 5 (2022): 726–33, www.ncbi.nlm .nih.gov/pmc/articles/PMC9483000.

rates of depression.[12] The accompanying figure reveals an alarming increase in adolescents (twelve to seventeen years old), from 13 to 17 percent and an even higher rise among young adults (eighteen to twenty-five years old), from 10 to 17 percent.

Mood disorders arise from a complex interaction of biological, psychological, and social factors. How these disorders show up in a person depends on many variables, including socioeconomic status, physical health, stress, support systems, and broad lifestyle behaviors, including sleep, diet, exercise, and exposure to alcohol and recreational drugs. The most significant risk factors are personal or family histories of mood disorder; major life changes, trauma, or stress; and certain physical illnesses and medications. The current biological, psychological, and sociological consensus is that vulnerable people exposed to overwhelming stress with less-than-adequate coping resources are at greatest risk for developing a mood disorder. The figure below illustrates how risk factors intersect with stressful events and an individual's personal and family's biological and psychological predisposition to cause or worsen a mood disorder.[13]

Mood disorders are classified into numerous categories, including major depressive disorder (MDD) and bipolar disorders. For our purposes in considering Kevin's case, we will limit ourselves to two diagnoses: MDD and dysthymia, also known as persistent depressive disorder (PDD).

How Risk Factors Interact to Cause or Exacerbate Mood Disorders.

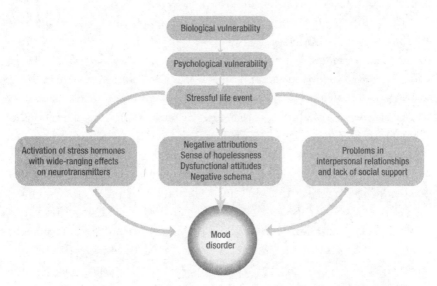

Source: https://www.slideserve.com/kelly-moody/abnormal-psychology-psy-120-prof-south-11-21-08.

The symptoms of MDD include these:

- Persistent sad, anxious, or "empty" mood
- Feelings of irritability, frustration, or restlessness
- Feelings of hopelessness or pessimism
- Feelings of guilt, worthlessness, or helplessness
- Loss of interest or pleasure in hobbies and other activities
- Decreased energy, fatigue, or feeling "slowed down"
- Difficulty concentrating, remembering, or making decisions
- Difficulty sleeping, early-morning awakening, or oversleeping
- Changes in appetite or unplanned weight changes
- Thoughts of death or suicide, or suicide attempts
- Aches or pains, headaches, cramps, or digestive problems that have no clear physical cause and that do not ease, even with treatment

To receive this diagnosis, a person must experience five or more of these symptoms most of the day, nearly every day, for at least two weeks. The symptoms must also be causing significant distress for the person and interfering with their ability to function in usual daily activities.[14]

The symptoms of PDD include depressed and irritable mood for at least *two years*, along with at least two of the following symptoms: poor appetite or overeating, insomnia or hypersomnia, low energy or fatigue, low self-esteem, poor concentration or decision-making, and hopelessness.[15]

Treatment for MDD and PDD includes antidepressant medications, psychotherapy, brain stimulation therapies, or a combination of these. As with all mental health conditions, treatment needs to be tailored to the person's unique situation and individual needs and preferences. Most antidepressants take up to four to eight weeks to work, and the vegetative symptoms, such as poor sleep or loss of appetite, usually improve before the mood symptoms. The choice of antidepressant is usually based on the patient's and their family's prior experience with medications, the efficacy and safety profile, and potential side effects. The prescriber must spend time explaining how the medication works, how and when to take it, and what side effects to watch for, and then contacting the prescriber if it appears to be having adverse effects. Most important, it's vital to talk with the prescriber about how to reduce the medication safely if the person wants to discontinue it. A variety of evidence-based psychotherapy treatments, such as cognitive behavioral therapy, interpersonal therapy, insight-oriented therapy, and acceptance and commitment therapy (discussed in Chapter 8), are widely available for MDD and PDD.

Kevin's case represents an example of double depression. He had long-standing PDD before the onset of his current depressive episode. The co-occurrence of PDD and MDD is harder to treat than either condition alone. In addition, evidence suggests that people who experience double depression are at high risk for becoming chronically depressed. That's why it's important to treat PDD as early as possible.

"HOW HARD IS THIS GOING TO BE?" UNEXPECTED TWISTS ON THE ROAD TO RECOVERY

Kevin returned the following week for an individual session. Our primary goal was to assess his depressive symptoms and their impact on his functioning. We planned to give him information about his diagnosis and to explore what he was ready to do about treatment alternatives. Our hope was that he was entering the preparation stage of change and would be willing to look at a menu of options. We could help him examine the pros and cons of each, reflect on his motivations to pursue therapy or medication or both, and strengthen his commitment to change. We could also provide him with a road map for getting started on the road to recovery. Taking care to avoid being too prescriptive or directive, we stuck to a motivational interviewing framework that emphasized his autonomy and respected his decision-making.

We learned that Kevin was in the throes of a severe depressive episode. He had the majority of the symptoms of depression, including feeling down and empty most of the day, and being much less interested in most things and less able to enjoy things he used to enjoy. What's more, his appetite was diminished, he had trouble sleeping, and he felt restless and fidgety but tired. He also felt worthless and guilty, had trouble concentrating and making decisions, and occasionally thought he would be better off dead. With respect to suicidal thoughts, Kevin did not actively think about ending his life but admitted that he sometimes wished he could go to sleep and never wake up. He never experienced suicidal intentions or conceived of plans to commit suicide, and he agreed to let his parents know if he were to start having active suicidal thoughts or intentions.

After confirming for Kevin that he met criteria for severe depression, we asked him if he was ready to talk about doing something about it.

"I guess so," he replied, "but how hard is this going to be? I don't really feel like talking about my feelings at the moment. If anything, it makes me feel worse to think about them at all. I'd rather just ignore them, to be honest."

We acknowledged that depression makes people feel helpless and hopeless and that the thought of talking about feelings might be too much to take on at the moment. So, we suggested some other options: "You're saying you aren't up for talk therapy at the moment. That's fine. Maybe when you're feeling up for it, you'll reconsider. But for now, what do you think you'd be willing to do differently? Would you be willing to try changing your medications? We can modify your regimen a bit and see if that helps your mood.

To this we added, "And would you be willing to engage in something called behavioral activation? It turns out that increasing one's physical activity can reduce the symptoms of depression. It's not like you have to immediately go and work out for hours a day. But in addition to going to work, you could begin by getting out of your room and going for some walks. Maybe you could take your dog out for a stroll after you wake up and before you head to work. What sorts of steps would you be willing to take to begin tackling this depression?"

Kevin sat silently for a few moments and then replied, "I guess it makes sense to start taking my medication again. I didn't want to say anything when my parents were here with us, but I haven't been taking the fluoxetine for the past couple of months. I decided it wasn't helping me, so I just stopped it, but I never told anyone. I just didn't want my parents to get mad and start nagging me. Anyway, I probably should've said something sooner. I guess I can't do anything right, can I?"

"It sounds like you wanted to see what would happen if you stopped the fluoxetine, since you weren't sure it was working," we said, reflecting back what Kevin had just told us. "And you were concerned that your parents wouldn't respect your decision. Lots of people are ambivalent about taking medication, and if they can't see the benefits, they usually decide to stop without telling anyone. Is that what happened?"

Kevin nodded, and then added, "So you're not mad at me for not telling you?"

"No. It's good you're being fully disclosing now. And together, we can figure out whether to restart the fluoxetine or try something else. It's entirely up to you."

Our response to Kevin was aimed at building greater openness and trust.

Rather than saying "no problem" to his disclosure of stopping the medication, we recognized the motivation behind it and we affirmed that it was fundamentally his decision as to what to do next. We were meeting him where he was and supporting his autonomy.

After some more back-and-forth, we decided to start Kevin on a different medication—venlafaxine—which has a mechanism of action that is different from fluoxetine's and which is often used for treating depressive episodes that aren't responding to a selective serotonin reuptake inhibitor like fluoxetine. Coming from a different class of drugs, venlafaxine can offer additional benefits, such as improved concentration and reduced restlessness. After we described the potential advantages and side effects of the medication, Kevin seemed willing to give it a try. He also agreed to spend an hour each day walking his dog in the neighborhood. We made up to meet in two weeks to track his progress.

At the follow-up visit, Kevin reported no real change in his mood. He was still depressed and thought the medication was making little difference. He displayed all the same symptoms of depression that he had in the previous session. He also admitted that he hadn't gotten into the routine of walking his dog. He had tried going out once or twice but felt anxious and self-conscious strolling around the neighborhood during the daytime.

"It sounds like you're still having trouble motivating yourself to do much else besides go to work, come home, and play your video game," we noted. "Are you still taking the medication?"

Kevin nodded and replied, "Yeah. I'm taking it like you said to, but it's not doing much. And you're right, I'm still just dragging myself to work and just going through the motions. By the time I get home, all I want to do is get online and escape into the world of *Fortnite*. I also watch YouTube movies until about six a.m., when I finally drift off to sleep. When I wake up at around one p.m., I don't really have time to go for an hour walk with the dog. It's enough that I'm able to shower, get dressed, have breakfast, and head back out to work. That's my life. . . ."

"It's good to hear that you're still getting to work every day and that you're taking care of yourself," we said. "Lots of people with severe depression can't manage to get that much done. It's also important that you're taking the medication, but it sounds like the dose we started you on isn't quite enough to make much of a difference, at least not yet. Would you be willing to go up on the dose a little?"

Kevin agreed to an increase.

"What else do you think might help you to get more activated?" we asked. "It sounds like the bar was set too high when we recommended an hour of walking your dog. What would work for you?"

Kevin paused for a moment and then said, "Yeah, you're right. Maybe if I start with just fifteen minutes a day, I'll be able to make it work."

"That sounds more realistic," we said. "And what about when you're at work? Is there a way for you to get some physical activity while you're there?"

He thought for a moment. "I usually just sit around and check my phone while I'm in the lunchroom. I suppose I could spend part of my break time walking around the campus of the senior living facility. Do you think that would make much of a difference? I'm not sure it will."

"Well, it might, or it might not," we replied. "There's no way to tell without trying. But what's the worst that can happen? You try behavioral activation, and it doesn't work for you. Are you afraid of something else, maybe?"

"Yeah. Like it'll prove I'm not being responsible enough. Or that I'm a hopeless case."

"That's an understandable fear," we said. "It reflects the negative thinking your depression is inflicting on you. We call that a 'cognitive distortion,' and it leads people to magnify the negative and minimize the positive of any behaviors they undertake."

"Yeah, I remember that from my CBT sessions," Kevin replied. "I guess I just have to push through my doubts and do whatever I can to keep going in the right direction."

ANOTHER TWIST IN THE ROAD TO RECOVERY

Kevin canceled his next appointment at the last minute, saying he was called in to work an extra shift at the nursing home. He agreed to come in the following week but failed to show up and never called to cancel. We called and left him a message to make sure he knew we were concerned and hoping to reschedule, but we didn't hear back for another week—an urgent message from Jenny telling us that things were not good with Kevin. She told us he was looking more depressed, had started to miss work, and was keeping more to himself than usual. We agreed to schedule an urgent family visit for the next day.

Kevin looked considerably more depressed than before, looking down at the floor and avoiding eye contact with us. Jenny and Adam sat together, appearing extremely concerned. This time, Adam began the session.

"It turns out Kevin's been holding out on all of us about what he's really been up to," he said. "We discovered he's been drinking on a regular basis without telling us about it. Jenny and I had some suspicions but no proof. Whenever we asked him if he was smoking weed or drinking alcohol, he'd always deny it. But we started wondering if he was covering something up. So yesterday, I had to come home to pick something up that I'd left in my home office. It was just after one p.m., and I expected to run into Kevin getting up and ready for work. Instead, he was still asleep in his room. I knocked on the door, and there was no answer. I opened it and walked in.

"He was passed out on his bed, still in his clothes, and there was an almost empty bottle of Jim Beam on the floor next to him. I shook him awake and asked him what the hell was going on. He started yelling at me and telling me to mind my own business and get out of his damn room immediately. I stood there, looked right at him, and told him that I had every right to know what was happening with him and that I wanted him to get cleaned up and come out to talk with me."

Clearly, Adam had reached his limit. He'd been doing his best up until then to be less judgmental or critical, to hang back and refrain from nagging Kevin about his responsibilities, and to respond rather than react to the young man's difficulties. But this breach of trust was too much for Adam.

As Adam spoke, Kevin shifted his gaze up to his stepfather, his eyes filled with tears. "You're right," Kevin said. "I've been holding out on you and Mom. I'm not going to lie about it. It's true. I've been drinking a little bit more than I should be. But it's not really that bad. I'm not an alcoholic or anything. I just got carried away the other night. It's really fine. I'm sorry to worry you both. But trust me, I've got this under control—"

"Is that right?" Jenny demanded. "You think it's nothing to worry about? How can you say that? You're depressed and you're not taking care of yourself the way you need to be. I know about alcohol and mood disorders. It makes things much worse. It not only makes you more depressed, but it interferes with the medication's antidepressant effects. Plus, it takes away people's motivation to get better. Here we were, proud of the fact that you were finally getting help after months of us worrying about you and hopeful that things would improve soon. But instead, you're just sabotaging yourself and preventing yourself from getting better.

She then confided, "I know what I'm talking about. I had to live through my father's drinking bouts and his endless apologies and rationalizations that he had it all under control. It was awful to see how his problem drinking ultimately destroyed him and the family. We're not going to sit by and let you ruin your life, Kevin. We love you too much, and we aren't going to put up with your hazardous drinking behavior for another day. You really need more intensive help."

At this point, Kevin turned to us and asked if he could speak to us alone. In the ensuing conversation, we learned Kevin had been drinking more heavily over several months but had hidden it from his parents. He described his drinking routine. When he came home from work, he'd have a few shots of bourbon while playing on his computer. Typically, his online video-game friends were drinking or getting high as well. Kevin explained it as their typical way of loosening up and having a good time. When pressed about the amount of alcohol he was consuming each night, Kevin estimated four to five drinks. He insisted that this amount was well within the norms of his friendship circle and that he was able to keep it under control.

We continued to explore how Kevin's drinking behavior had changed over the prior few months by asking open-ended questions. What did drinking do for him? How did he feel the next day? Did it affect his sleep or his mood? Had his drinking patterns changed over the past few months, and if so, how? We came to learn that Kevin gradually began consuming more alcohol as he felt more depressed about his life. As he put it, "It's the only thing that helps me to relax and forget about my misery. But I guess it's not working much to help my depression." We acknowledged that he was even more stuck than before, and we suggested that it might now be time for him to come up with a better plan for dealing with his problems. Kevin agreed.

The remainder of the session centered on helping Kevin and his parents come up with a game plan to address this new twist on his road to recovery. At first, Kevin resisted his parents' insistence that he get more intensive treatment. He acknowledged that his drinking had become a problem, but he insisted he could handle it himself. At this point, we supported his parents' position that things needed to change, but we avoided blaming Kevin for sabotaging his care plan. Instead, we reframed it as an effort to self-medicate his depression with alcohol. We believed this new information about his problem-drinking behavior suggested that a different strategy was needed to help him with his dual diagnosis: depression and alcohol use disorder.

Using a motivational interviewing framework, we asked Kevin and his family to consider all the alternatives they had before them, ranging from acute hospitalization at a dual-diagnosis hospital program to a day/partial hospital program to seeking a second opinion from an expert in substance use disorders and depression. We suggested that they go online and look at the various options available to them, given their insurance coverage. We agreed to meet again the next day to help them come up with a plan.

We ended the visit by first turning to Kevin and reminding him that this was his choice and that he needed to take the step that made the most sense to him. We expressed our firm belief that if he was ready to make a commitment to dealing with his dual diagnosis, he could see results in a short time. We then told Jenny and Adam how vital it was that they were part of this discussion and that we were ready to help them cope with this crisis.

After much discussion at home, Kevin agreed to enter a day/partial hospital program as long as he had the option of leaving if it wasn't meeting his needs. Located at a site not far from his home, the facility operated weekdays from 9 a.m. to 4 p.m. Kevin was expected to participate in all aspects of the program: medical visits, individual and group therapy, and recreation activities.

Before we return to the next phase of the Chapman family's treatment, let's review some key concepts about young adults' substance use and substance use disorders (SUD) and the role that families can play in helping them in recovery. Although we are keenly aware of the public health crisis regarding opiate use disorder and the deadly impact of the opioid epidemic on young people, our review will primarily focus on alcohol use disorder, the most common substance use disorder. Much of this review is applicable to opiate use disorder, but we urge readers to consult other resources to gain a deeper understanding of this potentially fatal disorder (see the appendix).

YOUNG ADULTS AND SUBSTANCE USE

Alcohol and marijuana top the list of substances used by young adults aged nineteen to thirty, according to the 2021 *Monitoring the Future* annual report, sponsored by the National Institute on Drug Abuse (see the accompanying table on the next page).[16]

Notably, binge drinking was reported by 32 percent of the subjects surveyed, and daily marijuana use by almost 11 percent. In 2021, alcohol consumption in this age group had declined to prepandemic levels, whereas marijuana use reached historic highs. This data clearly shows that the regular use of alcohol, marijuana, and other substances is quite common in this age group.

So, when does substance usage become an SUD? The definitions in the surgeon general's 2016 report *Facing Addiction in America* offer a starting point (see box on next page).[17]

TABLE 9.1: EXECUTIVE SUMMARY

The most prevalent substances used by young adults ages 19 to 30 in 2021 were:

	PAST 12 MONTHS	PAST 30 DAYS
Alcohol	81.8%	66.3%
Marijuana (any mode)	42.6%	28.5%
Vaping Nicotine	21.8%	16.1%
Vaping Marijuana	18.7%	12.4%
Cigarettes	18.6%	9.0%
Other Drugs	18.3%	7.5%

In addition, binge drinking (having 5+ drinks in a row in the past 2 weeks) was reported by 32.0%, and daily marijuana use (20+ occasions in the past 30 days) was reported by 10.8% of young adults in 2021.

DEFINITIONS FOR SUBSTANCE USE AND ABUSE
(U.S. DEPARTMENT OF HEALTH AND HUMAN SERVICES)

ADDICTION: The most severe form of substance use disorder, associated with compulsive or uncontrolled use of one or more substances. Addiction is a chronic brain disease that has the potential for both recurrence (relapse) and recovery.

BINGE DRINKING: Binge drinking for men is drinking five or more standard alcoholic drinks, and for women four or more standard alcoholic drinks, on the same occasion at least one day in the past month.

HEAVY DRINKING: Defined by the CDC (Centers for Disease Control and Prevention) as consuming eight or more drinks per week for women and fifteen or more drinks per week for men, and by the Substance Abuse and Mental Health Services Administration (SAMHSA), for research purposes, as binge drinking on five or more days in the past month.

SUBSTANCE: A psychoactive compound with the potential to cause health and social problems, including substance use disorders (and their most severe manifestation, addiction).

SUBSTANCE MISUSE: The use of any substance in a manner, situation, amount, or frequency that can cause harm to users or to those around them. For some substances or individuals, any use would constitute misuse (e.g., underage drinking, injection drug use).

SUBSTANCE MISUSE PROBLEMS OR CONSEQUENCES: Any health or social problem that results from substance misuse. Substance misuse problems or consequences may affect the substance user or those around them, and they may be acute (e.g., an argument or fight, a motor vehicle crash, an overdose) or chronic (e.g., a long-term substance-related medical, family, or employment problem, or chronic medical condition, such as various cancers, heart disease, and liver disease). These problems may occur at any age and are more likely to occur with greater frequency of substance misuse.

SUBSTANCE USE DISORDER: A medical illness caused by repeated misuse of a substance or substances. According to the Fifth Edition of the *Diagnostic and Statistical Manual of Mental Disorders* (DSM-5), substance-use disorders are characterized by clinically significant impairments in health and social function, and impaired control over substance use, and are diagnosed through assessing cognitive, behavioral, and psychological symptoms. Substance use disorders range from mild to severe and from temporary to chronic. They typically develop gradually over time with repeated misuse, leading to changes in brain circuits governing incentive salience (the ability of substance-associated cues to trigger substance-seeking), reward, stress, and executive functions like decision-making and self-control. Multiple factors influence whether and how rapidly a person will develop a substance use disorder. These factors include the substance itself; the genetic vulnerability of the user; and the amount, frequency, and duration of the misuse. Note: Severe substance use disorders are commonly called addictions.

Source: Facing Addiction in America: The Surgeon General's Report on Alcohol, Drugs, and Health (Washington, D.C.: U.S. Department of Health and Human Services, 2016), https://store.samhsa.gov/sites/default/files/d7/priv/surgeon-generals -report.pdf.

The DSM-5 lists eleven criteria of an SUD. As the accompanying box shows, the severity of the disorder is characterized by the number of criteria that apply.

DSM-5 CRITERIA FOR SUBSTANCE USE DISORDER*

1. Taking the substance in larger amounts and for longer than intended

2. Wanting to cut down or quit but being unable to do so

3. Spending a lot of time obtaining the substance

4. Craving the substance

5. Repeated inability to carry out major obligations at work, school, or home because of substance use

6. Continued use despite persistent or recurring social or interpersonal problems caused or made worse by the substance

7. Stopping or reducing important social, occupational, or recreational activities because of substance use

8. Recurrent use of the substance in physically hazardous situations

9. Consistent use of the substance despite acknowledgment of its persistent or recurrent physical or psychological difficulties

10. Tolerance (defined as a need for markedly increased amounts to achieve intoxication or markedly diminished effect from continued use of the same amount)

11. Withdrawal in one of two forms: the characteristic withdrawal syndrome or in instances when the substance is used to avoid withdrawal

* 2–3 symptoms = mild severity, 4–5 = moderate, and ≥ 6 symptoms = severe

---

Current scientific views consider SUDs as medical conditions characterized by "compulsive or uncontrolled use of one or more substances." With an SUD, alterations in the brain's circuitry lead the affected person to become progressively less able to limit their consumption of the substance. This is not to say that all people with SUDs have no control whatsoever over the behavior. Rather, their degree of self-control over their substance use depends on the duration and severity of the illness, the nature of the substance, and bio-

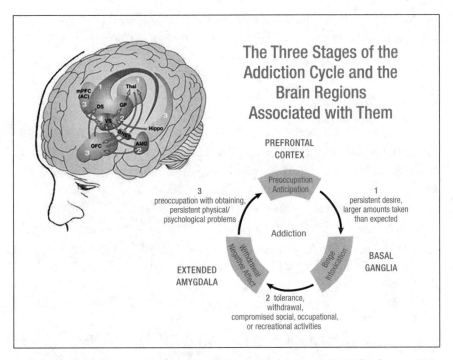

Source: *Facing Addiction in America: The Surgeon General's Report on Alcohol, Drugs, and Health* (Washington, D.C.: U.S. Department of Health and Human Services, 2016), figure 2.3, https://store.samhsa.gov/sites /default/files/d7/priv/surgeon-generals-report.pdf.

logical, psychological, and environmental factors. The figure above shows the three stages in the development of SUDs.[18]

Over time, a person moves from binge episodes of intoxication to chronic overuse so as to avoid withdrawal symptoms and ultimately to a constant preoccupation with, and anticipation of, obtaining the substance. Alterations in brain circuitry occur with changes in the thinking-feeling-behaving cycle. The person consequently has progressively greater difficulty maintaining their usual level of functioning. The progression of an SUD almost invariably leads to the onset or worsening of other mental conditions, such as anxiety, depression, and thought disorders.

The association between mental conditions and SUD is strong. For example, up to 41 percent of adults with SUDs have an anxiety disorder—a considerably higher proportion than in the general population.[19] Around 30 percent have a mood disorder, and nearly 7 percent have schizophrenia. Similarly, among people seeking clinical treatment for alcohol use disorder, 41 percent had a co-existing mood disorder, and 33 percent had an anxiety disorder.[20]

THE CHICKEN OR THE EGG?

For many people with SUDs, the cyclic nature of addiction makes it difficult to tease out the root cause. For example, the role binge drinking played in Kevin's onset of depression, or the role depression played in his uptick in binge drinking, is uncertain. More than likely, there was a bidirectional feedback loop. Clearly, the combined conditions had a major impact on his level of functioning and played a role in his poor response to treatment. We characterized the severity of his alcohol use disorder as moderate: He met criteria for symptoms 1, 2, 5, and 6. By the time we referred him for more intensive treatment, however, his depressive episode had become severe.

FAMILIES MAKE A DIFFERENCE: WAYS TO HELP

Experts have long known that families can play a crucial role in helping young people with SUDs reduce their harmful behaviors, engage with treatment, and maintain their recovery. But learning how to fill this role can be a challenge. The simple truth is that it's hard to be the parent of someone exhibiting problematic substance use. It takes great patience, skill, and emotional resilience to remain constructive, nonreactive, and helpful to them. There's no one-size-fits-all methodology. We encourage parents to practice the dos and don'ts of improved communication outlined in Chapter 4. Then, layer those baseline skills with those more specifically oriented to substance use treatment.

So, where can families learn to master these skills and find real support from others who are going through the same struggles? Among the most promising and effective approaches is one that comes out of the University of New Mexico.[21] Called Community Reinforcement Approach and Family Training (CRAFT), the model was first developed by Dr. Robert Meyers and popularized by his colleagues in their best-selling book *Beyond Addiction: How Science and Kindness Help People Change.*[22] CRAFT focuses on training concerned significant others to change how they interact with the substance-using person in ways that promote positive change. Research into the efficacy of CRAFT, funded in part by the National Institute on Alcohol Abuse and Alcoholism, has shown that over 70 percent of families who receive the training get their loved one into treatment, and that the majority of them report less anxiety, less anger, and more positive interactions with the substance user after completing the program. Typically, the training is carried out in a weekly group therapy or workshop format lasting roughly eight to twelve weeks. The participants are taught the basic principles of CRAFT and, through demonstrations, role-playing, and facilitated group discussions, are instructed in specific techniques for changing how they interact with their loved one. Family members are also taught ways to reduce their enabling behaviors, improve their communication skills, and take better care of themselves.

The goals of CRAFT are to reduce the loved one's harmful substance use, to engage them in treatment, and to improve the functioning (emotional, physical, and relational) of friends and family members. The model emphasizes the vital importance of relationships with family and friends in helping people change, and it offers an optimistic framework for participants (see box below).

TEN REASONS TO HAVE HOPE

- You can help.
- Helping yourself helps.
- Your loved one isn't crazy.
- The world isn't black-and-white.
- Labels do more harm than good.
- Different people need different options.
- Treatment isn't the be-all and end-all.
- Ambivalence is normal.
- People can be helped at any time.
- Life is a series of experiments.

Another important dimension of CRAFT is the simplicity and directness of its messages. The fundamentals of the approach are highly practical, direct, and accessible. Robert Meyers and Jane Ellen Smith encapsulated the method's guiding principles in a series of ten basic messages:[23]

1. Research has shown that family members can successfully learn techniques to help get their substance-abusing loved ones into treatment. *We cannot emphasize this enough!*

2. *You are not alone.* As isolated as you may feel as you cope with your loved one's substance abuse, the fact is that you are not alone. Millions of families are at this very moment suffering from problems just like yours. Although knowing that others suffer certainly doesn't lessen your pain, you may take hope from knowing that many have "solved" their problems and learned to live more satisfying lives.

3. *You can catch more flies with honey than vinegar.* Research has shown that it is easier to get your loved one to listen to loving words than to criticism. So, choose ways to discuss *what you do like about him or her and what positive changes please you.*

4. *You have as many tries as you want.* Relationships are a *process*: they exist over time. One event or discussion rarely defines an entire relationship, so you have as many tries at improving your relationship as you wish to take. CRAFT is designed to move at the pace you choose—you are in control. People can be helped at any time.

5. *You can live a happier life whether or not your loved one becomes abstinent.* An important part of CRAFT is learning to take care of yourself, regardless of your loved one's behavior.

6. When you help yourself, you help your family. You become a positive role model for the whole family. Our resilient, upbeat, and healthy attitude can be infectious, in a good way.

7. Neither you nor your loved one is crazy. All people have problems, and substance misuse is just that—a problem. You did not cause it, your loved one did not set out to be an abuser, and problems have solutions.

8. The world is not black-and-white. Most problems vary in degree and difficulty. One should think of changing a bad habit in successive approximations. Change may be easier for an individual if they have more than one option.

9. Scientific studies have shown that labels, such as addict or alcoholic, are a major barrier to people seeking help for substance use.

10. You have nothing to lose and a lot to gain by getting involved.

We encourage parents of young adults with substance use problems to follow the recommendations similar to those in *Beyond Addiction*. Although a full set of lessons and training lies beyond the scope of this book, parents can use the CRAFT or similar models to engage their young adults in nonconfrontational discussions about the unanticipated consequences of their addictive behaviors. We share their perspective that you can't help your loved one to change until you take better care of yourself. This includes learning mindfulness practices, like self-awareness, acceptance, and tolerance of suffering. It's also vitally important to know your own limits, respect them, and recognize when you're reaching them.

The CRAFT model also gives people specific ways to engage their loved ones in nonconfrontational, constructive dialogue rather than pointless arguments or screaming matches. With these skills, parents and other family or friends begin to understand their loved one's triggers for substance use. They learn positive-communication techniques and positive-reinforcement strategies, such as rewarding nonusing behavior; problem-solving; safety training; and getting a loved one to accept help. These methods, derived from cognitive behavioral therapy and family therapy, have been manualized in a way that enables people to practice the skills without requiring them or their loved ones to be in therapy.

The CRAFT module on positive communication, for instance, offers seven basic steps to keep in mind when engaging your twentysomething in a discussion: (1) be positive, (2) be brief, (3) be specific, (4) label your feelings, (5) offer an understanding statement, (6) accept partial responsibility, and (7) offer to help. Before starting a conversation, you'll want to follow some of the preparatory steps we've already described in Chapter 4, especially those involved with checking your own defensiveness, slowing things down, and taking the other's perspective.

We have offered here no more than an outline of CRAFT's method for empowering families to help loved ones with problematic substance use behavior. Nor are we suggesting that CRAFT is the only valid approach out there. But this widely accepted and well-tested approach is highly effective and relatively easy to access via online and in-person training workshops. We've included additional information about it in the appendix. Let's turn back to Kevin and his parents' next phase of the journey.

"HOPE HELPS A LOT, AND SO DOES TREATMENT!"

Kevin entered a partial hospital program with a great deal of anxiety and skepticism. He imagined he was going to be lectured about how bad it was for him to be drinking. He anticipated being put into an Alcoholics Anonymous (AA) group, where he'd have to admit that he was a hopeless alcoholic who had ruined his life and who had to put his faith in a higher power in order to change. These are among the self-stigmas and negative distortions that many substance users hold about AA or Narcotics Anonymous. Instead, he found a warm and accepting team of therapists and doctors who spent time evaluating him and learning about his struggles with depression, internet gaming disorder, problem drinking, and ADHD. Rather than being judgmental, his care providers were kind and supportive. They were knowledgeable about people who are dealing with multiple mental health conditions, and they were respectful of Kevin's values, opinions, and priorities for treatment. Best of all, they acknowledged his strengths and gave him options regarding his care plan.

Jenny and Adam were equally impressed with the program's outreach to them. From the outset, they were invited to meet with the treatment team social worker, who wanted to learn about their experiences with their son. They were introduced to other parents who attended twice-weekly group sessions in which the CRAFT model was explained and taught. And they participated in weekly family therapy sessions with Kevin. During these sessions, Jenny and Adam learned about Kevin's treatment progress and shared their new insights into how they could better support him in his pursuit of his goals.

Within a few weeks, the climate in the Chapman home had considerably improved. Although he still had periods of irritability and negativity, Kevin was in a visibly better mood. Now that he was on leave from work, his sleep-wake cycle normalized. He cut way back on his video-gaming and spent much less time alone in his room. He started joining the family for dinner and spending time with them afterward, watching movies and playing board games. He was playing basketball regularly and maintaining a healthier diet. And he began reconnecting with friends from the past with whom he had lost touch.

For their part, Jenny and Adam made great strides in taking better care of themselves. Jenny returned to her regular yoga classes and enrolled in a mindfulness-based meditation course. Adam returned to his regular workouts at the local gym and rejoined a weekly softball game that he had stopped attending during the crisis. Both parents were considerably less anxiety-ridden about Kevin and, hence, less reactive to his continuing mood fluctuations.

At a follow-up family session, a month after Kevin had started the partial hospital program, we reviewed how things were going for the Chapmans. Kevin spoke up first.

"You know," he said, "I really didn't know what to expect when I started at the program. It turns out that going there was the best decision of my life. I'm in a much better place now. I'm learning a lot about depression and problem drinking and video-gaming and how they all interact to make things worse for me. I'm finally figuring out how to get myself unstuck from all the negative stuff I've been doing. And I'm thinking about maybe going to community college so that I can make something more of my life than just being a nursing assistant. Best of all, I'm getting along better with my parents, and I'm starting to get together with old friends. It's not like everything is perfect, but I feel like I have a game plan to move ahead."

Jenny and Adam nodded while their son talked. Jenny spoke next and shared how proud she was of Kevin and how impressed she was with the way the program had included them as participants in his treatment. "We feel like we're partners in the process!" she said.

When it was Adam's turn to speak, he teared up. "It's like we have our son back," he said. "I'm overjoyed. And you know what? I'm back to believing there's a good future for him and for us. Hope helps a lot, and so does treatment!"

10

Parents as Mental Health Advocates

IN THE NEW NORMAL OF DELAYED ADULTHOOD, WE'VE NOTED PARENTS ARE OF-
ten embedded in every step of their emerging adult's ramble to self-sufficiency.
While this extension of parenting into young adulthood is new, many of its
roles are quite familiar: parent as nurturer, provider, and counselor for things
great and small. These forms of support are especially important during uncertain times, when parents and young adults are interconnected, and the new
norm is multigenerational living. However, one unexpected and unfamiliar
new parental role is added when an emerging adult develops signs of a mood
disturbance or substance misuse. The formidable developmental demands of
young adulthood increase their vulnerability to mental illness. Its onset may
result from a stressful situation, a hereditary predisposition, or both. That's
when parents need to become mental health advocates.

Part II has acquainted you with the commonly experienced mental health
stumbling blocks for young adults. The importance of family involvement
has focused on effective communication and treatment strategies. But what
do parents or young adults do when they don't know whose door to knock on
to get help? Some 35 percent of adults who needed but didn't receive mental
health services said it was because they didn't know where to go.[1] According
to Jennifer Snow, director of public policy at the National Alliance on Mental
Illness (NAMI), the problem is that the U.S. has no unified system of mental
health care but rather an individual patchwork that varies widely by state and
county.[2] This situation has worsened since Covid-19, with an increase in adults
seeking treatment for anxiety or depression.

This chapter begins with a look at the cottage industry of parents as mental health advocates. There are different levels of involvement within the role: from the more common experience of emotional support to a search navigator to the "right" therapist, to the less familiar occurrence of a sometime caregiver. To illustrate the many challenges that parents face, we introduce Sheila, who joined the ranks of parent as mental health advocate on behalf of her daughters. Sheila's family drama explores the sometimes-conflicting concerns and motivations of parents and their young adults regarding psychotherapeutic treatment. We'll also consider the complexity of determining the appropriate level of parental inclusion in, or exclusion from, a young adult's psychotherapy.

The chapter concludes with encouragement and suggestions for your self-care. Parents who have put their needs on hold for the sake of their children and adolescents may now need to rebalance their own care with the needs of their young adults.

PARENTS AS THE EMOTIONAL SUPPORT: A TALE OF TWO SIBLINGS

Sheila requested a consultation from us for guidance, a direction, and a plan. In a brief phone call, she introduced the problem in this way: "I have two young adult daughters. Emily lives independently but won't let go of the apron strings. She calls daily, which some mothers would love, but it's always an exhausting romp through the problem du jour. Honestly, this level of support is above my pay grade. Then there's Kayla, my younger daughter, who lives at home with me, rather miserably. No one's flourishing around here." Like many mothers of her generation, Sheila has been the primary emotional parent since their early childhoods. Following her husband's (and their father's) death five years ago, Sheila became increasingly isolated with her worries about her daughters, who insisted that she not disclose their personal issues to anyone in the extended family.

In theory, family therapy incorporates the perspectives of all relating family members. In practice, sessions may convene the willing, available, and relevant members for assessment purposes only, or meetings may be ongoing. Because both Emily and Kayla declined to attend a family session, we initially offered a three-session consult to Sheila. When only a young adult or parent attends a separate confidential session, it can be particularly useful to discuss conflicts, challenge and correct misinterpretations, and so improve relationships. The bottom line: There are many options for resolving long-standing tensions.

When we met Sheila for a three-session consult, we gathered a quick history by making a family genogram noting developmental, health, mental health, and relationship histories. Next, Sheila, clearly an Anglophile, related her experiences of motherhood by drawing on the House of Windsor. She told us, "I used to feel so lucky, like King George VI, who said Princess Elizabeth was his pride and Margaret was his joy. That was my Emily and Kayla. Now Emily's pride has turned into perfectionism and Kayla's a killjoy, to put it mildly. While Emily looks great on paper—her emotional CV is a high-wire act—I'm on speed dial with her three times a day. Each time Emily calls, she's in distress. It's just one fire drill after another. You'd think she'd know how to manage by now. And since Kayla returned home after finishing college a year ago, she's just completely stalled out in a dead-end, part-time job as a barista. I'm still footing her food, clothing, shelter, cell phone, and therapy bills. Our relationship is mostly by text, where Kayla disses my concerns with 'fexts'—you know, fighting on text. Like—'OMG, I told you I'm ok, LMA.'"

"I've tried to get help for each of them," Sheila continued, "but they put up major obstacles. Emily sounds insulted that I would even suggest that she get therapy. 'That's a hard no,' she says. Kayla goes to an individual therapist, but I'm shut out of everything that's going on. I'm supporting each of them in one way or another, and giving them a wide safety net. I've heard that their situation is called 'privileged dependence.'[3] Does that make me an enabler or just 'a sucker'? It feels crazy to keep doing the same thing and expecting a different result, but what am I supposed to do?" Sheila sighed.

Like Sheila, most parents want to support appropriate mental health treatment if their young adults are agreeable. However, these two sisters illustrate a few of the unanticipated barriers that young adults can use to block parental involvement. Our therapeutic goal was to offer creative ways to advise Sheila on her options, despite the obstacles she described. We began the consult with Sheila's concern about Emily.

I Don't Need Help. Instagram Says So.

Sheila reported that Emily had always relied on her as a sounding board. The frequency and intensity of Emily's outreach had increased in the years since her father's death. Initially, Sheila assumed that her daughter would spontaneously outgrow the frequency of contact. Emily's emotional dependence was both a tribute to the security that Sheila had provided and a signal of Emily's difficulty managing her daily anxiety. Now the mother fretted that at age twenty-eight, Emily needed professional guidance.

We reassured Sheila that young adults who are not in a partner relationship do contact their parents and lean on them more often for emotional support. However, in view of the mother's description of Emily's chronic perfectionistic tendencies and accompanying distress, we agreed that she could benefit from a therapeutic assessment. But how to encourage Emily to reconsider her rejection of therapy? We suggested that Sheila ask Emily to share her reasons for not wanting to get help. As expected, Emily's comments included: "I don't have time" and "I looked it up on Instagram—I'm just stressed, not mentally disturbed." She followed this up with guilt-inducing resistance: "You understand me better than anyone, Mom. I don't want to talk to some stranger."

The pressure of Emily's distress made Sheila's protective stance understandable. While some might view Sheila through the lens of helicopter parenting, our emphasis was on the leverage and resources for change rather than on pathology. We credited Sheila for her many years of dedication to Emily's needs. Yet, we encouraged Sheila to step back from being "on call" so that Emily could step up the hard work of emotional individuation.

Sheila could be the change agent to promote her daughter's growth. To reduce Emily's resistance, we suggested that Sheila have a heart-to-heart talk and tell Emily that a mother's love is not a substitute for the professional guidance that could help to treat her perfectionistic anxiety. Now, equipped with our support, Sheila had ready responses to her daughter's rationalizations. After many tears and protests, Emily agreed to her mother's request to seek treatment. Sheila's loving but firm insistence helped her daughter overcome her mental health stigma. Emily had finally accepted that she needed more support than willpower and phoning home could provide. Next, Sheila planned to help Emily identify a few therapists to consider. To streamline the process, we introduced the basics of search navigation.

PARENTS AS SEARCH NAVIGATORS: QUESTIONS AND QUALITIES TO LOOK FOR IN A THERAPIST

Parents are accustomed to the role of a health advocate for their children when they find a pediatrician, attend a child's annual checkup, or seek medical advice when a child's fever spikes. But mental health search navigator? What's that? In certain ways it shares similar features with a health advocate: Find a professional you trust, provide history and context for any new or alarming problem, evaluate treatment options, and follow up.

Unlike your earlier quest, you are a stranger in a strange land. You are no longer surrounded by other parents of same-age children who can give word-of-mouth recommendations to their trusted health providers. You may not even know what kind of doctor you are looking for. A parent enters this foreign terrain when their adolescent or young adult shows behavioral or mood changes, or when strains between parent and child worsen, with no clear guidance or resolution in sight. Although most schools and colleges provide built-in health, wellness, and counseling referrals or services, those fall away once a diploma is in hand. Parents then often fill in the search role for their young adult. No matter the age, whenever an individual is struggling with a mental or behavioral disorder, their ability to find appropriate treatment will be constrained by their illness. This is especially true for young adults who lack the health system experience or resources that middle-aged parents have acquired.

Because there are over four hundred kinds of psychotherapy, it takes a search navigator to find a good match. Compared to those seeking a medical consult, it takes longer to find and get mental health care, and there are fewer choices of providers. But where do you start, and how do you know what to look for? Then, how do you know when you've found it? Multiple phone calls may mark the beginning of a search for the appropriate therapist. Whether that therapist provides individual, couples, or family therapy, the search can feel like a real-life version of *Mission Impossible*. Your assignment, should you choose to accept it, is to sort through an array of treatment modalities, clinical approaches, professional credentials, and communication styles.

Like the hardest multiplayer online game, you have entered what one mother describes as the "dysfunction of the mental health system." She summed up her discouraging experience in this way: "My thirty-year-old son lives with me—his dad and I have been divorced for many years. My son is depressed and also abusing alcohol and weed. It's been really hard to find someone who does 'one-stop shopping' to treat him." She described a confusing search for an appropriate therapist within a fragmented system of mental health specialists. "One specialist prescribes psychoactive medications; another provides talk therapy; another specializes in substance use problems; another treats executive functioning and attention deficits. If someone like my son is unlucky enough to have what they call co-occurring substance use with another disorder, good luck getting the different doctors to talk with each other. After more weeklong searches for someone accepting new patients, he got an appointment for a month later. That appointment was canceled due to an office error. In all, he waited six weeks to get seen. At first, I thought it was my fault that it took so long to find someone—like I had missed the 'where to get help' memo. Eventually, I understood that other families had similar experiences, and I wasn't to blame."

Because this mother persisted, her son eventually received the treatment he needed. Despite the search confusion and systemic service challenges, try to resist feeling defeated. It may help to remember that you are giving voice on behalf of your loved one. To help you know where to start, NAMI offers practical guidance on this process.[4] We summarize NAMI's recommendations.

FINDING A MENTAL HEALTH PROFESSIONAL

Follow these steps to make sure you connect with the right mental health professional for your own needs and preferences.

Think about whom you're looking for:

- If you need a professional who can prescribe medications, then you'll want to find a psychiatrist or clinical nurse specialist in mental health. Otherwise, you might want to consider a therapist or counselor for "talk" therapy. To be sure, many psychiatrists also provide psychotherapy.

- If you have a specific type of mental health condition, consider looking for someone who has experience dealing with it.

- If appointments are not readily available, there are online resources with information about self-help and support groups sponsored by NAMI.

Gather referrals:

- If you are going to use your personal health insurance, call the company and get the names of mental health providers who accept your insurance.

- You'll also want to get clarity on the benefits that your plan pays for. For example, what is the likely copay for visits, and what specific types of therapy are covered by your in-network plan? It's important to know how much you will be reimbursed if you go "out of network."

- If your health plan has poor mental health benefits or if the provider(s) you're most interested in don't accept your insurance, you can inquire if they are willing to accept a reduced payment on a sliding scale (based on your income level). If not, ask them if they have a payment plan.

Make the call:

- Once you have the necessary information, start calling the mental health professionals on your recommended list. Expect delays before new appointment slots are available.
- Place your name on a wait list if one is available.
- If your first choices are unavailable, find out if they can recommend other practitioners.

Ask questions:

- Be very clear about what you are looking for and learn as much as you can about the practitioner's approach to treatment, including their preferred modality of care (individual, family, group) and therapeutic orientation (cognitive behavioral, intergenerational, psychodynamic, interpersonal, etc.).
- Ask about their training and prior experience working with young adults and their families.
- Ask the therapist to describe what you can expect if you begin working together.

Build a relationship:

- Give the relationship time to develop.
- Make sure the therapist appreciates where you're coming from and addresses your concerns.

Source: "Finding a Mental Health Professional," National Alliance on Mental Illness, accessed September 25, 2023, https://www.nami.org/Your-journey/Individuals-with -mental-illness/finding-a-mental-health-professional.

To further clarify, we summarize the many types of mental health professionals and their myriad credentials. Psychiatrists, who are M.D.s, are medically trained and can offer medical treatment and psychotherapy (although many prefer to focus primarily on psychopharmacology). The psychiatrist should be board certified, meaning they have passed a qualifying examination sponsored by the American Board of Psychiatry and Neurology. Advanced practice nurses have received additional clinical training beyond their R.N. degree and must be licensed by the state. They generally focus on medication management, although many have additional training in psychotherapy.

Psychologists most often have doctorates (a Ph.D. or a Psy.D.) and should be licensed to practice by your state's licensing board. State boards also license: clinical social workers (LCSW), marriage and family therapists (LMFT), and professional counselors (LPC), each of whom is a master's-prepared professional and has received sufficient supervised training.

Beyond their credentials, you will want to learn more about the practitioners' experience working with young adults. How familiar are they with the kinds of issues your emerging adult is experiencing? Have they received additional clinical training since finishing their formal education? What is their reputation among former patients and among their peers? Do they come highly recommended? Are they affiliated with an academic institution, and are they engaged in clinical teaching?

Other questions concern their approach to young adult mental health treatment. Is a therapist wedded to a particular type of therapy, or are they flexible in their treatment methods? What is their clinical orientation? How do they incorporate family members into their assessment and treatment planning? Do they welcome parental input, and do they explain their diagnostic impressions and treatment recommendations in ways that make sense? What are their expectations of the patient and family throughout treatment? Will they provide guidance to parents who are seeking ways to support the young adult in achieving their treatment goals? And are they willing to offer sessions to bring everyone together to review progress—or lack thereof?

A final set of qualities to consider when you are choosing a therapist relates to trust. Keep in mind these important questions: Does the therapist have the specific skills, credentials, and professional training to most effectively address your issues? Do they communicate and relate well, and are they genuinely respectful of everyone in the family? Are they willing to make themselves available if problems arise in between sessions? Will this therapist modify the original treatment plan if needed and remain flexible and open to the individual's and family's input? Regrettably, it is important not to assume that a particular therapist will view parents as an intrinsic source of care and support. Our own mental health professions have too often reflexively excluded parents from a young adult's treatment. Finally, do you have a gut feeling that this is someone who can help?

Occasionally, there is a less-than-optimal fit between the therapist and the patient or family. This incompatibility may be due to a variety of factors: lack of sufficient trust between patient and therapist, poor communication between therapist and family, a patient's or family's resistance to change, or some other barrier to effective therapeutic engagement that impedes progress. If you do encounter these roadblocks, you and your young adult need to discuss these issues with the therapist. Hopefully, you'll come up with a game plan to get around the obstacles before ending the therapy. If there is no resolution, we encourage you to search for a new therapist.

Local NAMI support groups can help you persevere (for information, see appendix). We next turn to the role of parents as mental health caregivers for young adults as we return to Sheila and Kayla.

PARENTS AS CAREGIVERS TO YOUNG ADULTS

The situation may be familiar to you or someone you love—a young adult without a living-wage job, sufficient "manage your life" skills, poor coping, or significant depression is living back home. Their parent may very well be a mental health caregiver.

The word *caregiver* evokes the image of a middle-aged adult caring for an elderly parent. This powerful association elicits our concern and compassion for their dutiful if exhausting fulfillment of a valued generational payback. Elder care is a predictable burden of aging, whose onset often occurs in the sixth or seventh decades of life. In contrast, the pattern of mental illness across a life span is the opposite of that seen in physical illness. For mental illness, the most common age of onset is adolescence and early adulthood. Parents of young adults might not have expected and are rarely prepared for the caregiver role of someone so young.

Yet a surprising number of parents, more often single mothers, assumes this unique caregiver role. A recent survey shows that parents are much more often mental health caregivers to their young adult children than to their elderly parents.[5] These young adults often reside with their parents during their treatment and recovery.[6] Many parents report that it's difficult to talk to others, whether family or friends, about their loved one's condition. As a result, they feel isolated and experience self-stigma.

In the United States, home-based care for a floundering young adult is largely a family concern with very limited public support, with the exception of those eligible for social security disability insurance. Despite the growing prevalence of youth mental illness, the vast majority of federal and local programs to support family caregivers are oriented toward the geriatric population. Parents, stepparents, and siblings are often on their own to manage the contagious effects of emotional burnout and interpersonal distress. Many marriages struggle around the uncertainties and persistent challenges of parenting an emotionally vulnerable young adult. The exhausting toll that their mental health challenges may place on a parent or family is largely invisible except to those directly involved.

Parents who are mental health caregivers for their young adult assume one of the very few jobs for which there is a pervasive feeling of enormous emotional responsibility and guilt about their child's problems. For no pay, parents are on call 24-7 for transportation, groceries, meals, and medication supervision as they also endure anxiety-ridden uncertainty with little support.

Sheila's situation with an irritable and resentful daughter living at home, while making few inroads toward independence, was troublesome, but without an indication of a serious mental illness. Nonetheless, Sheila had become a mental health caregiver. Although Kayla attended weekly therapy, her mother reported, "Kayla tells me that it's private and none of my business. She acts like I'm an intrusive and nosy mom with no clue about how hard her life is. I'm convinced she's telling her therapist that I've ruined her life and that I'm to blame for all her problems. Her therapist probably thinks it's all my fault."

We continued our consult with Sheila by acknowledging the challenge of giving voice to parental worries when they are excluded from a young adult's individual therapy. Parents understandably feel frustrated, particularly when a young person like Kayla is unhappily living at home with them, stalled out, without a future plan. We gave Sheila a peek behind the therapeutic curtain to reassure her that the well-worn bias of therapists as parent-bashers is inaccurate, and to offer her an overview of how therapists manage client confidentiality.

A Therapist's Dilemma

It's true that therapists often inquire about the early and the current parent-child relationship. After all, childhood is a crucial formative period in which parents imperfectly meet children's needs. No matter how hard parents try to avoid it, and even when they improve on the prior generation's efforts, parents emotionally injure their children at times. Children present a variety of behavioral, emotional, academic, and social issues that may overwhelm a parent's ability to recognize and appropriately respond to them. At times, parents may also be overcome by their own personal problems or lack of resources. Less often, parents have undiagnosed or untreated mental illnesses that impact a child's experiences.

We assured Sheila that competent therapists, whether individual or family-based, are trained to take a nuanced neutral stance toward an adult child's anger at, or disappointment in, their parents. Professionals understand these feelings as one aspect of a complex relationship. In fact, they appreciate the ambivalence a young adult often feels as they seek to separate from parents (as we discussed in Chapter 2). Once a therapist has achieved a solid relationship with a young adult client, the therapist often encourages them to consider the parents' viewpoints and motives from a more objective perspective. The therapist may raise questions like "What might be motivating your parents to be so concerned about you?" or "How do you imagine your parents feel when they see you struggling to figure out your life issues?" Such questions nudge the young adult to deeper insights into how they themselves may be contributing to the parent-child conflicts in the family.

Because we neither wish to idealize families nor pathologize them, we need to note a few reasons for keeping a family out of treatment altogether. Individual therapy, without parents or other family members, is appropriate when the goal is to preserve a therapeutic alliance with the client, particularly to draw needed boundaries in cases of physical or sexual violations or other family violence. Of course, individual therapy is also appropriate when the client or the family is unwilling to participate fully in family treatment.

One such example arises from one of the most painful parental situations—when young adult children are estranged or alienated from their parents. We also treat parents who want to be there for their young adults but who are shut out of their lives. The search for *the* cause is often a complex mystery that a parent can only guess at. Was it a nasty divorce, promises made but not kept, a vault full of misunderstandings, unfinished business from the earlier parent-child relationship, or unmet expectations on both sides?

There may be neither a good nor correct answer, and an exhaustive treatment of parent-child estrangement lies outside the scope of this book. However, our field does provide resources for this unique parental pain. Psychologist Joshua Coleman, who has traveled this path personally, is the author of two books we recommend: *When Parents Hurt* and *The Rules of Estrangement*. As comforting and informative companions, these books can ameliorate the grief, sadness, and worry that hurt or estranged parents may feel.

Fortunately, that was not the situation between Kayla and her mother. However, Kayla's opposition to granting her mother therapeutic access put not only Sheila but also the therapist in a bind.

What parents may not fully appreciate is the conflict therapists find themselves in when a young adult like Kayla is adamant about maintaining their privacy. Therapists are familiar with this dilemma of being stuck in the middle. A therapist has a professional, legal, and ethical mandate to protect a client's confidentiality, barring rare, strict, and legal exceptions involving a client's danger to self or others. What Sheila didn't know was that therapists are free to hear (if not respond to) parental concerns by way of call, voicemail, email, or letter. We consider it a therapeutic responsibility both to respect the client-therapist boundary of confidentiality and to hear the concerns of involved family members.

Good individual therapy will prevent an adult child from blaming all their woes on parents. The blind parent-bashing that Sheila imagined would be counterproductive to a client. It would chip away at their loyalty to their parents and to the love they may feel despite their hurt. In parallel, if the parent is in therapy, the therapist provides the support and insight needed to help them cope with their family relationships. That can include understanding the part they may play in an adult child's difficulties and how to relate most constructively. Of necessity, therapists must tread lightly, taking care to avoid reinforcing negative family patterns and generational stereotypes.

Reassured, Sheila wondered, "But should I let Kayla know I'm reaching out to her therapist?" Transparency builds trust; secrecy erodes it. Following our guidance, Sheila informed Kayla that she planned to leave a message for the therapist to share her specific parental goals and concerns. In parallel, Sheila could expect that the therapist would tell Kayla that she had received her message. In this way, a therapist can protect client confidentiality and observe a limited protocol of parental involvement. We hoped that if the individual therapist had the training to do so, they might persuade Kayla to have her mother join periodically or refer Kayla and Sheila to a family therapist. Either way, Sheila could give input to guide Kayla's therapist on behalf of her daughter's well-being.

At a follow-up visit, Sheila let us know that she had informed Kayla of her call to the individual therapist. As expected, Kayla was quite annoyed by what she regarded as her mother's interference. Still, Sheila felt relieved that she had made the call and could introduce her concerns to Kayla's therapist as needed.

One interpretation of the daughter's repeated displays of anger was an unconscious cover for her developmental bind. Anger allowed Kayla to assume a pseudo-adult power stance while also maintaining her dependent position. It's that push-me-pull-you developmental struggle of loss before gain, more commonly seen in adolescence, when emotional distancing precedes greater independence.

We offered additional parenting sessions to support Sheila's efforts to reduce at-home accommodations in order to promote Kayla's autonomy. Over time, Kayla took the necessary steps to cross the Rubicon from childhood to adulthood.

While young adults like Kayla may discuss their family issues in individual therapy; it's important for parents to consider the uncomfortable possibility that they're sorting and unloading unfinished family baggage.

Beware of Your Baggage

We all have baggage that we bring to our relationships. If unresolved, that baggage gets carried to the next primary relationship of partner, coparent, or child, and we hope that they will unpack it for us. That is quite an ask. Yet this is such a common dynamic that it's the stuff of movies.

In the rom-com *Ticket to Paradise*, the acrimoniously divorced David and Georgia Cotton are compelled to clean up their unfinished business when their daughter Lily suddenly announces plans to marry a young man, native to Bali, with whom she's fallen in love while vacationing. Her parents initially seek to disrupt the wedding plans because they fear she's throwing away her chance at happiness—which amounts to their preferred professional career plans for her in a middle-class American lifestyle. Their shared belief and distortions largely stem from their unresolved anger and blame of each other over their failed marriage. Now each is determined to rescue Lily from making similar mistakes. Lily has, in fact, made a very solid decision about her life partner and her vision of a good life. By eventually accepting their daughter's healthy but different choices, David and Georgia also grow up emotionally.

Unlike in the movies, young adults may not be teaching their parents to grow up. If anything, the young person's own delayed development keeps parents actively involved. Enter the family therapist, whose role is to facilitate the healing of individual relationships. Family dynamics are shaped by circular feedback loops. Anxious youth can precipitate overprotective parents. Reactive parents can contribute to anxiety or anger in their young adults.

Disagreements about parenting their children can impact a marriage and inform a young adult's determination to make the kind of opposite choices that Lily, the movie character, did. Long-playing family patterns from childhood often crystallize in parent–young adult relationships. When individuals don't work out these dynamics, they play them out in their lives and across generations. When family therapy is not possible, individual or couples therapy can help people break free of many negative feedback patterns and resolve unfinished business—they agree to hold and be held to mutual accountability. The result can be a more compassionate understanding of self and each other, lighter baggage, and improved relationships.

Remember to Take Care of Yourself

Over the course of several sessions, Sheila had made significant changes on behalf of facilitating her daughter's transitions to full adulthood. However, they were not the only ones who needed support. In our concluding sessions, we reminded Sheila that it was important to practice her own self-care.

The mental health of middle-aged parents is not a headline grabber. Yet this age group has experienced a steep rise in rates of anxiety and depression over the past several years. As we described earlier in the book, living with rapid sociohistorical changes, coupled with the additional burden of supporting a struggling young adult, is bound to make a parent feel vulnerable and distressed. Yet how can parents, who have made so many choices and sacrifices on behalf of their children, sometimes prioritize their own needs when their young adult is experiencing health, financial, or work concerns; mental health problems; or substance misuse?

The often-used phrase "Take care of yourself" can be maddening to parents who are worried about their young adult's well-being. What, after all, is the term "self-care," other than a spa-like bromide used as a marketing promotion? Self-care, as a buzzword, can too often provide a rationalization to think only of yourself, even at the expense of another.

Clinically, we define self-care as an action. It is the act of focusing on your own physical and mental well-being. For mothers, fathers, and other family caregivers who are accustomed to making their needs a distant second to those of a child of any age, self-care can seem a selfish indulgence. Instead, we encourage you to focus on the difference between self-interest and selfishness—best illustrated by the standard preflight instruction "Put the oxygen mask on yourself first before helping others." This metaphor applies best to a crisis, but we can extend its usefulness by practicing activities that boost our resilience while maintaining our commitment to care for others. The decision to explore new healthy mind-body habits involves change.

You Can't Meditate Your Way Out of Their Problems

Self-care is important for your own physical and mental health. However, you must recognize that it won't solve your twentysomething's problems. When you are worried about your young adult, especially when you are their care-giver during a temporary or more serious setback or mental illness, self-care will neither eliminate your feelings of helplessness and hypervigilance nor restore your sleep disturbed by bouts of wakeful worry. Among the hardest lessons parents grapple with is this: No matter how much you've done and how hard you've tried, there is only so much that you can do for, and only so much influence you can have with, your young adult children. Your loved ones will have to figure things out for themselves as they live their choices and experience the resulting consequences. Our young adults make decisions we would not make, but we cannot control them. Self-care is a form of allowing yourself to rest in that truth.

If you accept that premise, self-care can ease the demands of ongoing caregiving and enable a parent to regain their equilibrium. Your next action is to identify the activities that you enjoy and reduce those that drain you. All of us need both sustaining individual interests and the support of communities of care. Recall past hobbies or current enjoyable pursuits. Refocus on yourself. Look around at the many things you can do to help you achieve well-being. We've started a list as a prompt for your review. Select an easily accessible pastime to add to your daily or weekly routine. Add others as you can.

SUGGESTED SELF-CARE ACTIVITIES

- Take a walk in nature.
- Read or listen to a book.
- Watch an enjoyable show.

- Invite someone to join you for a walk, a run, a cup of coffee.
- Spend time with people you enjoy.
- Listen to a guided meditation.
- Do yoga or Qigong in person or by watching a video on YouTube.
- Join an interest group.
- Draw or paint.
- Take a class.
- Talk to friends on the phone.
- Keep a journal.
- Sit outside when the weather allows.
- Take a shower or bath.
- Listen to or play soothing or upbeat music.
- Light candles.
- Work in a garden.
- Cook and enjoy good food.

Now make a list of people or activities that drain you. Imagine saying no or reducing your frequency of contact or obligation to someone or something on this list. Allow yourself to consider and balance what you owe yourself and what you owe another. If you could change something, what would it be? How would you go about making that change happen?

Remember, to change your mood and lessen your state of worry, you must *do* something different. Typically, we recommend doing something that generates the opposite of a distraught mood. If you are sad, put on dancing music, a comedy, a silly YouTube cat video. Change the channel on your mood; even a temporary reset can be restorative.

Professional treatment is another form of self-care. We encourage parents to get psychotherapeutic help for themselves when they need it, regardless of whether their young adult is willing to enter treatment. Individuals, couples, parents, stepparents, and stepfamilies benefit when parents develop the resources and resilience needed for themselves *and* others. Psychotherapy can assist you in generating a plan for how to enhance your resilience. It can also helpfully align your acceptance of what is and is not in your control.

Possibly even more important than individual activities are those that connect you to a community of caring others. The community may be an organized support group, a place of worship, or friends with whom you feel close. You'll want to be with people or in a place where you can share your concerns. In the appendix, we list national organizations that provide education, support, and a community of caring others and direct you to local chapters.

A LEGACY OF HOPE

Parenting is a long game, and it has just grown longer. Your parental involvement has intensified and now extends into the life of your young adult, who needs your support more than ever. In this age of uncertainty, an exciting opportunity emerges as you and your young adult child strengthen your relationship. But neither the young person's transition into a productive, emotionally mature adult nor a greater emotional closeness between you happens automatically. Both processes take work.

In this longest era of parenthood, we've touched on the common misunderstandings and challenges as the parent-child relationship matures.

The stories of today's families reside on a continuum from young adults who enjoy relatively smooth sailing to those with substantial and persistent difficulties navigating the voyage. Many young people will weather times of financial uncertainty, work concerns, housing needs, and the ups and downs of peer and romantic relationships. Wherever they lie along this continuum, the basic premise of this book is that you have an invaluable role to play in supporting their passage from emerging to full adulthood. Your perspective, guidance, emotional support, and financial assistance are vital to your young adult's well-being.

You're Not Done Yet identifies key catalysts of this growth as you emerge from your earlier parental role. We've named a few of the adjustments you'll need to make to gain a more peer-like relationship with your young adult. You must shift away from a closed and directive mindset—the one that communicates "I've got all the answers"—and in its place substitute an open-minded, creative, and flexible capacity to learn as much as you can from youth and young adults. Along the way, you may need to challenge your expectations, biases, and stereotypes of the younger generations. But what you'll lose in certainty you'll gain in self-awareness. You'll become better able to constructively address and resolve differences, misunderstandings, and hurts between you and your emerging adult. And if you cannot resolve the conflicts right away, perhaps you can tolerate them for as long as it takes for reconciliation. The generations are different, yet they share many goals. Older and younger generations alike share the most important family goal—encouraging a youth to become an autonomous, capable, and caring adult.

That goal can be especially challenging when tough times present themselves to both generations. It's tougher still when a young adult experiences painful setbacks, is stalled, or needs to overcome and manage a mental health stumbling block. Hang in there, parents. With your support, their goals and yours will align over time.

Live in the here and now, learning and sharing small activities together. Cherish the laughs and moments of fun. Live each day to the fullest and end each day with an appreciation of what went right. All of us need these times to feel more connected to one another and to get through life's uncertainties.

As you turn your focus to the relationship you want with your adult child, your new lifetime role will emerge—that of collaborative partner. Coming to respect and know each other beyond your early familial roles, you will grow beyond a dusty, obligatory relationship to one of deepened connection as you honor, relate with, and learn from each other. For both generations, that is a powerful legacy to leave and a tradition worth passing on.

ACKNOWLEDGMENTS

We are enormously grateful to Anna deVries at St. Martin's. Anna's unwavering belief in the book as it evolved was crucial to our ability to play with ideas and synthesize important concepts in search of the balance between scientific and clinical perspectives. Her incisive, wise, and candid refinements were a hallmark of her kind and generous attentiveness to our process. Many thanks to Laura Clark, the incredibly talented and organized associate publisher of nonfiction, who heads up our team at St. Martin's, including: the cover designer, Soleil Paz, who patiently tolerated our many "what-abouts?" Along with Tom Cherwin, our meticulous copy editor; senior production editor Kiffin Steurer; designer Nicola Ferguson; and publicist nonpareil Rebecca Lang; and cheers to Erica Martirano in marketing.

Our agent, Jennifer Weis, encouraged us to grapple with the seismic shifts and barrage of unexpected changes that parents and young adults had encountered during the Covid-19 era, underscored by the search for the new normal. Early in the book's conceptual development, Allan Fallow, expert editor of *The Stressed Years of Their Lives*, introduced us to fellow editor Patty Boyd, who organized chapter substructure, swept aside clunky phrasing, and invaluably "got" the book. Patty was as sharp-eyed as she was sympathetic to and supportive of our fledgling efforts. We took her indispensable advice, "Bad luck to say 'final,'" as we wrote and rewrote drafts.

We also relied on the deep and ongoing investment of Vanessa Smith, award-winning documentary filmmaker, who filmed interviews with us for *The Stressed*

Years of Their Lives and again during the early pandemic lockdown. Her encouragement continued as she, Christine Biddle, and Audrey Zinman formed a book group to provide feedback to an early draft. They gently suggested additional topics and shared poignant life experiences that helped us to formulate some key principles of the text. In memory of and deep appreciation for Peter Doris, friend, mental health advocate, career coach, and former head of human resources for a Fortune 500 company, who advanced our knowledge of the educational to employment linkages, along with his introductions to Steve Greene, New York director of the Johnson O'Connor Research Foundation, and business executive and author Bill Holland. Thanks to you each for generously contributing interviews to the book. Judy Green, LCSW, a dedicated and nationally certified trainer for the NAMI Family-to-Family Education Program, very helpfully contributed valuable input from her many years at NAMI.

A final note of thanks from each of the authors.

To Tony Rostain, my coauthor, who embodies the rarest combination of joie de vivre with deeply caring, invested, and compassionate psychiatrist as practitioner/scientist/humanist. Tony, my deep appreciation for embracing the serendipity of this unforeseeably demanding, stimulating, and rewarding experience of being coauthors. Your thoughtful insights, courage, and friendship have been invaluable to me both professionally and personally over the last many years. Our book talks and trips have been especially gratifying and always memorable. As coauthors, we were enthusiastically in sync to make this *our* book—and one that would make a difference in the lives of youth and parents alike. Together, we did it!

I owe a great debt of thanks to my readers. My sister, Gwenn, was my alpha reader. She contributed research on inequities and societal shifts while steadfastly offering substantive comments. Gwenn filled the gaps in my thinking, as only a sister can, with "I think you really meant this . . ." and made the book the better for it. More thanks to readers and good friends: Susan LaDuca, who read with clinical familiarity and a three-generational ear. "Would kids really say that?" Lisa Nicholson and Steve Gruelich, who thoughtfully commented on an early draft and decluttered jargon. Thank you each for your kind and astute reading. To Libby Mosier, wonderful essayist and friend, many thanks for your early and patient tutelage on the craft of memoir and for your enthusiastic encouragement.

More thanks to dear friends who both kindly tolerated my obsessive focus on the book and gave me a two-year pass while I was "in the den." Among them: Jane Buhl, Claire and Michael Robinson, Mark and Patti Stanish, Beth and Carl Holden.

Our beloved young adults, Jared and S. E., and William, were a source of deep inspiration and my reason for writing this book. Your generational perch, voices, lived experiences, and spot-on memes provided a depth of understanding that was both treasured and irreplaceable. Jared and S. E. gave us a bright memory of a pandemic's eve celebratory wedding and generously remained on standby for ready analyses of online games. William's return home during Covid's lockdown generated many thoughtful talks about the brave new world of twenty-somethings. Thank you each for sharing your perspectives and your wisdom.

To Earl Sr., and to the parent generations that have enriched my life, I am deeply grateful. To those who are with us in spirit—Nana Ruth, and my own maternal great-grandmother, grandparents, and parents, Jeannette and Max, whose hopes, dreams, and sacrifices imbue cherished memories. I have endeavored to live your legacies of doing better, generation by generation.

Deepest gratitude to my husband, Earl, for your gracious and generous support over many years, book after book, of "being there." I am blessed with your unwavering belief in the mission and meaning of my writing. Feeling known and understood by you is such a gift. Beyond the ineffable, many thanks for being the omega reader, who spent days spotting what I dubbed my "glaring stupidities." Your loving care was steadfastly served with a side of delicious meals and occasional escapes. I am forever thankful for who you are in my life.

—B. Hibbs,
May 30, 2023

This book was conceived in the second year of the Covid pandemic, in the immediate aftermath of the tragic death by suicide of my beloved son, Julian, in May 2021, a few months before his thirty-third birthday. It is difficult to describe the profound and enduring effects his sudden departure has had on me and on his family and friends. My journey through grief and mourning has taken many turns, and I am still learning, and struggling, to come to terms with the loss. I continue to feel profound gratitude for the incredible spirit Julian brought to the world, and for the many lessons he taught me about being a father to a remarkable son. I'm also blessed to be surrounded by the love and devotion of my family, friends, colleagues, and community who have generously shared their love, compassion, companionship, and solidarity. Without this support, I would not have been able to dedicate myself to writing this book.

I want to thank my coauthor, colleague, and friend, B. Hibbs, whose original invitation to write *The Stressed Years of Their Lives* started us on an intellectual journey that has profoundly enriched my life. Our years of working and writing together about the challenges of parenting adolescents and young adults has afforded me the opportunity to explore new ideas and reformulate my approach to the science and art of clinical practice. Your generosity of spirit and your loving-kindness during the early days of our discussions about *You're Not Done Yet* helped me to find the confidence I wanted to embark on this second book. With your encouragement, I was able to take the time I needed to grieve the loss of my son before dedicating myself to undertaking this important project. I deeply value the time we spent conceptualizing the book and discussing the critical issues we address in it. Our conversations were always stimulating and thought-provoking, and they helped us sort out the most salient issues we wanted to address. Finally, the opportunity to travel together and share our ideas with audiences across the U.S. and Canada has been especially fun and professionally gratifying.

I am especially grateful to my patients and their families for entrusting me with their care. I feel fortunate to have a career that affords me the opportunity to work with people daily who are struggling to come to terms with myriad mental health challenges. Their willingness to engage in a treatment process that can be both demanding and frustrating at times, and their honest efforts to find solutions to the problems they are facing are a constant source of inspiration for me. I hope my descriptions of their stories helps them and others find ways to live better lives.

I want to acknowledge the ongoing support of my dear friends Michael Felsen, Matthew Alexander, Robert Hoffnung, Robert Schiller, Richard Summers, David Kaye, Eugene Beresin, Louis Freedberg, Jim Wright, Maureen Rush, Jacqueline Hudak, and Edwin Harrari, each of whom offered me much-needed shelter from the storm and encouraged me to keep moving forward. I give thanks to Michael Baime, Ralph Ciampa, and John Ehman for their spiritual companionship and reflective wisdom. I appreciate the special camaraderie I've shared with J. Russell Ramsay, Lisa Tuttle, Mary Solanto, Sarah O'Neill, Lenard Adler, Jeffrey Newcorn, and Cathy Budman in the work of treating young adults with ADHD and related disorders. I'm grateful to Eric Kupersmith and my other colleagues at Cooper University Health Care for providing me with a warm and caring professional home. I thank my bandmates from Pink Freud and from House. And I'm especially indebted to Syd Pulver for his remarkable therapeutic skills, which enabled me to navigate the troubled waters of these past two years.

Finally, I am forever grateful for the ongoing love and devotion of my family who had to put up with the fact that I spent much of my personal time over the past two years working on this book. To Michele: Thank you for being my life partner for twenty-five years. Your love is a constant source of inspiration and your encouragement through this writing process is greatly appreciated. To my daughter, Isabelle; her husband, Jeff; my stepdaughter, Genevieve; her husband, Jim; their kids, Isaiah and Jake; and my stepson, Sam: Thank you for being incredibly loving kids and grandkids! You give me real hope for the future. To my sister Carine and Phil: Thank you for "being there" through the good and bad times, and for taking care of me when I most needed it. And to my sisters, Tanina and Laura, and their husbands, Richard and Chris: Your love has strengthened me in the face of tragedy. Thank you, thank you, thank you.

—A. Rostain

May 30, 2023

APPENDIX

INTERNET RESOURCES

Authors' website: https://www.macmillanspeakers.com/speaker/drs-b-janet
   -hibbs-anthony-rostain/

Finding Resources for Yourself and Your Young Adult

Skills Training and Upward Mobility Resources for Young Adults

Major Nonprofits Serving Mainly Underrepresented Groups

- NPower: https://www.npower.org
- Per Scholas: https://perscholas.org
- Year Up: https://www.yearup.org

Educational and Skills Groups Expanding Nationally

- AmeriCorps: https://americorps.gov/serve
- Ascendium Education Group: https://www.ascendiumeducation.org
- Bill & Melinda Gates Foundation: https://www.gatesfoundation.org
- CareerOneStop, partner of American Job Center Finder and sponsored

by U.S. Department of Labor: https://www.careeronestop.org/localhelp /americanjobcenters/find-american-job-centers.aspx
- The Chronicle of Higher Education: Different Voices of Student Success Resource Center: https://www.chronicle.com/featured/student -success
- ECMC Foundation: https://www.ecmcfoundation.org
- Gener8tor Upskilling: https://www.gener8tor.com/skills
- Goodwill Industries, Goodwill Rising Together: https://www.goodwill.org
- The Kresge Foundation: https://kresge.org
- Linked Learning Alliance: https://www.linkedlearning.org
- Lumina Foundation: https://www.luminafoundation.org
- Pathways to Prosperity Network: https://archive.jff.org/what-we-do/ impact-stories/pathways-to-prosperity-network/
- P-Tech: https://www.ptech.org
- Rework America Business Network: The Markle Foundation https:// markle.org/about-markle/news-release/RABN/
- Strada Education Foundation: https://stradaeducation.org

Resources for Parents as Mental Health Caregivers

Being a mental health caregiver can be lonely and isolating, full of worry and confusion about where to turn for help and guilt feelings. Support has been proven to combat these feelings. There are support groups to educate yourself about mental illness, to offer a community of compassionate parents, and to gain support when needed. These types of resources can supplement individual or family counseling.

Family Caregiver Alliance: https://www.caregiver.org/
National Alliance on Caregiving: The Circle of Care Guidebook for Mental Health Caregivers: https://www.caregiving.org/guidebook-for-mental -health-caregivers/
National Alliance of Mental Illness: Support Groups for Parents: Family and Friends; Family Support Group; Family-to-Family; Homefront. https://nami.org/

Finding an Effective Provider

Firsthand Referrals

If your family has joined any of the many support groups for parents dealing with mental illness during your young adult's illness, seek firsthand referrals and experience from other parents dealing with the diagnosis.

You may also seek information from the local branch of the National Alliance for Mental Illness (NAMI), the largest grassroots mental health organization dedicated to helping those affected by mental illness. NAMI's local branches in a state or region often retain lists of providers recommended by those families who are members of NAMI and make them available to all inquirers. This referral service does not require membership. NAMI also offers advice on a range of issues on mental health and legal issues via the NAMI Help-Line: https://www.nami.org/Find-Support/NAMI-HelpLine/NAMI-HelpLine-Top-Ten-FAQs, Monday through Friday; and a Crisis Text Line 24/7 for families in crisis: https://www.crisistextline.org.

Professional Organizations

The websites of the major professional organizations that deal with mental health issues provide information on the particular profession, assistance with getting a therapist, and information on mental health problems.

American Association for Marriage and Family Therapy: http://www.aamft.org/iMIS15/AAMFT

American Psychiatric Association: https://www.psychiatry.org

American Psychological Association: http://www.apa.org

Attention Deficit Disorder Association: https://add.org

Children and Adults with ADHD (CHADD): https://chadd.org

Mental Health America (MHA): https://www.mhanational.org

National Association of Social Workers: https://www.socialworkers.org

National Institute of Mental Health: https://www.nimh.nih.gov

National Institute on Alcohol Abuse and Alcoholism: https://www.niaaa.nih.gov

National Institute on Drug Abuse: https://www.drugabuse.gov and www.nida.nih.gov

Anxiety & Depression Association of America (ADAA): https://www.adaa
.org/

Depression and Bipolar Support Alliance (DBSA): https://www.dbsalliance
.org

National Eating Disorders Association (NEDA): https://www.nationaleatingdisorders
.org

International OCD Foundation (OCDF): https://www.iocdf.org

For many more resources, see NAMI's list of top HelpLine resources: http://
www.nami.org/Find-Support/NAMI-HelpLine/Top-25-HelpLine-Resources

U.S. Department of Health and Human Services:

- MentalHealth.gov: https://www.mentalhealth.gov
- The Substance Abuse and Mental Health Services Administration
  (SAMHSA) (https://findtreatment.samhsa.gov) provides an online map-
  based program visitors can use to find facilities in their vicinity. SAMHSA
  Treatment Services Locator provides referrals to low-cost and sliding-scale
  mental health care, substance abuse, and dual diagnosis treatment. Phone
  800-662-4357 to learn more about treatment and services. https://www
  .findtreatment.samhsa.gov
- On May 23, 2023, the Surgeon General issued an advisory on the mental health effects of social media: https://www.hhs.gov/surgeongeneral/
  priorities/youth-mental-health/social-media/index.html
- National Registry of Evidence-Based Programs and Practices (NREPP)
  is a searchable database of mental health and substance abuse interventions to help the public find programs and practices that may best meet
  their needs and learn how to implement them in their communities.
  All interventions in the registry have been independently assessed and
  rated for quality of research and readiness for dissemination. http://
  www.samhsa.gov/nrepp
- Eating Disorders Treatment and Reviews: This site contains the largest
  database on reviews for treatment centers, from both consumers and
  professionals. https://www.edtreatmentreview.com

Critical Resources and Helplines

Mental Health Support and Suicide Prevention

The American Foundation for Suicide Prevention provides referrals to support groups, mental health professionals, resources on loss, and suicide-prevention information. Phone: 1-888-333-2377. https://afsp.org

Mental Health America (MHA), https://www.mhanational.org, has an excellent website with screening tools for early detection and intervention and connections to local services.

NAMI Crisis Text Line: Text NAMI or START to 741-741. The Crisis Text Line will connect a family with a trained crisis counselor to receive free 24-7 crisis support via text message. https://www.crisistextline.org

National Suicide Prevention Lifeline at 1-800-273-TALK and http://suicide preventionlifeline.org. Calls made to this twenty-four-hour hotline are routed to the caller's nearest crisis center. https://suicideprevention lifeline.org

YouMatter, http://www.youmatter.suicidepreventionlifeline.org, is a National Suicide Prevention Lifeline site for young adults, complete with a blog where visitors can share problems and receive support.

What If a Young Adult Needs Hospitalization?

Specific questions to ask your doctor: "Questions to Ask Before Psychiatric Hospitalization of Your Child or Adolescent," available at http://www .aacap.org/AACAP/Families_and_Youth/Facts_for_Families/FFF-Guide /11-Questions-To-Ask-Before-Psychiatric-Hospitalization-Of-Your-Child -Or-Adolescent-032.aspx

Recovery from Psychosis

National Institute of Mental Health (NIMH): https://www.nimh.nih.gov /index.shtml

NAVIGATE—first episode psychosis treatment: https://navigateconsul tants.org/

RAISE—Recovery After an Initial Schizophrenia Episode: https://www
.nih.gov/news-events/news-releases/team-based-treatment-first
-episode-psychosis-found-be-high-value

APPS

What's the Right App for You?

There are a million and a half apps available for download from the Apple
App Store, Google Play Store, and the individual phone's app store. Around
35,000 of those apps are health related, including apps to track wellness, exercise, diet, and nutrition; then a few thousand mental health apps from which
to choose. As we write this, new apps are added, modified, or removed daily.
While apps provide highly accessible and inexpensive nudges to prompt wellness behaviors and mental health takeaways, the downside, with rare exceptions, is that developers provide no information on the quality or efficacy of
an app beyond users' reviews, star ratings, and testimonials. Only a few apps
have any kind of research to support their effectiveness. Apps are likely to be
more effective when adopted into f2f (family to family) therapy.

We offer a short list of commonly agreed upon "good" mental health apps,
and then identify curated libraries of apps for more in-depth search.

Libraries of Apps

While the app stores have search tools, selecting an app to try will be a cumbersome process, as there are thousands of apps available to evaluate. Fortunately,
there are several libraries of curated and limited collections of apps and relevant
search methods (filters). When you find an app, you will usually have to copy
its name and search the app stores. Here are a few app resources to consider.

1. NYC WELL

https://nycwell.cityofnewyork.us/en/app-library

Only thirteen apps, but the most popular are listed, with clear simple descriptions, evaluations, and links to the stores. A good starting place to see the
variety of approaches, goals, and methods among apps. NYC Well also has "free

digital mental health resources for the duration of the Covid-19 pandemic" at https://nycwell.cityofnewyork.us/en/covid-19-digital-mental-health-resources/. While some of the thirteen programs overlap the above, they are all worth a look.

2. ONE MIND

https://onemindpsyberguide.org

One Mind reviews about 250 mental health apps, utilizing user-friendly multiple search terms (conditions, treatments) and filters (cost, audience, etc.). One Mind also provides app tool kits, which are a collection of fourteen apps, each opening to an infographic with three to fifteen apps showing their names, logos, and a brief description (https://onemindpsyberguide.org/resources/app-toolkits).

3. MIND-M-HEALTH INDEX AND NAVIGATION DATABASE

https://mindapps.org

This website offers a brief background on how they evaluate apps. It nicely explains how their experts apply the 105 objective criteria from the American Psychiatric Association to apps to create the MIND database of 687 apps. To find an app, it offers eighty-eight search filters and so will take time to learn, but if you need something specialized, it is worth the time investment.

4. UCSF DEPARTMENT OF PSYCHIATRY AND BEHAVIORAL SCIENCES

https://psych.ucsf.edu/copingresources/apps

Links to seventeen popular apps and therapeutic programs of which an app is a part: eight for meditation and relaxation, eight for coping with anxiety and depression, and one on insomnia.

5. PRO.PSYCOM

https://pro.psycom.net/clinician-lifestyle-practice/mental-health-apps-how -to-use-in-treatment

The article "Mental Health Apps: How to Use Apps as Treatment Adjuncts" by Alexis Pellek. Pellek summarizes issues such as privacy, choosing apps, and integrating apps into one's practice, and offers descriptions and links to apps and programs for half a dozen of conditions we think of as chronic: posttraumatic stress disorder, eating disorders, schizophrenia, substance use, and serious mental illness.

Next Steps

Download and test an app or three. Adopt a try-and-discard approach and enjoy your continual learning about how developers have handled the demands of the problem. Road test the app with a colleague or trapped family member. Better reactions and feedback will allow recognition and response to the app's limitations. Remember both you and the client must buy in to continue to use it. Do not focus on curing the problem. Apps are not therapy (yet?). However, an app that supports fuller understanding and amelioration is valuable.

REFERENCES

Pooja Chandrashekar, "Do Mental Health Mobile Apps Work: Evidence and Recommendations for Designing High-Efficacy Mental Health Mobile Apps." *mHealth* 4, no. 6 (2018): doi: 10.21037/mhealth.2018.03.02.

Statista, "Most Popular Apple App Store Categories in March 2015, by Share of Available Apps" (2015), http://www.statista.com/statistics/270291/popular-categories-in-the-app-store/.

Android and iPhone Apps for Mood Disorders

Apps recommended by the APA (2014):

Bipolar disorder: Healthline.com lists the best iPhone and Android apps for bipolar disorder, including apps to monitor sleep, medication, and mood over time, and apps to explain the diagnosis. For the complete list, see "The Best Bipolar Disorder Apps of 2017," http://www.healthline.com/health/bipolar-disorder/top-iphone-android-apps#1.

Breathe 2 Relax: Breathing techniques to relieve stress. https://itunes.apple.com/us/app/breathe2relax/id425720246

CBT*ABC way: Cognitive-behavioral therapy apps in Spanish and English, iTunes, $6.99. Go to TikalBayTek: http://www.tikalbaytek.com

Headspace: A meditation app that helps people begin and establish a meditation practice. https://www.headspace.com

PRIME (Personalized Real-Time Intervention for Motivation Enhancement):
A Facebook-like mobile app that connects members to a circle of peers
and professional clinicians who can assist as needed. Its goal is to inspire
young people (ages fourteen to thirty) who have recently been diagnosed
with schizophrenia to increase social connection to reduce depression
and symptoms. May be adapted to other mental disorders. https://itunes
.apple.com/us/app/ucsf-prime/id1031402495?mt=8

PTSD Coach: https://itunes.apple.com/us/app/ptsd-coach/id430646302?mt=8

ReliefLink: An app developed by Emory University for suicide prevention
and more general support for improving mental health. iTunes, free:
https://itunes.apple.com/us/app/relieflink/id721474553?mt=8

Step Away: Mobile intervention for alcohol addiction. iTunes, $4.99: http://
stepaway.biz

What's My M3: This app offers a free three-minute checklist and assessment for several mental health problems. Better monitoring of mood
and mental health can be an important tool. https://whatsmym3.com

Online Young Adult Peer Support & Therapy

7 Cups: https://www.7cups.com

Instant support through text and online with trained peer listeners, licensed
therapists, and peer support for a variety of problems.

Mindstrong Health: https://mindstronghealth.com

Former NIMH director Dr. Tom Insel is involved in smartphone-based behavioral health care to intervene preventatively in the treatment of a
range of behavioral health disorders.

Evidence-Based Education on
Mental Health and Interventions

Mental Health First Aid (http://www.mentalhealthfirstaid.org/cs/about/research)
is a peer-reviewed, international, and evidence-based program. This eight-hour
course teaches laypeople how to identify, understand, and respond to signs of
mental illnesses and substance use disorders. A search tool helps people identify courses near their location: https://www.mentalhealthfirstaid.org/cs/take
-a-course/find-a-course/.

Mental Health First Aid USA is also listed on the Substance Abuse and

Mental Health Services Administration's National Registry of Evidence-Based Programs and Practices (NREPP), http://nrepp.samhsa.gov/02_about.aspx.

The NREPP is an important resource as well, listing over seventy evidence-based programs with reliable information on mental health and substance abuse interventions. New program profiles are continually being added, so the registry is always growing. See https://nrepp.samhsa.gov/landing.aspx to access the latest updates.

UNDERSTANDING AND OVERCOMING STIGMA

Research

The National Academies of Science, Engineering, and Medicine in 2016 delivered to the Substance Abuse and Mental Health Services Administration a study outlining six recommendations urging them and other government agencies to focus more on reducing stigma.[1] The report found that, currently, U.S. public and private anti-stigma efforts are "largely uncoordinated and poorly evaluated."

The key recommendations are:

- The federal Department of Health & Human Services should take the lead on stigma-reduction initiatives.
- Research should explore how to design and test communications programs and large-scale surveys tracking people's beliefs.
- Leaders should gather input on initiatives from people who have experienced mental illness.
- Efforts should include grassroots work since research shows personal contact is more effective than education alone.
- Efforts should also include peer support services since evidence suggests that people who use these services are more likely to access other kinds of mental health care.

Resources for Families and Young Adults for Fighting Stigma

Active Minds: Originating in 2003 with campus outreach that began the conversation about mental health issues, Active Minds has expanded its mission and programs for young professionals at work and for communities. Through national programs, Active Minds aims to remove the stigma that surrounds mental health issues and create a comfortable environment for an open conversation about mental health issues for young people nationwide. Their mission is to empower youth and young adults to speak openly about mental health in order to educate others and encourage help-seeking. http://activeminds.org/programs

JED Foundation: https://www.jedfoundation.org/who-we-are. Also on Facebook at https://www.facebook.com/JedFoundation and Instagram at https://www.instagram.com/jedfoundation.

The NAMI StigmaFree campaign urges individuals, companies, organizations, and campuses to create an American culture in which the stigma that is often associated with mental health conditions is ended and replaced by hope and support for recovery. See more at: https://www.nami.org/Press-Media/Press-Releases/2015/National-Alliance-on-Mental-Illness-Launches-Stigm.

Autism Speaks: https://www.autismspeaks.org. Reducing stigma through global awareness and advocacy to increase research and access to care and support for affected individuals and their families.

Privacy Laws Affecting Information Privacy and Medical Care of Young Adults

There are two critical laws affecting the privacy of medical and education records: the Health Insurance Portability and Accountability Act (HIPAA) Privacy Rule related to the use and disclosure of information and the Family Educational Rights and Privacy Act (FERPA).

HIPAA is intended to protect the privacy of a medical patient's identifiable health records, including electronic health-care transactions. It gives patients the right to inspect their own medical records and request amendments to medical records. This law also restricts the release of confidential communication with the patient and the patient's medical records. To be in compliance with HIPAA, organizations must also protect students' health information.

FERPA, on the other hand, provides protection of students' educational records and is specific to education institutions that receive federal funds.

(FERPA also applies when a student studies abroad.) Simply being a student's parent won't allow you to sign tax returns or leases for the coming year on his or her behalf.

Clearly worded summaries of how HIPAA and FERPA affect students and families can be found on the website of the American School Counselor Association (ASCA), https://www.schoolcounselor.org/Magazines/July-August-2010/HIPAA-or-FERPA-or-Not, and the World Privacy Forum, https://www.worldprivacyforum.org/2015/02/student-privacy-101-health-privacy-in-schools-what-law-applies/.

Given that schools may have sensitive health information—or request such information from students and parents—it is important for families to understand which law covers health record privacy for school records. The answer is often complex, because both laws can apply to this information. In some cases, no privacy law applies to the health records. Basically:

- HIPAA, the Health Information Portability and Accountability Act, applies to some school health records some of the time. More generally, it prohibits sharing of medical information subject to patient consent outside the school records context once a student comes of legal age.
- FERPA, the Family Educational Rights and Privacy Act, applies to most school health records and academic records most of the time.
- No privacy law applies to some private school health records some of the time.

The Association of State and Territorial Health Officials (ASTHO) provides more detailed information about the interaction of these laws, along a chart displaying a snapshot of the rights, duties, and limitations imposed by FERPA and HIPAA. See the ASTHO Public Health Access to Student Health Data Issue Brief (http://www.astho.org/Programs/Preparedness/Public-Health-Emergency-Law/Public-Health-and-Schools-Toolkit/Public-Health-Access-to-Student-Health-Data/) and the text of the federal laws and regulations for more detailed information.

ASTHO is the national nonprofit organization representing public health agencies in the United States, the U.S. Territories, and the District of Columbia, and over 100,000 public health professionals these agencies employ.

Advance Directives for a Young Adult

The eighteenth birthday has many implications, but one of the most important—and most often overlooked—is that parents no longer have any inherent legal authority over the young adult. While medical professionals have discretion to share information without the patient's permission, some who are risk averse will not. So, in an emergency, telling medical professionals that you are someone's parent will not allow you to make medical decisions for them. And if a young adult is abroad, simply being his parent won't allow you to sign tax returns or leases on their behalf.

There is a simple solution. By age eighteen, parents should help every young adult either download and sign free forms or consult with an attorney and have three important documents drafted for them: a durable power of attorney, a health-care proxy, and a HIPAA authorization. These documents allow a young adult to decide who should have the power to make which decisions for them if needed and will provide both the young adult and the parents with a great deal of peace of mind.

To record his or her medical preferences, your teen will need to complete written documents called advance directive forms. There are two types of advance directives, and it's important to have both:

1. A living will spells out what types of medical treatment a person wants at the end of life if they're unable to speak for themselves. It tells medical professionals a person's wishes regarding specific decisions, such as whether to accept mechanical ventilation.

2. A health-care power of attorney appoints someone to make health-care decisions—and not just decisions regarding life-prolonging treatments—on one's behalf. The appointed health-care agent (also called an attorney-in-fact or proxy) becomes the patient's spokesman and advocate on a range of medical treatments the patient sets out in the document. Of course, the health-care agent makes decisions only when the patient can't communicate on their own. This type of document is sometimes referred to as a health-care proxy, appointment of a health-care agent, or durable power of attorney for health care. It is different from a regular durable power of attorney, which typically covers only financial matters.

If a young adult has a history of a mental disorder, parents may also want to ask about a psychiatric advance directive (PAD). This legal document permits a second party to act on a young adult's behalf if they become acutely ill and unable to make decisions about treatment. The PAD is written by your loved one when they are currently "competent." It details the individual's preferences for treatment should they become unable to make such decisions due to their mental health condition.

For more information on advance planning, see NAMI's website on crisis planning at http://www.nami.org/Find-Support/Family-Members-and-Caregivers /Being-Prepared-for-a-Crisis#sthash.94I5iwsr.dpuf and the AARP fact page, How to Prepare With Your Adult Child for Emergencies, at http://www.aarp .org/home-family/friends-family/info-2016/how-to-prepare-with-your-adult -child-for-emergencies-mq.html.

NOTES

INTRODUCTION

1. Elena G. van Stee, "Parenting Young Adults Across Social Class: A Review and Synthesis," *Sociological Compass* 16, no. 9 (August 2022): 1–16, https://doi.org/10.1111/soc4.13021.

2. Richard Fry, Jeffrey S. Passel, and D'Vera Cohn, "A Majority of Young Adults in the U.S. Live with Their Parents for the First Time Since the Great Depression," Pew Research Center, last modified September 4, 2020, https://www.pewresearch.org/short-reads/2020/09/04/a-majority-of-young-adults-in-the-u-s-live-with-their-parents-for-the-first-time-since-the-great-depression/.

3. Cecilia M. W. Livesey and Anthony L. Rostain, "Involving Parents/Family in Treatment During the Transition from Late Adolescence to Young Adulthood: Rationale, Strategies, Ethics, and Legal Issues," *Child Adolescent Psychiatry Clin N Am* 26, no. 2 (April 2017): 199–216, https://doi.org/10.1016/j.chc.2016.12.006.

4. Stella Sechopoulos, "Most in the U.S. Say Young Adults Today Face More Challenges Than Their Parents' Generation in Some Key Areas," Pew Research Center, last modified February 28, 2022, https://www.pewresearch.org/short-reads/2022/02/28/most-in-the-u-s-say-young-adults-today-face-more-challenges-than-their-parents-generation-in-some-key-areas/#:~:text=About%20seven%2Din%2Dten%20Americans,survey%20conducted%20in%20October%202021.

5. Scott R. Eliason, Jeylan T. Mortimer, and Mike Vuolo, "The Transition to Adulthood: Life Course Structures and Subjective Perceptions," *Social Psychology Quarterly* 78, no. 3 (2015): 205–27, www.ncbi.nlm.nih.gov/pmc/articles/PMC4591543.

6. Van Stee, "Parenting Young Adults," 1–16.

7. Stephanie Coontz, *The Way We Never Were: American Families and the Nostalgia Trap* (New York: Basic Books, 2016).

8. Steven Mintz, *The Prime of Life: A History of Modern Adulthood* (Cambridge, MA: Belknap Press of Harvard University, 2015).

9. Kim Parker and Ruth Igielnik, "On the Cusp of Adulthood and Facing an Uncertain Future: What We Know About Gen Z So Far," Pew Research Center, last modified May 14, 2020, https://www.pewresearch.org/social-trends/2020/05/14/on-the-cusp-of-adulthood-and-facing-an-uncertain-future-what-we-know-about-gen-z-so-far-2/.

10. Frank J. Infurna et al., "Historical Change in Midlife Health, Well-Being, and Despair: Cross-Cultural and Socioeconomic Comparisons," *American Psychologist* 76, no. 6 (2021): 870–87, https://doi.org/10.1037/amp0000817.

11. "Americans Anticipate Higher Stress at the Start of 2023 and Grade Their Mental Health Worse," American Psychiatric Association, last modified December 21, 2022, https://www.psychiatry.org/news-room/news-releases/americans-anticipate-higher-stress-at-the-start-of.

12. Ashley M. Ebbert, Nina L. Kumar, Suniya S. Luthar, "Complexities in Adjustment Patterns Among the 'Best and the Brightest': Risk and Resilience in the Context of High Achieving Schools," *Research in Human Development* 16, no. 1 (2019): 21–34, https://doi.org/10.1080/15427609.2018.1541376.

1. THE NEW NORMAL

1. Kurt Lewin, *Field Theory in Social Science: Selected Theoretical Papers* (New York: Harper & Row, 1951).

2. National Student Clearinghouse Research Center. PDP Insights, August, 2022. https://nscresearchcenter.org/wp-content/uploads/PDPInsightsReport.pdf?utm_source=Iterable&utm_medium=email&utm_campaign=campaign_4792089_nl_DailyBriefing_date_20220803&cid=db&source=ams&sourceid=

3. Sigmund Freud, *Analysis Terminable and Interminable*, sect. 5 (1937); reprinted in *The Standard Edition of the Complete Psychological Works of Sigmund Freud,* vol. 23, ed. James Strachey and Anna Freud (London: Hogarth Press, 1964), quoted in *The New Penguin Dictionary of Modern Quotations* by Robert Andrews (New York: Penguin Books, 2001).

4. Jeffrey Arnett, "Emerging Adulthood: A Theory of Development from the Late Teens Through the Twenties," *American Psychologist* 55 (2000): 469–80.

5. Jeffrey Arnett, ed., *The Oxford Handbook of Emerging Adulthood* (New York: Oxford University Press, 2016).

6. Belle Liang and Tim Klein, *How to Navigate Life: The New Science of Finding Your Way in School, Career, and Beyond* (New York: St. Martin's Press, 2022), 25.

7. Liang, *How to Navigate Life*, 25.

8. Liang, *How to Navigate Life*, 25.

9. Soraya Hakimi, Elaheh Hejazi, and Mosoud Lavasani, "The Relationships Be-

tween Personality Traits and Academic Achievement," *Procedia—Social and Behavioral Sciences* 29 (2011): 836–845, https://pdf.sciencedirectassets.com/277811/1-s2.0-S1877042811X00228 /1-s2.0-S187704281102773X/main.pdf.

10. Thomas J. Schofield et al., "Parent Personality and Positive Parenting as Predictors of Positive Adolescent Personality Development Over Time," *Merrill-Palmer Quarterly* 58, no. 2 (April 2012): 255–83, https://doi.org/10.1353/mpq.2012.0008.

11. Diana Baumrind, "Patterns of Parental Authority and Adolescent Autonomy," *New Directions for Child and Adolescent Development* 108, no. 61 (2005).

12. Robert Kegan, *The Evolving Self: Problem and Process in Human Development* (Cambridge, MA: Harvard University Press, 1983).

13. Bobby Duffy, "The Bunk of Generational Talk," *The Wall Street Journal*, last modified October 22, 2021, https://www.wsj.com/articles/the-bunk-of-generational-talk-11634914564.

14. Bobby Duffy, "Who Cares About Climate Change? Attitudes Across the Generations," The Policy Institute, King's College London (September 2021), https://www.kcl.ac.uk/policy-institute/assets/who-cares-about-climate-change.pdf.

15. Duffy, Bobby. *The Generation Myth: Why When You're Born Matters Less Than What You Think.* (New York: Basic Books, 2021).

16. Mintz, *The Prime of Life.*

17. Alison Gopnik, *The Gardener and the Carpenter: What the New Science of Child Development Tells Us About the Relationship Between Parents and Children* (New York: Farrar, Straus and Giroux, 2016): 23.

18. Arielle Eiser, "The Crisis on Campus," *American Psychological Association* 42, no. 8 (September 2011): 18, https://www.apa.org/monitor/2011/09/crisis-campus.

19. Katherine Newman, *The Accordion Family: Boomerang Kids, Anxious Parents, and the Private Toll of Global Competition* (Boston: Beacon Press, 2012).

20. Robin Marantz Henig, "What Is It About 20-Somethings?" *The New York Times Magazine*, last modified August 18, 2010, www.nytimes.com/2010/08/22/magazine/22Adulthood-t.html.

21. Stephanie Saul, "College Enrollment Drops, Even as the Pandemic's Effects Ebb," *The New York Times*, last modified May 26, 2022, https://www.nytimes.com/2022/05/26 /us/college-enrollment.html#:~:text=Overall%2C%20enrollment%20at%20public%20 colleges,351%2C000%20students%20or%207.8%20percent.

22. Elissa Nadworny, "College Enrollment Plummets During the Pandemic. This Fall, It's Even Worse," NPR, last modified October 26, 2021, https://www.npr .org/2021/10/26/1048955023/college-enrollment-down-pandemic-economy.

23. "Some College, No Credential Student Outcomes, Annual Progress Report— Academic Year 2020/21," National Student Clearinghouse Research Center, last modified May 2022, https://nscresearchcenter.org/wpcontent/uploads/SCNCReportMay2022.pdf.

24. "The Lancet: COVID-19 Pandemic Led to Stark Rise in Depressive and Anxiety Disorders Globally in 2020, with Women and Younger People Most Affected," The

Institute of Health Metrics and Evaluation, last modified October 8, 2021, https://www
.healthdata.org/news-events/newsroom/news-releases/lancet-covid-19-pandemic
-led-stark-rise-depressive-and-anxiety#:~:text=First%20global%20estimates%20of%20
impact,were%20due%20to%20the%20pandemic.

25. Scott Keeter, "Many Americans Continue to Experience Mental Health Difficulties as Pandemic Enters Second Year," Pew Research Center, last modified March
16, 2021, https://www.pewresearch.org/facttank/2021/03/16/many-americans-continue
-to-experience-mental-health-difficulties-aspandemic-enters-second-year/.

26. V. J. Felitti et al., "Adverse Childhood Experiences and Health Outcomes in
Adults: The Ace Study," *Journal of Family and Consumer Sciences* 90, no. 3 (Fall 1998): 31.

27. Suniya Luthar, Lucia Ciciolla, and Bin Suh, "Adverse Childhood Experiences from
High-Achieving High Schools: Appraising Vulnerability Processes Towards Fostering Resilience," *American Psychologist* 72, no. 2 (2021): 300–313, https://doi.org/10.1037/amp0000754.

2. EMERGING ADULTHOOD AS A DEVELOPMENTAL STAGE

1. Jeffrey Arnett, "Emerging Adulthood: A Theory of Development from the Late
Teens Through the Twenties," *American Psychologist* 55, no. 5 (2000): 469–80.

2. M. W. Pratt and M. L. Mastuba, *The Life Story: Domains of Identity and Personality Development in Emerging Adulthood* (New York: Oxford University Press, 2018).

3. Erik Erikson, *Childhood and Society* (New York: W. W. Norton & Co., 1950).

4. Arnett, *Emerging Adulthood*.

5. Stella Sechopoulos, "In Which Key Areas Do US Adults Think Life Is Harder for
Younger Generations?" World Economic Forum, last modified March 10, 2022, https://
www.weforum.org/agenda/2022/03/young-adults-future-finance-housing-inflation.

6. https://iop.harvard.edu/youth-poll/41st-edition-spring-2021.

7. Mroz M. Lind et al., "Emerging Adults' Outlook on the Future in the Midst of
COVID-19: The Role of Personality Profiles," *Journal of Adult Development* 29 (2022): 108–120.

8. See, for example, G. H. Elder Jr. and M. J. Shanahan, "The Life Course and Human Development," in *Handbook of Child Psychology: Theoretical Models of Human Development*,
ed. R. M. Lerner and W. Damon (Hoboken, NJ: John Wiley & Sons Inc., 2006), 665–715.

9. Mark McConville, *Failure to Launch* (New York: G. P. Putnam's Sons, 2020): ch. 4.

10. McConville, *Failure to Launch*, ch. 5.

11. D. P. McAdams, "Life Authorship in Emerging Adulthood," in *The Oxford Handbook of Emerging Adulthood*, Jeffrey Arnett, ed. (New York: Oxford University Press, 2014).

12. Larry J. Nelson and Laura M. Walker, "Flourishing and Floundering in Emerging Adult
College Students," *Emerging Adulthood* 1 (2012): 67–78, https://doi.org/10.1177/2167696812470938.

3. TRUTH OR TRUTHY

1. T. S. Fiske, "Prejudice, Discrimination, and Stereotyping," in *Noba Textbook Series: Psychology*, ed. R. Biswas Diener and E. Diener (Champaign, IL: DEF Publishers, 2022), http://noba.to/jfkx7nrd.

2. Hugo Mercier and Dan Sperber, *The Enigma of Reason* (Boston: Harvard University Press, 2019).

3. Nathan Rabin, "Stephen Colbert," AV Club, last modified January 25, 2006, www.avclub.com/stephen-colbert-1798208958.

4. B. Duffy, *The Generation Myth* (New York: Basic Books, 2021): 33.

5. P. Tough, *The Years That Matter Most: How College Makes or Breaks Us* (New York: Houghton Mifflin Harcourt, 2019).

6. Everytown Research & Policy, "Child & Teen Gun Safety," Everytown for Gun Safety Action Fund, accessed May 14, 2022, https://everytownresearch.org/issue/child-teen-safety.

7. Duffy, "The Bunk."

8. Jean M. Twenge, *iGen: Why Today's Super-Connected Kids Are Growing Up Less Rebellious, More Tolerant, Less Happy—and Completely Unprepared for Adulthood—and What That Means for the Rest of Us* (New York: Atria Books, 2017).

9. Duffy, "The Bunk."

10. "Generational Divide over Climate Action a Myth, Study Finds," King's College London, last modified September 15, 2021, https://www.kcl.ac.uk/news/generational-divide-over-climate-action-a-myth-study-finds.

11. U.S. millennials homeownership—statistics & facts. https://www.statista.com/topics/4403/millennials-and-real-estate-in-the-us/

12. Debra Kamin, "The Market for Single-Family Rentals Grows as Homeownership Wanes," *The New York Times*, last modified October 22, 2021, https://www.nytimes.com/2021/10/22/realestate/single-family-rentals.html.

13. Duffy, "The Bunk."

14. Tara Westover, "I Am Not Proof of the American Dream," *The New York Times*, last modified February 6, 2022, https://www.nytimes.com/2022/02/02/opinion/tara-westover-educated-student-debt.html?searchResultPosition=6.

15. H. L. Mencken, "The Divine Afflatus," *New York Evening Mail*, November 1917.

16. Daniel Kahneman, *Thinking, Fast and Slow* (New York: Farrar, Straus and Giroux, 2011).

17. Duffy, "The Bunk."

18. Chris Mooney, "Stephen Colbert, Scientific Pioneer," *Huffpost*, last modified April 5, 2012, www.huffpost.com/entry/stephen-colbert-truthiness_b_1405153; and Chris

Mooney, "The Science of Why We Don't Believe Science," *Mother Jones*, May–June 2011, www.motherjones.com/politics/2011/04/denial-science-chris-mooney.

19. Association of Executive Search and Leadership Consultants, "Checking Your Blind Spot: Ways to Find and Fix Unconscious Bias," *Executive Talent*, accessed May 7, 2022, www.aesc.org/insights/magazine/article/checking-your-blind-spots.

20. Kahneman, *Thinking, Fast and Slow.*

21. Alison Gopnik, "Why Children Learn Better than Adults," *The Wall Street Journal*, November 6, 2021.

22. Alison Gopnik, *The Gardener and the Carpenter: What the New Science of Child Development Tells Us About the Relationship Between Parents and Children* (New York: Farrar, Straus and Giroux, 2016).

23. Gopnik, "Why Children Learn."

4. CHANGING THE RULES

1. Duffy, "The Bunk."

2. Susan Pinker, "Do We Really Get Mellower with Age?" *The Wall Street Journal*, January 7–8, 2023, C5.

3. Steven Stosny, "Blind Spots," *Psychology Today*, last modified May 13, 2018, https://www.psychologytoday.com/us/blog/anger-in-the-age-entitlement/201805/blind-spots.

4. Andrew Solomon, *Far from the Tree: Parents, Children, and the Search for Identity* (New York: Simon & Schuster, 2012).

5. Stella Chess and Alexander Thomas, *Temperament in Clinical Practice* (New York: Guilford Press, 1986).

6. Nellie Bowes, "How to Feel Nothing Now, in Order to Feel More Later: A Day of Dopamine Fasting in San Francisco," *The New York Times*, last modified November 7, 2019, www.nytimes.com/2019/11/07/style/dopamine-fasting.html.

5. GET A JOB

1. Fiona Hill, *There Is Nothing for You Here: Finding Opportunity in the Twenty-First Century* (New York: HarperCollins, 2021).

2. Andrew Cherlin, *Labor's Love Lost: The Rise and Fall of the Working-Class Family in America* (New York: Russell Sage Foundation, 2014).

3. J. Fuller, C. Langer, and M. Siegelman, "Skills-Based Hiring Is on the Rise," *Harvard Business Review*, last modified February 11, 2022, https://hbr.org/2022/02/skills-based-hiring-is-on-the-rise.

4. Jeffrey R. Young, "How Childhood Has Changed (and How That Impacts Edu-

cation)," EdSurge, last modified July 11, 2017, https://www.edsurge.com/news/2017-07-11
-how-childhood-has-changed-and-how-that-impacts-education.

5. Van Stee, "Parenting Young Adults," 1–16.

6. Completing College: National and State Reports, National Student Clearinghouse Research Center, last modified October 2, 2023 https://nscresearchcenter.org/
completing-college/completions_report_2021/ access date: 10/2/23

7. Van Stee, "Parenting Young Adults," 1–16.

8. "Some College, No Credential Student Outcomes: Annual Progress Report 2020–
2021," National Student Clearinghouse Research Center, issued May 10, 2022, https://
nscresearchcenter.org/wp-content/uploads/SCNCReportMay2022.pdf.

9. Elissa Nadworny, "In 'Never Too Late,' Finally, a Guide for Adults Going to College," NPR, last modified December, 23, 2018, https://www.npr.org/2018/12/23/678799694
/in-never-too-late-finally-a-guide-for-adults-going-to-college.

10. National Student Clearinghouse Research Center, "Some College."

11. National Student Clearinghouse Research Center, "Some College."

12. J. S. Hacker, *The Great Risk Shift: The New Economic Insecurity and the Decline of the American Dream* (New York: Oxford University Press, 2019).

13. "Total Fall Enrollment in Degree-Granting Postsecondary Institutions, by Attendance, Status, Sex of Student, and Control of Institution: Selected Years, 1947 through
2019," National Center for Educational Statistics, last modified October 2, 2023. https://
nces.ed.gov/programs/digest/d19/tables/dt19_303.10.asp.

14. Margaret Calahan and Laura Perna, "Report: Low-Income, First-Generation
Students Growing Barriers to Success," Indicators of Higher Education Equity in the
United States, 2019, http://pellinstitute.org/indicators/reports_2019.shtml.

15. Peter N. Stearns, "A 'Crisis' of Student Anxiety? The Challenges to Student Mental
Health Are Real. They Are Also Decades in the Making," *The Chronicle of Higher Education,* last
modified September 1, 2022; https://www.chronicle.com/article/a-crisis-of-student-anxiety.

16. Kevin Carey, "The College Degree Is in Shambles," *The Chronicle of Higher Education,* last modified November 26, 2021, https://www.chronicle.com/article/the-college
-degree-is-in-shambles?.

17. Richard Fry and Amanda Barroso, "Amid Coronavirus Outbreak, Nearly Three-
in-Ten Young People Are Neither Working Nor in School," Pew Research Center, last
modified July 29, 2020, https://www.pewresearch.org/short-reads/2020/07/29/amid-corona
virus-outbreak-nearly-three-in-ten-young-people-are-neither-working-nor-in-school/.

18. National Student Clearinghouse Research Center, "Some College."

19. "The Hidden U.S. COVID-19 Pandemic: Orphaned Children," Centers for Disease Control and Prevention, last modified October 7, 2021, https://www.cdc.gov/media
/releases/2021/p1007-covid-19-orphaned-children.html.

20. Saul, "College Enrollment."

21. "Spring 2023, Current Term Enrollment Estimates," National Student Clearinghouse, last modified May 24, 2023, https://nscresearchcenter.org/current-term-enrollment-estimates/.

22. Lee Gardner, "What's a College Degree Worth? Better Data Is Coming to a Dashboard Near You. Will Students Use It?" *The Chronicle of Higher Education* 69, no. 19 (May 2023): 22–25.

23. Steve Lohr, "A 4-Year Degree Isn't Quite the Job Requirement It Used to Be," *The New York Times*, last modified April 8, 2022, https://www.nytimes.com/2022/04/08/business/hiring-without-college-degree.html.

24. National Student Clearinghouse Research Center, "Some College."

25. Van Stee, "Parenting Young Adults," 1–16.

26. Video interview conducted and recorded with Mr. Steve Greene, Johnson O'Connor Research Foundation, https://www.jocrf.org/, by B. Janet Hibbs on April 25, 2022.

27. Telephone interview conducted and recorded with Mr. Peter Doris by B. Janet Hibbs on May 20, 2022.

28. Video interview conducted and recorded with Mr. Bill Holland by B. Janet Hibbs on March 25, 2022.

29. Ryan Craig, "A Brief History (and Future) of Online Degrees," *Forbes*, last modified June 23, 2015, https://www.forbes.com/sites/ryancraig/2015/06/23/a-brief-history-and-future-of-online-degrees/?sh=55eec4f248d9.

30. Mintz, *The Prime of Life*.

31. Van Stee, "Parenting Young Adults," 1–16.

32. Lohr, "A 4-Year Degree."

33. Michael Itzkowitz, "The Accreditation in College Is Broken: Lax Standards Threaten Higher Education's Credibility," *The Chronicle of Higher Education* 68, no. 13 (March 2022), https://www.chronicle.com/article/the-accreditation-system-is-broken.

34. Julie Jargon, "For College Students, LinkedIn FOMO Is Real—These Tips Will Help," *The Wall Street Journal*, last modified March 12, 2022, https://www.wsj.com/articles/for-college-students-linkedin-fomo-is-realthese-tips-will-help-11647045049.

35. Emma Goldberg, "All of Those Quitters? They're at Work," *The New York Times*, last modified May 15, 2022, https://www.nytimes.com/2022/05/13/business/great-resignation-jobs.html?searchResultPosition=1.

36. Belle Liang and Tim Klein, *The Five Purpose Principles* (New York: St. Martin's Press, 2022).

37. Kate Holton and Sinead Cruise, "Onboarding During COVID: New Hires Grapple with Office Politics from Home," Reuters, last modified September 28, 2020, https://www.reuters.com/article/us-health-coronavirus-companies-onboardi/onboarding-during-covid-new-hires-grapple-with-office-politics-from-home-idUSKCN26F2GV.

38. "ECMC Survey: 4-Year College Has Lost Its Luster Among Teens," Contractor,

accessed July 9, 2022, https://www.contractormag.com/around-the-web/article/21181560/ecmc-survey-4year-college-has-lost-its-luster-among-teens.

39. Georgia Goble, "Gen Z Dread: Why Are Young People So Scared?" Varsity, last modified September 12, 2020, https://www.varsity.co.uk/features/19780.

40. Lohr, "A 4-Year Degree."

6. EXECUTIVE FUNCTIONS AND YOUR TWENTYSOMETHING'S PATH TOWARD SELF-ACTUALIZATION

1. Russell Barkley, *ADHD and the Nature of Self-Control* (New York: Guilford Press, 1997).

2. "Remarkable Case of Injury," *American Phrenology Journal* 13 (1851): 89, cited in Fred G. Barker II, "Phineas Among the Phrenologists: The American Crowbar Case and Nineteenth-Century Theories of Cerebral Localization," *Journal of Neurosurgery* 82 (1995): 672–82.

3. Russell Barkley, *Barkley Deficits of Executive Functioning Scale (BDEFS) for Adults* (New York: Guilford Press, 2011).

4. Robert M. Roth, Peter K. Isquith, Gerard A. Gioia, "Behavior Rating Inventory of Executive Function®—Adult Version," PAR, https://www.parinc.com/Products/Pkey/25.

5. https://www.additudemag.com/executive-function-disorder-in-adults-symptoms/
https://add.org/executive-function-disorder/
https://ldaamerica.org/disabilities/executive-functioning/

6. Joel Nigg, *Getting Ahead of ADHD: What Next-Generation Science Says About Treatments That Work—and How You Can Make Them Work for Your Child* (New York: Guilford Press, 2017).

7. Joel Nigg, "Beyond Genes: Leveraging Sleep, Exercise and Nutrition to Improve ADHD," *ADDitude Magazine*, July 13, 2022, https://www.additudemag.com/adhd-lifestyle-changes-food-sleep-exercise-genes-environment/.

8. "Empowering the World Through Coaching," International Coach Federation, https://coachingfederation.org.

9. Frances Prevatt and Joel Young, "Recognizing and Treating Attention Deficit/Hyperactivity Disorder in College Students," *Journal of College Student Psychotherapy* 28 (June 2014): 182–200.

10. Frances Prevatt and Sherry Yelland, "An Empirical Evaluation of ADHD Coaching in College Students," *Journal of Attention Disorders* 19 (August 2015): 666–77.

11. Elizabeth Ahmann et al., "A Descriptive Review of ADHD Coaching Research: Implications for College Students," *Journal of Postsecondary Education and Disability* 31, no. 1 (2018): 17–39.

12. For the US groups, see Solanto, Safren, Rostain & Ramsay. For the United Kingdom, see Young and Branham. For Europe, see Hessinger & Phillipsen, Virta.

13. Anthony L. Rostain and J. Russell Ramsay, *Cognitive-Behavioral Therapy for Adult ADHD: An Integrative Psychosocial and Medical Approach* (New York: Routledge/Taylor Francis Group, 2015).

14. Anthony L. Rostain and J. Russell Ramsay, *The Adult ADHD Tool Kit: Using CBT to Facilitate Coping Inside and Out* (New York: Routledge/Taylor Francis Group, 2015).

15. J. Russell Ramsay, *Rethinking Adult ADHD: Helping Clients Turn Intentions into Actions* (Washington, D.C.: American Psychological Association, 2020).

16. Ramsay, *Rethinking Adult ADHD*, 89–93.

17. Edmund Sonuga-Bark et al., "Computer-Based Training for ADHD: A Review of Current Evidence," *Child Adolescent Psychiatric Clinics of North America* 23, no. 4 (October 2014): 807–24, doi: 10.1016/j.chc.2014.05.009.

18. Scott Kollins et al., "A Novel Digital Intervention for Actively Reducing Severity of Paediatric ADHD (STARS-ADHD): A Randomized Controlled Trial," *Lancet Digital Health* 2, no. 4 (February 2020): https://doi.org/10.1016/S2589-7500(20)30017-0.

19. Scott Kollins et al., "Effectiveness of a Digital Therapeutic as Adjunct to Treatment with Medication in Pediatric ADHD," *NPJ Digit Med* 4, no. 1 (March 2021): https://doi.org/10.1038/s41746-021-00429-0.

20. Livesey and Rostain, "Involving Parents/Family," 199–216.

7. SHINY SCREENS EVERYWHERE

1. Brooke Auxier and Monica Anderson, "Social Media Use in 2021," Pew Research Center, last modified April 7, 2021, http://pewresearch.org/internet/2021/04/07/social-media-use-in-2021/.

2. Laura A. Stockdale and Sarah M. Coyne, "Bored and Online: Reasons for Using Social Media, Problematic Social Networking Site Use, and Behavioral Outcomes across the Transition from Adolescence to Emerging Adulthood," *J Adolesce* 79 (February 2020): 173–83, doi: 10.1016/j.adolescence.2020.01.010.

3. Chirag Gupta, Sangita Jogdand, and Mayank Kumar, "Reviewing the Impact of Social Media on the Mental Health of Adolescents and Young Adults," *Cureus* 14, no. 10 (October 2022): doi: 10.7759/cureus.30143.

4. Jean Twenge and Gabrielle Martin, "Gender Differences in Associations Between Digital Media Use and Psychological Well-Being: Evidence from Three Large Data Sets," *Journal of Adolescence* 79 (February 2020): 91–102, doi: 10.1016/j.adolescence.2019.12.018.

5. Amy Orben, Tobias Dienlin, and Andrew K. Przybylski, "Social Media's Enduring Effect on Adolescent Life Satisfaction," *Proceedings of the National Academy of Sciences* 116 (May 2019): 10,226–10,228, https://doi.org/10.1073/pnas.1902058116.

6. Sarah M. Coyne et al., "Does Time Spent Using Social Media Impact Mental Health? An Eight Year Longitudinal Study," *Computers in Human Behavior* 104 (March 2020): 106160.

7. "Surgeon General Issues New Advisory About Effects Social Media Use Has on Youth Mental Health," U.S. Department of Health and Human Services, last modified

May 23, 2023, https://www.hhs.gov/about/news/2023/05/23/surgeon-general-issues-new
-advisory-about-effects-social-media-use-has-youth-mental-health.html.

8. Adam Gazzaley and Larry Rosen, *The Distracted Mind: Ancient Brains in a High-Tech World* (Cambridge, MA: MIT Press, 2016).

9. John D. Eastwood et al., "The Unengaged Mind Defining Boredom in Terms of Attention," *Perspectives on Psychological Sciences* 7, no. 5 (September 2012): 482–95, doi: 10.1177/1745691612456044.

10. "This Is Water," http://bulletin-archive.kenyon.edu/x4280.html.

11. Piya Choudhury, "How Different Generations Use Social Media (Updated)," WP Social Ninja, last modified May 10, 2021, https://wpsocialninja.com/how-different -generations-use-social-media.

12. The International Classification of Diseases (ICD) has established guidelines for the diagnosis of Gaming Disorder: https://www.who.int/standards/classifications /frequently-asked-questions/gaming-disorder.

13. Regina J. J. M. van den Eijnden, Jeroen S. Lemmens, and Patti M. Valkenburg, "The Social Media Disorder Scale," *Computers in Human Behavior* 61 (August 2016): 478–87, https://doi.org/10.1016/j.chb.2016.03.038.

14. Adam F. Aldhawyan et al., "Determinants of Subjective Poor Sleep Quality in Social Media Users Among Freshman College Students," *Nature and Science of Sleep* 12 (May 2020): 279–288, doi: 10.2147/NSS.S243411.

15. Van den Ejinden, "The Social Media Disorder," 478–87.

16. Marshall McLuhan, *Understanding Media: The Extensions of Man* (New York: McGraw Hill, 1964).

17. Vance Packard, *The Hidden Persuaders* (New York: Pelican Books, 1957).

18. *The Social Dilemma*, directed by Jeff Orlowski, written by Vickie Curtis, Davis Coombe, and Jeff Orlowski-Yang, aired September 9, 2020, on Netflix, https://www .netflix.com/title/81254224.

8. WHEN DISTRESS BECOMES A WAY OF LIFE

1. Chloe Garnham, "The Gen Z Mental Health Wave: What Is Causing the Surge?" HealthMatch, last modified September 1, 2022, https://healthmatch.io/blog/the-gen -z-mental-health-wave-what-is-causing-the-surge.

2. Nirmita Panchal et al., "The Implications of COVID-19 for Mental Health and Substance Use," Kaiser Family Foundation, last modified March 20, 2023, https://www. kff.org/mental-health/issue-brief/the-implications-of-covid-19-for-mental-health-and -substance-use/.

3. "Youth Mental Health," U.S. Department of Health and Human Services,

accessed November 23, 2023, https://www.hhs.gov/surgeongeneral/priorities/youth-mental-health/index.html.

4. Maia Niguel Hoskin, "Moms Are Feeling More Anxious and Burned Out Than Ever, Even as the Pandemic Recedes," What to Expect, last modified October 12, 2022, www.whattoexpect.com/news/first-year/survey-moms-feel-more-pressure-pandemic.

5. Sechopoulos, "Most in the U.S."

6. Elena G. van Stee, "Privileged Dependence, Precarious Autonomy: Parent/Young Adult Relationships through the Lens of COVID-19," *Journal of Marriage and Family* 85, vol. 1 (November 2022): 215–232, https://doi.org/10.1111/jomf.12895.

7. Anthony Rostain and B. Janet Hibbs, *The Stressed Years of Their Lives: Helping Your Kid Survive and Thrive During Their College Years* (New York: St. Martin's Press, 2019): 151.

8. Aaron T. Beck, *Cognitive Therapy and the Emotional Disorders* (New York: International Universities Press, 1976).

9. M. McGoldrick, N. G. Preto, and B. Carter, "The Life Cycle in Its Changing Context: Individual, Family and Social Perspectives," in *The Expanding Family Life Cycle: Individual, Family and Social Perspectives*, ed. Monica McGoldrick, Betty Carter, and Nydia Garcia Preto (Boston: Pearson Education, Inc.), 20.

10. Adapted from Hibbs and Rostain, *The Stressed Years of Their Lives.*

11. Livesey and Rostain, "Involving Parents/Family," 199–216.

12. *The Diagnostic and Statistical Manual of Mental Disorders*, 5th ed., American Psychiatric Association (Washington, D.C.: AMA Publishing, 2013).

13. Stephen P. Becker et al., "Report of a Work Group on Sluggish Cognitive Tempo: Key Research Directions and a Consensus Change in Terminology to Cognitive Disengagement Syndrome," *Journal of the American Academy of Child and Adolescent Psychiatry* 62, no. 6 (June 2023): https://doi.org/10.1016/j.jaac.2022.07.821.

14. Russ Harris, *ACT Made Simple: An Easy-to-Read Primer on Acceptance and Commitment Therapy* (Oakland, CA: New Harbinger Publications, 2019).

15. Steven C. Hayes, "Acceptance and Commitment Therapy, Relational Frame Theory, and the Third Wave of Behavioral and Cognitive Therapies—Republished Article," *Behavior Therapy* 47, no. 6 (November 2016): 868–85, doi: 10.1016/j.beth.2016.11.006.

16. Harris, *ACT Made Simple.*

17. Yuen Yu Chong, "The Framework of Acceptance and Commitment Therapy," ResearchGate, last modified August 2021, https://www.researchgate.net/figure/The-framework-of-Acceptance-and-Commitment-Therapy_fig1_353665422.

18. Russ Harris, "FACE COVID: How to Respond Effectively to the Corona Crisis," TheHappinessTrap.com, last modified March 2020, www.actmindfully.com.au/wp-content/uploads/2020/03/FACE-COVID-eBook-by-Russ-Harris-March-2020.pdf.

9. SOLUTIONS FOR COMPLEX DISORDERS

1. American Psychiatric Association, *Diagnostic and Statistical Manual of Mental Disorders,* 5th ed. (Australia: American Psychiatric Association Publishing, 2013).

2. Andrew K. Przybylski, Netta Weinstein, and Kou Murayama, "Internet Gaming Disorder: Investigating the Clinical Relevance of a New Phenomenon," *The American Journal of Psychiatry* 174 (November 2016): 230–36, https://doi.org/10.1176/appi.ajp.2016.16020224.

3. Clifford J. Sussman et al., "Internet and Video Game Addictions: Diagnosis, Epidemiology, and Neurobiology," *Child and Adolescent Psychiatric Clinics of North America* 27, no. 2 (April 2018): 307–26, doi: 10.1016/j.chc.2017.11.015.

4. Kristy Carlisle, "Utility of *DSM-5* Criteria for Internet Gaming Disorder," *Psychological Reports* 124, no. 6 (October 2020): 2613–32, https://doi.org/10.1177/003329412096547.

5. Lu Liu et al., "The Comorbidity Between Internet Gaming Disorder and Depression: Interrelationship and Neural Mechanisms," *Front Psych* 9 (April 2018): 154, https://doi.org/10.3389/fpsyt.2018.00154.

6. Doug Hyun Han and Perry F. Renshaw, "Bupropion in the Treatment of Problematic Online Game Play in Patients with Major Depressive Disorder," *Journal of Psychopharmacology* 26, no. 5 (May 2012): 689–96, doi:10.1177/0269881111400647.

7. David N. Greenfield, "Clinical Considerations in Internet and Video Game Addiction Treatment," *Child and Adolescent Psychiatric Clinics of North America* 31, no. 1 (January 2022): 99–119, https://doi.org/10.1016/j.chc.2021.09.003.

8. J. O. Prochaska, C. C. DiClemente, and J. C. Norcross, "In Search of How People Change: Applications to the Addictive Disorders," *American Psychologist* 47 (1992): 1102–14.

9. Rostain and Hibbs, *The Stressed Years*, 145.

10. W. M. Miller and S. Rollnick, *Motivational Interviewing: Helping People Change*, 3rd ed. (New York: Guilford Press, 2013).

11. K. Hall, T. Gibbie, and D. I. Lubman, "Motivational Interviewing Techniques Facilitating Behaviour Change in the General Practice Setting," *Australian Family Physician* 41, no. 9 (September 2012): 660–67.

12. Renee Goodwin et al., "Trends in U.S. Depression Prevalence From 2015 to 2020: The Widening Treatment Gap," *American Journal of Preventive Medicine* 63, no. 5 (November 2022): 726–33, doi: 10.1016/j.amepre.2022.05.014.

13. "Mood Disorders and Suicide," SlidePlayer, last modified 2015, https://slideplayer.com/slide/4928270/.

14. "Depression," National Institute of Mental Health, last updated April 2023, https://www.nimh.nih.gov/health/topics/depression.

15. Raj K. Patel and Gregory M. Rose, "Persistent Depressive Disorder," National

Library of Medicine, last modified June 26, 2023, https://www.ncbi.nlm.nih.gov/books/NBK541052/.

16. U.S. Surgeon General, "Protecting Youth Mental Health," 2021. https://www.hhs.gov/surgeongeneral/priorities/youth-mental-health/index.html.

17. "Facing Addiction in America: The Surgeon General's Report on Alcohol, Drugs, and Health," U.S. Department of Health and Human Services, accessed September 25, 2023, https://www.ncbi.nlm.nih.gov/books/NBK424857/pdf/Bookshelf_NBK424857.pdf.

18. "Facing Addiction," 2–7.

19. J. D. Schulden and C. Blancom, "Epidemiology of Co-occurring Psychiatric and Substance Use Disorders," in *Textbook of Substance Use Disorder Treatment*, 6th ed., ed. K. T. Brady, F. R. Levin, M. Galanter, and H. D. Kleber (Arlington, VA: American Psychiatric Association Publishing, 2021), 672.

20. Schulden and Blancom, "Epidemiology," 672.

21. "The CRAFT Approach: Encouraging Healthy, Constructive, Positive Changes for Your Family," Partnership to End Addiction, accessed September 25, 2023, https://drugfree.org/article/craft-community-reinforcement-family-training/; https://helpingfamilieshelp.com/about-craft.

22. J. Foote et al., *Beyond Addiction: How Science and Kindness Help People Change—A Guide for Families* (New York: Scribner, 2014).

23. Robert J. Meyers and Jane Ellen Smith, "CRAFT: Community Reinforcement and Family Training," slide presentation, Department of Psychology, University of New Mexico and Center on Alcoholism, Substance Abuse, and Other Addictions, September 6, 2014.

10. PARENTS AS MENTAL HEALTH ADVOCATES

1. "SAMHSA Announces National Survey on Drug Use and Health (NSDUH) Results Detailing Mental Illness and Substance Use Levels in 2021," Substance Abuse and Mental Health Services Administration, last modified January 4, 2023, https://www.samhsa.gov/newsroom/press-announcements/20230104/samhsa-announces-nsduh-results-detailing-mental-illness-substance-use-levels-2021.

2. Adriana Belmonte, "Why Mental Health Care in America Is So Shoddy," Yahoo! News, last modified July 27, 2021, https://news.yahoo.com/why-mental-health-care-in-america-is-so-shoddy-183448311.html.

3. Van Stee, "Parent/Young Adult," 215–32.

4. "Finding a Mental Health Professional," National Alliance on Mental Illness, accessed September 25, 2023, https://www.nami.org/Your-journey/Individuals-with-mental-illness/finding-a-mental-health-professional.

5. Doris A. Fuller, "Mental Health Caregivers under 'High Emotional Stress,'" *Re-

search Weekly (Treatment Advocacy Center), last modified March 1, 2016, https://www
.treatmentadvocacycenter.org/fixing-the-system/features-and-news/3025-research
-weekly-mental-health-caregivers-under-qhigh-emotional-stressq.

6. "Caregivers of Younger Adults: A Focused Look at Caregivers of Younger Adults,"
Caregiving, https://www.caregiving.org/wp-content/uploads/2020/05/Report_Caregivers
_of_Younger_Adults_11–12–09.pdf.

APPENDIX

1. National Academies of Sciences, Engineering, and Medicine, *Ending Discrimination
against People with Mental and Substance Abuse Disorders: The Evidence for Stigma Change* (Washington, D.C.: The National Academies Press, 2016), https://doi.org/10.17226/23442,
http://www.nap.edu/catalog/23442/ending-discrimination-against-people-with
-mental-and-substance-use-disorders.

INDEX